Visual Basic® Developer's Guide to the Win32 API

Visual Basic® Developer's Guide to the Win32 API

Steve Brown

SYBEX®

San Francisco • Paris • Düsseldorf • Soest • London

Associate Publisher: Richard Mills
Contracts and Licensing Manager: Kristine O'Callaghan
Acquisitions & Developmental Editor: Denise Santoro
Editor: Galen Miller
Project Editor: Colleen Wheeler Strand
Technical Editor: Greg Guntle
Book Designer: Kris Warrenburg
Graphic Illustrator: Tony Jonick
Electronic Publishing Specialist: Grey Magauran
Project Team Leader: Jennifer Durning
Proofreader: Jennifer Campbell, Kimberly August
Indexer: Ted Laux
Cover Designer: Design Site
Cover Illustrator/Photographer: Jack D. Myers

SYBEX is a registered trademark of SYBEX Inc.

Screen reproductions produced with Collage Complete.
Collage Complete is a trademark of Inner Media Inc.

TRADEMARKS: SYBEX has attempted throughout this book to
distinguish proprietary trademarks from descriptive terms by following the capitalization style used by the manufacturer.

Library of Congress Card Number: 99-66825
ISBN: 0-7821-2559-X

Manufactured in the United States of America

10 9 8 7 6 5 4 3 2 1

This book is dedicated to the many programmers who have struggled with the Windows API, where even the simplest ideas can become complex undertakings and not everything is what it seems.

ACKNOWLEDGMENTS

Many thanks go to the people who helped make this book a success. Thanks to Greg Guntle for his technical editing expertise. Thanks to Galen Miller for editing the content. Other thanks go out to Jennifer Durning, Grey Magauran, Ted Laux, and all of the other people who had a part in making this book, and the series, a reality. Special thanks go out to Denise Santoro, Richard Mills, and Colleen Strand, who assisted and prodded me when necessary.

I would like to thank my wife and daughter for putting up with my long hours and general unavailability during this project. Also, there are many others who supported me through this project: J.C., Mom and Dad, Denise, Doug, J.J., Joe, Alice and the kids, Jeff, Cathy, John, Don, Wanda, Mel, Joyce, Bob, Jono, Giovanna, Sean, Julie, Giovanni, Kyle, Dana, Ruth, Jim, Lee, Scott, Henry, Dean, Alan, Jack, Zak, Elaine, Darleen, Rick, and all of the others. Special thanks go to each and every one of you, and you know who you are! Thanks so much for your support, ideas, and motivation!

CONTENTS AT A GLANCE

TABLE OF CONTENTS

INTRODUCTION

Visual Basic is a very popular programming tool. Its simplicity is its power because you can develop extremely sophisticated and powerful applications without the headaches of traditional Windows development. But even as much as I enjoy using Visual Basic, there are certain aspects of the language that many programmers feel could be improved upon. Many of the controls are useful but lack the extra functionality that should have been included in the first place.

Programmers are often faced with the issue of either settling for Visual Basic's intrinsic controls or finding a third-party component that fits the bill. With the advent of ActiveX technology it has been easy for almost anyone to create ActiveX components and distribute them on the Internet. This is great if you need a component in a hurry, but what do you do if the company that developed the component disappears, or you can't find support for the component? You're back to square one.

Fortunately there is another answer and it's right at your fingertips. You can utilize the functionality already in your system by using the Windows API. The API consists of thousands of functions you can use to accomplish almost anything your heart desires. Unfortunately, the API isn't as easy to use in Visual Basic as it is in C. While Microsoft has included the API Viewer add-in within Visual Basic, many of the APIs are declared improperly, are outdated, or simply omitted, leaving you to fend for yourself.

So what do you do? You can use the included declarations and trust they will work, hack when they break, or consult the Microsoft Developer Network Library (MSDN). MSDN is a great resource to find out about APIs. Unfortunately, almost all of the APIs are documented in C.

You can rely on the Visual Basic samples included in MSDN to help you write your code or you can learn how to convert the API documentation into something more palatable in Visual Basic.

What Is Covered in This Book?

As you probably know, there are myriad books available that cover the Windows API. Some are very basic and others are quite extensive. Some cover the same material, while others break new ground.

In reality, the Windows API is so extensive that it is almost impossible to cover it adequately in a single text. And it changes so often that it is difficult to keep obtainable resources current. This book will help you understand the inner workings of the Windows environment and how to access them using the Windows API. This book is organized into four sections. By the end of the book you should know enough about the Windows API that you can "fly solo."

The first section introduces the Windows API and teaches you how to work with API declarations. In particular you will understand the structure of declaration statements and learn how to convert between C prototypes and Visual Basic declaration statements.

The second section deals with the internals of the Windows environment. You will learn how Windows uses messages and message handlers to control virtually every Windows object. You will also learn about Windows memory management. This particular section is extremely important to understand because you are left to manage your system's memory. Visual Basic insulates you from this.

The third section covers the basic Windows APIs. Each chapter is organized by functionality and contains all of the information required to use the APIs in that chapter.

The final section takes the API knowledge you have acquired and shows you how to wrap APIs in a class library. You will then utilize your class library developed throughout the book to develop a full-blown application, turbocharged by the Windows API.

Conventions Used in This Book

To use many of the Windows APIs you need to think like a C programmer. While the first section teaches you how to convert between C and Visual Basic, the C prototypes along with the Visual Basic declarations have been included so you can constantly see and understand why APIs are converted as they are.

Each API is broken down by description, C prototype, Visual Basic declaration, and their arguments. In addition, some APIs include further explanation when appropriate. This will allow you to immerse yourself in both Visual Basic and C.

Throughout this book the following conventions have been used to denote items that require special attention:

- Items in **bold** should be typed in exactly as they appear in the book.
- Items in *italics* denote new terms or phrases.
- Items in `Courier` represent keywords, commands, or other computer instructions.

Throughout the text you will find special notes, tips, and warnings that help clarify or simplify the topic you are reading.

Thank you for taking the time to read this book. I hope it makes working with the API easy for you and provides you with a good foundation for your future development efforts.

Who Should Read This Book?

If you have a solid understanding of Visual Basic conventions and usage and are able to create simple applications using any of the standard toolbar components, then this book will be of great assistance in your programming efforts. This book is intended for the intermediate and advanced programmer who wants to go beyond the basics of Visual Basic and start to add more flexibility, functionality, and power to their applications. By using the Windows APIs outlined in this book you will be able to bring new life to your Visual Basic applications.

System Requirements

The code samples included in this book were written as generically as possible so they can run on any Windows platform. If you have a computer with Windows 95, Windows 98, Windows NT, or Windows 2000, then you meet the first requirement to use the APIs in this book.

Although not a requirement, it is best if you have Visual Basic 6.0 on your system. The code samples should work on Visual Basic 5, however, all testing and development was done using Visual Basic 6.0 with Service Pack 3 installed. Most of the testing focused on Windows 98 and Windows 2000 platforms. But again, the code is generic enough to run on Windows 95 and Windows NT; it just wasn't tested in those environments.

The examples of code that were written for the Windows 95 or Windows NT platform are clearly marked in the book where they appear. Basically, if your computer is less than five years old you're in business!

C H A P T E R

O N E

1

The Windows API

- What Is the API?

- Static versus Dynamic Linking

- How to Find the Right API

- Using the API Viewer

- Moving On

The visual environment and BASIC syntax of the Visual Basic language have made complex Windows development easy for both the novice and advanced programmer. Visual Basic was designed to shield the programmer from some of the intricacies of Windows development, which makes it easy for all of us to use. For example, Visual Basic applications process a limited number of Windows commands, called *messages*, which are introduced in Chapter 3.

Although Visual Basic only exposes a subset of the functionality of Windows, it does provide a great foundation for most programmers. Almost any application you can think of can be written in Visual Basic. Even with its inherent limitations, Visual Basic provides a powerful mechanism that allows you to extend your applications in many ways by using the Windows API.

What Is the API?

The Application Programming Interface (API) is an interface to the many routines made available through Dynamic Link Libraries (DLLs). As you already know, Windows ships with hundreds of DLLs, and within these DLLs lie thousands of functions and procedures. Many of these routines are used by Windows and reused by other applications. Your applications can, and will, use some of these routines.

As you observe the Windows operating system you realize how many different tasks it is capable of performing. Using APIs, Windows manages memory, processes graphics, plays music, processes mouse events, accepts keyboard input, and many other things. Each of these tasks requires several subtasks to be completed successfully. Using the API, you can make your application mimic or, even better, reuse the functionality available in Windows.

You might think of the API as a giant toolbox with many drawers, bags, and tool belts, each containing several job-specific tools. For example, a tool belt would hold a hammer, tape measure, and several screwdrivers, while your toolbox might also have a bag of screws and a drawer full of bolts. Most likely your tools are organized so they are easy to carry and retrieve.

Using this example, DLLs would be the functional equivalent of toolboxes, racks, tool belts, etc. They are precompiled programming libraries that hold many, often related, programming tools.

FIGURE 1.1:

The API is like a toolbox.

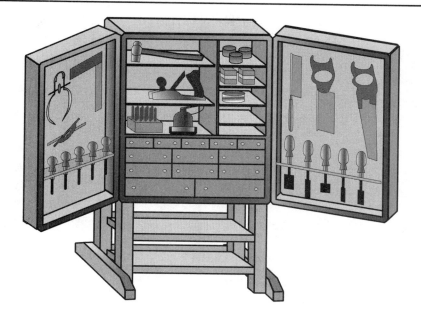

Like any programming language, Visual Basic provides a set of tools for the programmer to use. Although it doesn't provide the complete functionality of a language such as C++, it would be improper to equate Visual Basic to a child's toolbox. Actually, Visual Basic is more like a handyman's toolbox, which provides everything you need to accomplish your most common tasks. However, your normal supply of tools may be inadequate for a major task. For example, it doesn't make sense to dig your new backyard pool with a garden shovel. You need something with more horsepower, like a skip-loader or backhoe. Programming with Visual Basic is much the same. The API is the equivalent of using heavy equipment to accomplish the job.

There are several reasons why you would want to use the Windows API. Most likely it will be because Visual Basic doesn't provide enough tools to accomplish a specific task. For example, Visual Basic cannot easily play a wave file without another tool, such as the Multimedia control or the API.

There are some things Visual Basic can do, but the API can do it faster. An obvious example is rendering graphics on the screen. The reason is that the API contains better memory management routines and time-proven algorithms that are optimized for performance.

Another reason to use the API is when you have limitations on the number of files that can be sent or shipped as part of the product. For example, you could use the Common Dialog control in your project and ship its accompanying ActiveX control (OCX) file with your setup, however, there are many instances where you would not want to ship the control with your project. An alternative would be to use the API in your code and compile them directly into your executable.

Additional Functionality

As you may already know, or will soon discover, the API provides significant additional functionality that is lacking in Visual Basic. As mentioned earlier, it would be difficult to play a simple wave file without the help of another tool. Sure, the Multimedia control could do the trick, but it is an expensive tool for such a simple task. In this situation, the sndPlaySound API would serve you better.

Performance Gains

Using the pool-digging example, it is certainly possible to dig that pool with a garden shovel, while knowing that the shovel is obviously not the best method. It would be much better to use heavy equipment, which could do the job cleaner and faster. In this situation you would want to speed up the process. The API can provide many speed improvements for your development efforts.

Low Overhead

If you needed to use a drill at the end of your five-acre lot, you would be best served to buy a cordless drill, rather than connect hundreds of extension cords or buy a generator and lug it across the lot. ActiveX, formerly known as OLE automation, is much like the generator and extension cords. It's relatively easy to use and usually provides the functionality you need. It provides a great level of sophistication and flexibility…at a cost. As you read this book and develop your applications, you will see circumstances where it makes sense to use the API rather than that trusty control.

Static versus Dynamic Linking

Before we start using the APIs you should understand what is happening behind the scenes. Understanding how Visual Basic works with APIs will help you better utilize the API in your development efforts.

I'm sure by now you have heard the terms static linking and dynamic linking. Development languages like C and C++ make extensive use of static linking. In contrast, Visual Basic uses dynamic linking to extend its functionality.

Static Linking

Before Windows and other Graphical User Interfaces (GUIs) were developed, programming languages used static libraries to provide additional functionality within their applications. Static libraries were created that contained several routines you could include in your application during the linking process. Figure 1.2 shows the static linking process and how applications work with static libraries.

FIGURE 1.2:

The static linking process

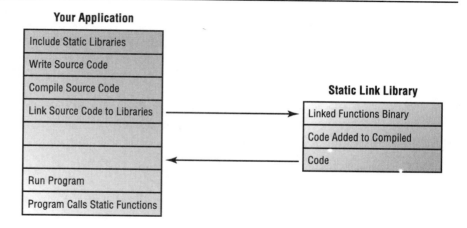

Static libraries consist of .OBJ files that contain object code. Libraries are generally loaded in their entirety. For example, a library called Graphics.obj could have many graphics routines, but your application only requires one to clear the screen. When your application is linked, all functions in Graphics.obj are actually included in your executable file. As a result, your executable code becomes larger, and if you wanted to change the functionality you would need to re-link your application with a new object library.

Dynamic Linking

Visual Basic provides extensibility through a process known as dynamic linking, which calls a routine within another program while your application is running.

The linking is dynamic because the link can be established almost any time. Figure 1.3 shows how dynamic linking works with your applications.

FIGURE 1.3:

The dynamic linking process

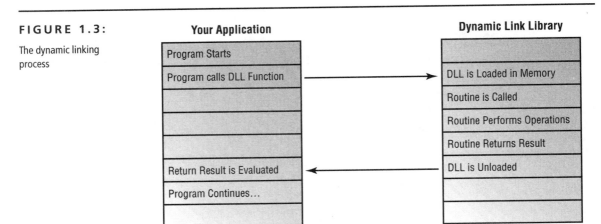

As you know, a DLL can contain many functions, which are both private to the DLL as well as public. Functions within a DLL that are available to your applications are said to be *exported*; that is, made available for use by other programs. This is much like public methods available through Visual Basic DLLs and classes.

If your application utilizes a function from a DLL, your application *imports* that function at run-time when it is actually required. Although dynamic linking makes your code run a little slower than statically-linked code, you are provided with significantly more functionality with a smaller application footprint. Even better, your applications can be upgraded easily when new versions of DLLs arrive. Since the DLLs are designed to be backward compatible, you won't need to re-compile and distribute your application because one library was upgraded.

How to Find the Right API

There are many resources available that document portions of the Windows API. Unfortunately, the API is so large that it is almost impossible to completely cover it in one text. In addition, new APIs are developed almost daily. This book will attempt to cover the most common and useful APIs for you as a Visual Basic programmer. The APIs are logically grouped together by chapter. There is also an

API quick reference in the appendix, which will give you quick access to APIs not be covered in this text.

Like an organized toolbox, APIs are generally stored neatly within DLLs. There are several DLLs common to all 32-bit Windows platforms. These include `Kernel32.DLL`, `User32.DLL`, and `GDI32.DLL`. There are many more system DLLs, but these three expose most of the functionality of the operating system.

`Kernel32.DLL` is responsible for handling most of the operating system's functionality, including memory management, device I/O, and most Windows environment functions. APIs such as `GlobalAlloc`, `GlobalLock`, `GlobalUnlock`, and `GlobalFree` allow you to allocate and lock memory for your applications. Other APIs, such as `GetWindowsDirectory` and `GetSystemInfo`, give you information about your operating environment.

`User32.DLL` is responsible for the GUI and window management. For example, `User32.DLL` exposes the `MessageBox` and `MessageBoxEx` APIs. These APIs display a message box just like the one created with Visual Basic's `MsgBox` command. APIs like `CreateWindow`, `GetForegroundWindow`, and `GetFocus` show you some of the more basic window management functions. `User32.DLL` is not just limited to screen interface functions. It also exposes APIs that allow you to retrieve information from input devices. For example, the `GetKeyboardState` API retrieves information about which keys are pressed on the keyboard.

`GDI32.DLL` is the library that handles most of the basic graphics functions. GDI stands for *Graphics Device Interface*, and `GDI32.DLL` handles graphics devices such as monitors and printers. Some of the more common APIs used in `GDI32.DLL` are `BitBlt`, which rapidly copies large chunks of graphics data; `RealizePallette`, which loads palette information into the current device context; and `GetBkColor`, which retrieves the current background color of a specific device context.

A good place to find information about APIs is to go directly to the source. In most cases this will be Microsoft, however, there are several third party components that have their own APIs. You should consult the manufacturers of these components to obtain their APIs.

Microsoft Developer's Network (MSDN) is a good place to obtain API declarations and Software Development Kits (SDKs) for most Windows components. You can access MSDN on the Internet at `http://msdn.microsoft.com`.

The most effective method for selecting the right API is to start with the API that satisfies the basic requirements of the task you wish to accomplish. Once you know the right API, careful scrutiny of its arguments will determine if other APIs are needed to satisfy the required arguments. For example, suppose you wanted to obtain the version of Windows you are running. After searching through this book, or MSDN, you come to the conclusion that the `GetVersionEx` API is the appropriate API. You insert the API declaration into your project, which looks like this:

```
Private Declare Function GetVersionEx Lib "kernel32" _
        Alias "GetVersionExA" _
        (lpVersionInformation As OSVERSIONINFO) As Long
```

By looking at the declaration you can see that the API requires one argument, a variable of the `OSVERSIONINFO` type. So your next step would be to look for a Type declaration, or structure, named `OSVERSIONINFO`. Once you obtain the Visual Basic declaration, you are ready to go!

Using the API Viewer

Before we progress further in the text, you will need to be familiar with using add-ins in Visual Basic. Specifically, you should know how to use the API Viewer add-in, shown in Figure 1.4.

FIGURE 1.4:

The API viewer add-in

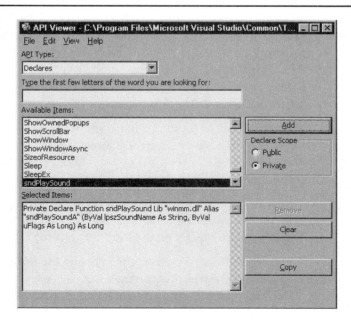

Assuming you know which API you want to use, the first step is to load the API Viewer. Once it is started, load the appropriate API file into the viewer, as follows:

1. From the Add-Ins menu, select API Viewer.

2. In the API Viewer, select Load Text File... from the File menu, or Load Database File... if you previously converted the file to a database.

3. Select the Winapi folder. This is where Visual Studio installs the API declaration files.

4. Within the Winapi folder you will see three API declaration files: `APILoad.txt`, `MAPI32.txt`, and `Win32API.txt`. The file you are concerned with is `Win32API.txt`.

TIP

The API Viewer runs faster if you convert the text file to a database. You can do this by loading the text file, then selecting Convert Text to Database... from the File menu. After the file is converted, the database file will automatically be loaded for you.

There are several areas of the API Viewer that deserve special attention, including the API Type selector, Available Items list, Selected Items list, Declare Scope section, and the various command buttons.

The API Type selector is used to narrow your list of choices. You can select from Constants, Declares, and Types. Selecting Constants lists all the Constants declared in the file. The Declares option lists all the API declarations in the Available Items list. Finally, selecting Types will list all the data structures, or Types, as they are known in Visual Basic, in the Available Items list.

Select the item you wish to use in the Available Items list. When you find the API, constant, or structure you want to use, click the Add button to add it to the Selected Items list.

The Selected Items list now shows you the information you selected from the various API categories. You can show the entire declaration or just the name by selecting Line Item or Full Text from the View menu.

Finally, there are the Add, Remove, Clear, and Copy buttons, which allow you to move declarations to and from the Selected Items list, as well as insert them directly into the Visual Basic IDE, or copy them to the clipboard.

Before inserting APIs into your project, make sure you set the proper scope for the declaration. Do this by selecting the appropriate Option button in the Declare Scope section. In general, API declarations should be declared as `Private` when inserted in form and class modules, and `Public` when inserted in basic modules. You will see when working with the class library throughout this book that the APIs are declared privately to their class modules.

TIP   After you insert declarations into your code, be sure to remove them from the Selected Items list. Otherwise they will get inserted again if you go back later and add more declarations.

To insert an API declaration into your code, follow these steps:

1. Select the appropriate API from the Available Items list.

2. Double-click the declaration or click the Add button to copy the declaration to the Available Items list.

3. Click the Insert button to insert the declarations into your code.

Now that you understand how to use the API Viewer, you need to understand the risks you will be taking once you start using the APIs. Although there are inherent risks, the rewards are even greater!

Moving On

Before we start working with the API, it is imperative to understand that with the API's power comes risks. Every aspect of the Visual Basic API declaration must be declared properly and match its C equivalent. This means that the API's name, number, and types of arguments, as well as the return type must all match appropriately. Failing to do so will either cause your program or your system to crash. You will learn more about this in Chapter 2, *Working with API Declarations*.

Even when you declare the APIs correctly, calling them incorrectly can also lead to catastrophic errors. There is one thing you can do to minimize the amount of risk to your code and operating system. Save your work often!

One thing you can do to help save your work is to configure your environment to automatically save the projects, or at least prompt you to do so. This option can be set on the Environment tab of the Options dialog. Open the Options dialog by selecting Options… from the Tools menu.

WARNING Although this point is obvious, it cannot be reiterated enough. When using the API, save your work often! Saving your work when using the API is like wearing safety goggles when using power tools. And I know you don't want to lose an eye!

CHAPTER
TWO

Working with API Declarations

- The Anatomy of an API Declaration

- Overview of Character Sets

- Converting Data Types

As you already know, there is a plethora of APIs out there. Most are directly related to the Windows operating system. In addition, third-party vendors may release APIs for their own controls. You may even do so with yours.

With so many different APIs, you may wonder how to use them all in your applications. Using most of the Windows APIs is easy. You determine which APIs to use and with the API Viewer, insert the declarations, data types, and constants into your code. Then you use them in much the same way you use intrinsic Visual Basic functions, like data types and constants.

This chapter covers the many aspects of including and properly declaring APIs within your projects. There is no single "holy grail" on how to include an API, but there are several guidelines you should know well before venturing out on your own.

By the end of this chapter you will know how to use the API Viewer to include API declarations in your code. In addition, you will have enough knowledge to convert other APIs from C notation to Visual Basic.

The Anatomy of an API Declaration

In this chapter, a single API declaration, SendMessage, will be dissected so you can see how Visual Basic interacts with the Windows API. Before dissecting the API declaration it is important for you to know what the API does, then you will understand what is required for the API to successfully carry out its task.

The SendMessage API is used to send messages to various windows in memory. These windows receive the messages and, if designed to do so, process them accordingly. Every event in Visual Basic is triggered by a message. For example, the KeyDown event of a textbox control is actually a handler for the WM_KEYDOWN message.

The SendMessage API is declared in Visual Basic as such:

```
Private Declare Function SendMessage Lib "user32" _
    Alias "SendMessageA" _
    (ByVal hwnd As Long, ByVal wMsg As Long, _
    ByVal wParam As Long, lParam As Any) As Long
```

As you can see, there are several keywords and arguments that make up the entire declaration. Let's examine these parts in greater detail.

Scope

The scope of the API declaration determines its availability within your project. You can declare an API as either `Public` or `Private`. Your selection is determined primarily by where the declaration is located. In our example, the API is declared as `Private` because it is only available to the form where it is declared.

When declaring APIs in standard modules, you can declare them either as `Public` or `Private`. Prior to Visual Basic 4, you would often see APIs included in standard modules and declared publicly, making them available to the entire project. These APIs would often be combined together in wrapper functions that combined the functionality of several APIs to build a complete function. This allowed the programmer to isolate all the initialization and cleanup routines required by the API from the rest of the project. Then the programmer would only need to call the wrapper function, rather than rewrite the code over and over again.

TIP

If you are including API declarations in your form's code, you must declare the API using the `Private` keyword. Visual Basic will not allow you to expose APIs publicly from within a form.

Although many programmers still declare APIs publicly in standard modules, it is often better to functionally group your APIs and wrapper functions into classes. APIs must be declared as `Private` within class modules so they are shielded from outside interference. To access the APIs from the rest of your code, simply create `Public` methods that wrap the APIs. Then you can call these methods from your projects.

If you attempt to declare an API publicly within a form or class module, Visual Basic will prompt you with a compile error like the one shown in Figure 2.1.

FIGURE 2.1:

Visual Basic's Compile error

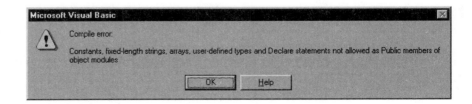

Microsoft Visual Basic

Compile error:

Constants, fixed-length strings, arrays, user-defined types and Declare statements not allowed as Public members of object modules

OK   Help

Declaration Type

The Declare keyword is what distinguishes the API from an intrinsic or user-defined function or subroutine. All API declarations must be in the (General)-(Declarations) section of your form, module, or class.

The API can take on one of two forms, depending on its declaration. The API is generally declared as a Function if it returns a value (as most do). If the API does not return a value, or you do not intend to use the return value, then the API is generally declared as a subroutine using the Sub keyword.

TIP   It is important to remember that you cannot call an API until you have declared it somewhere in your project.

API Name

Following the API declaration is the name of the API, as it will be known to Visual Basic. It is important to know that the name Visual Basic uses is not necessarily the true name of the API. There are many situations where you will want to reference the same API using different names. For example, the SendMessage API can take different parameter types depending on the message being sent. Some messages require a numeric parameter, whereas others require a string. For example, if you wanted to send string data using SendMessage, you could declare the API as follows:

```
Private Declare Function SendMessageString Lib "user32" _
    Alias "SendMessageA" _
    (ByVal hwnd As Long, ByVal wMsg As Long, _
    ByVal wParam As Long, ByVal lParam As String) As Long
```

Then you could create another declaration for numeric messages, as such:

```
Private Declare Function SendMessageLong Lib "user32" _
    Alias "SendMessageA" _
    (ByVal hwnd As Long, ByVal wMsg As Long, _
    ByVal wParam As Long, lParam As Long) As Long
```

Then you could call SendMessageString when you want to send text, or SendMessageLong when you want to send numeric data. Notice how both declarations actually call the same API, yet they pass different arguments. In Chapter 3, you will see many types of messages and learn how to pass them using both styles of API call.

Library

After you define the name of the API as it will be known within your Visual Basic project, you must specify in which library the API resides. This is done using the Lib keyword, followed by the library name in quotes. As you can see from our declaration, the SendMessage API resides in the User32 DLL.

There are a couple of things to note here. Many of the Windows APIs come from three core Windows services: the kernel, user interface, and Graphic Device Interface (GDI). APIs exposed by these three services can be declared by using kernel32, user32, or gdi32 after the Lib keyword.

APIs that lie outside the three main services will require the full name of the DLL where they reside. For example, the sndPlaySound API resides in the winmm.dll file and is declared using the Lib "winmm.dll" syntax.

When specifying a library, if you leave out the path to the DLL, Visual Basic will first search the application's path for the DLL. If it cannot find it there, it will search the current directory for the DLL. Next, Visual Basic will search your System directory, followed by the Windows directory. Finally, Visual Basic will search the directories specified in the Path environment variable.

Alias

As mentioned earlier, the name used within Visual Basic may not be the actual name of the API. Take another look at our sample declaration:

```
Private Declare Function SendMessage Lib "user32" _
    Alias "SendMessageA" _
    (ByVal hwnd As Long, ByVal wMsg As Long, _
    ByVal wParam As Long, lParam As Any) As Long
```

You can see that Visual Basic knows the API as SendMessage, however, the API's true name is SendMessageA. When declaring an API using a name other than its original, you must specify the API's original name using the Alias keyword.

There are two situations where you will want to use an alias for the API. The first is when there are multiple versions of the same API, and the second is when a single API can accept more than one data type for the same argument.

The first scenario is common to all APIs. Win32 now has an American National Standards Institute (ANSI) and a Unicode version of each API. The ANSI versions are denoted with the letter A after the API name, whereas the Unicode versions are denoted with the letter W. The W actually stands for *wide character*, which is another term for Unicode.

As mentioned in the previous section, the second and more common scenario is when an API can accept multiple data types for a single parameter. This is precisely why the SendMessage API was chosen for our dissection example. If you examine its argument list you will notice the argument lParam, which is declared as Any. The Any keyword allows you to pass any data type to the API. While this may sound convenient at first, it can actually cause more trouble than you might expect if you are not completely aware of what your arguments are.

If you are a seasoned VB programmer, you will rarely find an occasion when you are left with no option but to use the Variant data type (yes, I know there are actually some valid reasons, but they are the exceptions to the rule). Type casting is important for preserving the integrity of your data, as well as minimizing debugging efforts. As you will soon learn, or already know, working with APIs can be more unruly than working with the UNIX VI editor while wearing a blindfold. Don't get me wrong, the API is usable if you play by the rules, but if you break the rules, the API will show you how user-hostile Windows can be.

NOTE   You can change the name of your API declaration, as well as the data types, by using the Alias keyword appropriately in your declaration.

Arguments

Like a normal Visual Basic subroutine or function, APIs can accept arguments to perform calculations, retrieve values, set captions, and various other tasks.

Considering the volatility of the API, you need to have a good understanding of what is going on behind the scenes when using them. In particular, you need to understand how and why arguments are passed the way they are. The API declaration is where you define how arguments are passed.

To effectively understand what is happening when you pass arguments, you will need a basic understanding of how C handles various data types. While numeric arguments are fairly straightforward, passing strings back and forth is a bit trickier.

As you know from working with Visual Basic, arguments will either be passed *by value* or *by reference*. In Visual Basic, all arguments are passed by reference unless otherwise specified. When you declare APIs, the arguments also default to being passed by reference. When you pass an argument by reference, the called procedure can directly modify the value of the argument, and the calling procedure can see the results of that modification. Consider the following example:

```
Private Sub Command1_Click()
    Dim x As Integer

    x = 5
    Debug.Print x

    Add x, 5
    Debug.Print x
End Sub

Private Sub Add(var As Integer, nbr As Integer)
    var = var + nbr
End Sub
```

When you click the button, the value of x (5) is displayed in the Immediate window. Then the variable is passed to the Add subroutine. Since we did not specify otherwise, the variable is passed by reference. This means that the called procedure has direct access to the contents of the original variable.

When Add is called, the value of the variable var, which actually references x, is increased by the value passed through nbr, which is 5. Using simple arithmetic:

```
var = var + nbr
var = 5 + 5
var = 10
```

After the Add procedure is complete, the new value of x is displayed in the Immediate window. This time x equals 10. If you wanted to protect x from being modified by Add, you would need to pass it by value using the ByVal modifier, as shown:

```
Private Sub Add(ByVal var As Integer, nbr As Integer)
    var = var + nbr
End Sub
```

Using the C language, most numeric arguments are passed by value. Since Visual Basic defaults to passing arguments by reference, this means you will be using the ByVal modifier quite a bit.

Contrary to this, most strings are passed by reference. This is due to the way C manages memory: it doesn't. Memory management in C is left to the programmer. When working with the C language, you will truly understand what people mean when they say that a computer does *exactly* what it is told to do.

In contrast, Visual Basic manages memory for you. You don't need to understand how variables are stored in memory or how they are passed on the stack. Visual Basic does a good job of insulating you from the complexities of memory management. However, when you use the API, you are most certainly obligated to become not only educated, but proficient, in the ways of memory management. You will learn much more about memory management in Chapter 4.

So if strings are passed to APIs by reference, it should be easy to declare the API properly. Unfortunately, the folks up in Redmond threw us VB programmers a curve ball, as you will see in the next two sections.

The *ByVal* Modifier

Perhaps the biggest culprit of bad DLL calling conventions is the inadvertent use and misuse of the ByVal keyword. This keyword deserves some extra scrutiny, as its use with regard to APIs is somewhat different than when used strictly within Visual Basic.

As stated earlier, Visual Basic normally passes arguments by reference. This allows your functions to modify the values of arguments so the new value can be retrieved after the function is finished. In actuality, when the function is called, the argument's 32-bit memory address is passed to the function via the stack rather than its value, as shown in Figure 2.2. This allows the function to determine the location in memory where the variable resides and write directly to that memory location. This is how the called function can see the calling function's value, and how the calling function can retrieve a value from the called function.

The ByVal modifier tells Visual Basic to push the entire contents of an argument onto the stack so they can be retrieved by the API, or called function. If you wanted to insulate this memory location from the API, your VB experience would dictate that you use the ByVal modifier so the argument's value is passed to the stack, and not its memory address (Figure 2.3). When working within the confines of Visual Basic, this is the expected and predictable result. However, when used with the API, the ByVal modifier is overloaded to mean something else.

FIGURE 2.2:

Passing arguments by reference

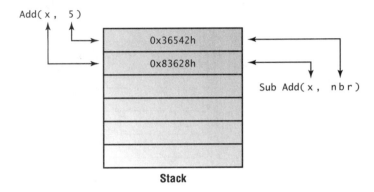

Stack

FIGURE 2.3:

Passing arguments by value

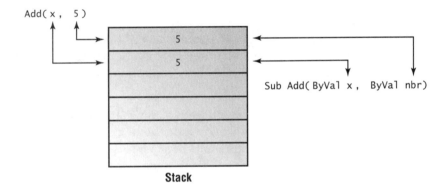

Stack

When using the API, ByVal is used to convert a Visual Basic string to a C string. Since C strings require a null-terminating character, Chr$(0), at the end of the string, ByVal was overloaded to produce this functionality. Even though you may think the argument's value is passed to the API, remember that all strings are passed by reference, even when you use ByVal. This can be confusing at first, but you will get the hang of this caveat by the end of this book.

So when working with the API, forget everything you learned in Visual Basic with regards to passing arguments and parameters. As you can see in Figure 2.4, the address of the variable is passed on the stack to the API, but a null-terminating character is added to the last byte of the memory address where the variable is stored.

FIGURE 2.4:

Passing string arguments to
an API with Byval

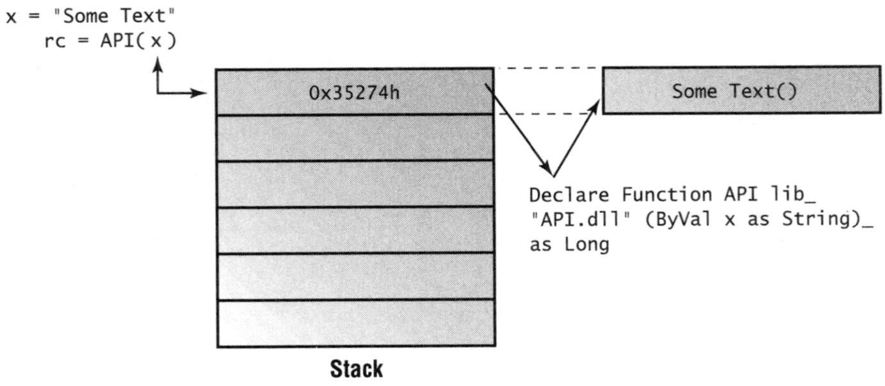

```
x = "Some Text"
  rc = API( x )
```

```
              0x35274h                              Some Text()

                              Declare Function API lib_
                              "API.dll" (ByVal x as String)_
                              as Long
```

Stack

If you are confused as to how this works, don't worry. At the end of this chapter I have included a table and some data type conversion guidelines to assist you through the conversion process. In addition, all API declarations described in this book are listed in both C notation, as you will most often find it, and in Visual Basic notation. This will allow you to constantly see how the parameters should be converted.

This is not all you will need to know about passing strings between APIs and Visual Basic. You will learn more of the caveats in a later section of this chapter that addresses the different character sets. After you learn how various character sets are handled, we will then cover data type conversions in detail, but let's finish covering the API declaration first.

Return Type

Referring back to the Declare statement, you know that the API can be declared as either a subroutine or a function. The API returns values from functions in much the same way as Visual Basic.

If the API you are declaring is a function, you will need to specify the return data type. Most often this will be a Long integer, but consult your API documentation to make sure.

Now you know what is involved in declaring APIs for use with Visual Basic. Before we go to the next chapter, you need to understand character sets and how they are handled in memory. These are the last gotchas that can make programming a nightmare if you don't understand exactly what is going on.

WARNING	When working with the API, make sure you declare the API properly. Make sure each argument is passed appropriately and that you use the right return type. And before you test the API, be sure to save your work! Otherwise you could lose it if the API call causes your program to crash, or worse, your system to hang.

Overview of Character Sets

Before we move on to converting data types, you should be aware of the various character sets used in the Windows API. By understanding which one is used, and why, you will be better equipped to correctly select APIs, declare them, and pass arguments to them.

There are three character sets that you will need to understand, and two that you will use with the Windows API. These are ANSI, the Multibyte Character Set (MBCS), and Unicode. You will most often use the ANSI character set, but when you start working with most of the APIs specific to Windows NT, you will work with the Unicode character set. Although you probably won't use it, the MBCS is covered to illustrate the transition from ANSI to Unicode.

ANSI

The original Windows API utilizes the ANSI character set when working with string data types. You are probably already familiar with ANSI, but here is a quick review.

The ANSI character set is the native character set of Windows 3.x and Windows 9x. It is an 8-bit character set that holds 256 characters. You have done most of your Visual Basic programming using this character set. It is the easiest character set to work with in Visual Basic, but also the most limited.

When an ANSI string is stored in memory, each character is stored using a single byte, and the whole string is comprised of an array of single-byte characters that make up the entire string. In Visual Basic you don't need to worry about how strings are stored in memory, because Visual Basic handles the memory management for you. In contrast, you are responsible to properly declare, store, and terminate the string in the C language. Since most APIs are written in C, you need to know how it works with strings.

The C language expects ANSI string parameters to be terminated with the null character, Chr$(0). So what is actually stored in memory is the array of bytes that makes up the actual string and a null-terminating character, as shown in Figure 2.5.

FIGURE 2.5:

Memory storage of ANSI string

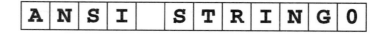

While ANSI is an easy character set to work with, its size limits its use, particularly when developing applications for different locales and languages. How could you represent the thousands of Chinese symbols with a character set that can only hold 256 characters?

Multibyte Character Set

There are thousands of different languages throughout the world, and they would be difficult to adequately represent using only 256 characters. Programmers recognized this issue and devised many ways of dealing with the problem. Some operating systems utilized multiple-code pages and others utilized multiple-byte character sets, such as the Double-Byte Character Set (DBCS).

Using DBCS, a character can be represented using either one or two bytes. The first 256 bytes are identical to the ANSI character set. However, additional characters are added for specific languages. Some of these characters use one byte, while others use two, one a leading and the other a trailing byte.

While it greatly expanded the possibilities, imagine trying to work with DBCS in all of your projects. Automatically, string manipulations become more complex because you need to manually parse each character to determine what it is. How would you handle a function such as Mid$() when you don't know if the extracted character is represented using a single byte or multiple bytes? You could have a string that contained five characters, but is eight bytes long. Imagine the headaches! Fortunately, another alternative was developed.

Unicode

Many of the limitations inherent in ANSI and DBCS are addressed in the Unicode character set. With Unicode, the programmer only needs to be concerned with one character set. Unicode takes MBCS a step further and uses two bytes (16 bits) to represent each character, regardless of which character it is. As a result, the Unicode character set can hold 65,536 distinct characters and symbols. The normal ANSI character set you are familiar with is still represented using two bytes per character. Using double bytes for every character allows Unicode to cumulatively represent all the languages in the world, as well as other symbols.

While this sounds like a great solution to address international issues, there are some drawbacks. First, all string data requires twice the amount of storage, as shown in Figure 2.6. As a result, your executables will be larger and text files will be twice as large.

FIGURE 2.6:

Memory storage of unicode string

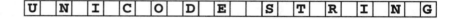

The second and more important drawback is that Unicode is not widely implemented, and this can make it difficult to distribute your application using a single-code base. This is apparent even with Microsoft's own operating systems. Unicode is supported natively in Windows NT, only somewhat in Windows 98, and unsupported in Windows 95. What does this mean for you the programmer? If you wish to develop an application that will run on all three platforms, you must program using APIs available on each platform. This means you should code your program using ANSI. The other option is to create individual projects, one for each platform, using different character sets for each.

Converting Data Types

As mentioned earlier, you will often have to convert C data types to their Visual Basic equivalents. This is a simple task when using numeric data, but is slightly trickier when working with strings. Working with strings is further complicated when you take various character sets such as ANSI and Unicode into account.

When working with arguments you will be passing numbers, strings, pointers, arrays, and structures. Each of these data types has their own declarations and calling conventions that you must understand before calling an API.

Numeric Data Types

There are several types of numeric arguments that you can pass to an API. You can pass integers, handles, device contexts, memory addresses, and many other Windows elements that are represented with numeric data.

If you are calling an API that does not modify the argument, precede the argument with ByVal in the declaration. For example, if you wanted to have the system sleep for a few seconds you could call the Sleep API, which is declared like this:

```
Declare Sub Sleep Lib "kernel32" _
    Alias "Sleep" _
    (ByVal dwMilliseconds As Long)
```

As you can see, the Sleep API requires the number of milliseconds to sleep. Since all it does is sleep, it does not modify dwMilliseconds, henceforth it is passed by value using the ByVal modifier.

Strings

Passing strings to DLLs is a bit tricky. To make a successful call, you must make sure you fully understand the requirements of the API and what it wants to do with the argument.

In C, strings are always passed by pointers. As such, strings will always be passed to the API by reference. Remember that the ByVal keyword is overloaded in Visual Basic. When it is used to pass strings between Visual Basic functions, the argument's value is passed. However, when it is used in an API declaration, it null terminates the string. Perhaps a C String modifier would have been better, as it precisely describes what is being passed. Maybe we can request it on the Visual Basic "wish list."

So why is the null-terminating character so important? The reason is that the C language, which most APIs were written in, needs to know where the end of the data is. Some APIs allow you to specify how long the string is, but others require the null character, which is actually Visual Basic's Chr$ (0). When the API receives the string parameter, remember that it is actually receiving an address. As a result, the API starts reading consecutive bytes starting at this memory location. As it reads each byte, it checks to see if the byte is the null-terminating character. If it finds one, the API stops reading bytes and returns the string data to the API. Otherwise, it concatenates the bytes together as it reads them. If the null-terminating character is omitted, the API will continue reading as far as it can.

Most likely the API, if not the entire program, will crash. So you can see why it is important to properly null-terminate your strings when the API expects it.

When an API requires a text buffer, you can either initialize a Visual Basic String data type or use a byte array.

Pointers

A pointer is a variable that contains the memory address indicating where the real contents of the variable are stored. As you learned previously, by default, Visual Basic passes arguments by reference. The same functionality is achieved in C by passing a pointer.

The Windows API only uses pointers to return values from the API. Since a function can only return one value, it is often necessary to return other values back through the arguments originally passed to the function. This is achieved by passing the arguments by reference.

When an API requires a pointer to a numeric value, such as LPHANDLE, LPD-WORD, or LPWORD, omit the ByVal modifier before the argument in the declaration.

All strings are passed to the API as pointers, so you don't need to do anything special with the declaration.

Some APIs require you to pass the address of a callback function. A callback is a Windows function called from within an API. You will see callbacks in many of the enumeration APIs, such as EnumWindows and EnumChildWindows. You pass this address using the AddressOf keyword.

Structures

C structures are the equivalent of Visual Basic's User-Defined Types (UDTs), which begin with the Type statement. When an API requires a structure, you need to make an equivalent UDT. In doing so, you also need to make sure you properly convert the individual elements from C to their equivalent Visual Basic data types. For example, the structure STARTUPINFO is shown below in C notation.

```
typedef struct _STARTUPINFO {
    DWORD cb;
    LPTSTR lpReserved;
    LPTSTR lpDesktop;
    LPTSTR lpTitle;
    DWORD dwX;
    DWORD dwY;
    DWORD dwXSize;
    DWORD dwYSize;
    DWORD dwXCountChars;
    DWORD dwYCountChars;
    DWORD dwFillAttribute;
    DWORD dwFlags;
    WORD wShowWindow;
    WORD cbReserved2;
    LPBYTE lpReserved2;
    HANDLE hStdInput;
    HANDLE hStdOutput;
    HANDLE hStdError;
} STARTUPINFO, *LPSTARTUPINFO;
```

The STARTUPINFO structure is represented in Visual Basic as:

```
Private Type STARTUPINFO
    cb As Long
    lpReserved As String
    lpDesktop As String
    lpTitle As String
    dwX As Long
    dwY As Long
    dwXSize As Long
    dwYSize As Long
    dwXCountChars As Long
    dwYCountChars As Long
    dwFillAttribute As Long
    dwFlags As Long
    wShowWindow As Integer
    cbReserved2 As Integer
    lpReserved2 As Long
    hStdInput As Long
    hStdOutput As Long
    hStdError As Long
End Type
```

When it comes time to declare the API, pass the structure by reference, as you can see in the following declaration:

```
Private Declare Function CreateProcessA Lib "kernel32" _
    (ByVal lpApplicationName As Long, _
    ByVal lpCommandLine As String, _
    ByVal lpProcessAttributes As Long, _
    ByVal lpThreadAttributes As Long, _
    ByVal bInheritHandles As Long, _
    ByVal dwCreationFlags As Long, _
    ByVal lpEnvironment As Long, _
    ByVal lpCurrentDirectory As Long, _
    lpStartupInfo As STARTUPINFO, _
    lpProcessInformation As PROCESS_INFORMATION) As Long
```

Note that the ByVal modifier is omitted for the lpStartupInfo and lpProcess-Information arguments. We want to pass the address to these structures so the API can access the structures' memory locations.

Arrays

Some APIs require arrays as arguments. Unlike Visual Basic, C doesn't know the size of an array. The programmer must inform the program what type of elements are in the array, and how many. The key to passing an array is to pass the array by reference. The argument's data type must also be defined. You pass the number of elements through another argument.

When you call the API, you pass the first element as an argument. For example, the GetPaletteEntries API retrieves a list of palette entries from the selected palette. These entries are returned through an array of PALETTENTRY structures, as follows:

```
Private Declare Function GetPaletteEntries Lib "gdi32" _
    Alias "GetPaletteEntries" _
    (ByVal hPalette As Long, _
    ByVal wStartIndex As Long, _
    ByVal wNumEntries As Long, _
    lpPaletteEntries As PALETTEENTRY) As Long
```

As you can see in the declaration, lpPaletteEntries is passed by reference, the starting entry is passed through the wStartIndex argument, and the number of entries requested is passed through the wNumEntries argument.

You would call this API as such:

```
          .
          .
          .
Dim lpPaletteEntries(256) as PALETTEENTRY
Dim rc as Long
          .
          .
          .
rc = GetPaletteEntries(hPalette, _
        wStartIndex, _
        wNumEntries, _
        lpPaletteEntries(0))
          .
          .
          .
```

WARNING   Be sure to pass the index of the first element when passing an array to an API. Omitting the index number will cause the API to fail and your system may crash!

Argument Conversion Table

If the preceding text seems overly complicated or is taking you awhile to digest, use Table 2.1 to assist you when working with API declarations.

TABLE 2.1: API Declarations

If the API requires...	Declare it as...
ATOM	ByVal *argument* as Integer
BOOL	ByVal *argument* as Long
BSTR (VB String)	*argument* as String
BYTE	ByVal *argument* as Byte
BYTE *	*argument* as Byte
char	ByVal *argument* as Byte

Continued on next page

TABLE 2.1 CONTINUED: API Declarations

If the API requires...	Declare it as...
char *	*argument* as Byte
DWORD	ByVal *argument* as Long
DWORD *	*argument* as Long
HANDLE	ByVal *argument* as Long
HANDLE *	*argument* as Long
int	ByVal *argument* as Long
INT	ByVal *argument* as Long
int *	*argument* as Long
LONG	ByVal *argument* as Long
LPARAM	ByVal *argument* as Long
LPBOOL	*argument* as Long
LPBYTE	*argument* as Integer
LPHANDLE	*argument* as Long
LPDWORD	*argument* as Long
LPWORD	*argument* as Integer
LPINT	*argument* as Long
LPUINT	*argument* as Long
LRESULT	ByVal *argument* as Long
LPSTR (C String)	ByVal *argument* as String
short	ByVal *argument* as Long
UINT	ByVal *argument* as Integer
UINT *	*argument* as Long
WORD	ByVal *argument* as Integer
WORD *	*argument* as Integer
WPARAM	ByVal *argument* as Long

After looking at the table, you may have noticed that many of the C data types have an asterisk after them. Also, most of the data types are actually different between languages.

You may see a data type with an asterisk after it in a C prototype. The asterisk indicates that the API expects a pointer to a variable of the type described. For example, if an API required a `char` data type, then you would declare the API with `ByVal char`. This would pass the value of `char` to the API. However, if the API wanted a pointer to a character (`char *`), then you could probably assume the API wants a string, and you are actually passing the address of the first byte. Most often, however, you will see a variable prefaced with something like `lp`, which means *long pointer*.

You may have noticed that most of the data types don't necessarily correspond as you might think they would. For example, when an API requires an unsigned integer (`UINT`), declare the parameter as a `Long` in Visual Basic. So why is there this difference?

As you will see throughout this book, there are several data types in C that have no equivalent in Visual Basic. Unsigned integers and unsigned `Long` integers are just a couple. You may have also noticed that an integer in C is equivalent to a `Long` in Visual Basic. In some situations you will need a way to convert data types between the two languages for the APIs to function properly.

So if some data types don't exist in Visual Basic, you need a way to convert data types back and forth. As mentioned previously, unsigned numeric values require special consideration when being converted. For example, an unsigned integer in C must be converted to a `Long` in Visual Basic because the unsigned integer has a maximum value of 65535. This may not seem like a problem until you realize that Visual Basic's `Integer` data type has a minimum value of –32768 and a maximum value of 32767. This gives the `Integer` an effective range of 65535, but a maximum upper limit of 32767, which is not enough if the unsigned integer returns a value equal to or higher than 32768.

This same theory applies to unsigned `Long` integers in C. You must use Visual Basic's `Double` data type, since it is the only data type large enough to accommodate the unsigned `Long`.

As you progress through the book, you will see both the C prototype and the corresponding Visual Basic declaration so you can compare their parameter types. After seeing them over and over you should have a better grasp of how the data types are converted. By the time you reach the end of this book, everything in this chapter should be second nature to you.

Now that you have had some theory, let's get our hands dirty and start wielding some code!

CHAPTER

THREE

Windows Messages

- Overview of Windows Messages

- Sending Messages

- Subclassing Windows

- Message Categories

- Combo Box Messages

- Edit Control Messages

- Windows Messages

- But Wait, There's More!

3

The fundamental process that makes Windows tick is called messaging. Almost every object within Windows is a window. You may think of Visual Basic forms as windows, and they are. But did you know that a button is also a window? So is a list box and many other controls you work with in Visual Basic.

When dealing with messages, you need to think in terms of windows rather than controls.

Overview of Windows Messages

Almost every window has an identifier called a *handle*. A handle is a 32-bit integer assigned to the window. You can obtain the handle to most Visual Basic controls through the hWnd property. In fact, hWnd actually stands for "handle to a window." When working with the Windows APIs, don't think of controls and windows like you do in Visual Basic. Instead of addressing them by their Name property, you will address them by their handle. In fact, most APIs require a handle of some sort, as you will see throughout this book.

Notice the form in Figure 3.1. To Visual Basic it is known as Form1. To Windows it is known as 876. To Visual Basic the button is known as Command1. To Windows it is known as 992. These numbers are examples and will probably be different on your system.

FIGURE 3.1:

Visual Basic uses Names, Windows uses Handles

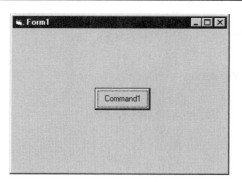

Every window has a message handler that processes Windows messages. Even Visual Basic forms have message handlers, you just don't see them. The events you are familiar with, such as Load, Activate, MouseDown, and Resize are procedures called by an internal message handler. A command button has a message handler as well. Its handler responds to messages such as WM_LBUTTONDOWN and WM_RBUTTONDOWN, which in turn fire the MouseDown event of the button. For every control that has an event, it also has a message handler.

A message handler is actually very simple. As you can see in Figure 3.2, the handler receives a message and responds to it or discards it, depending on the design of your application.

FIGURE 3.2:

The message handler

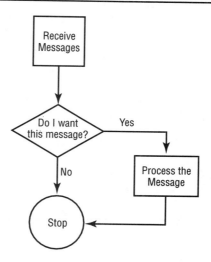

The code listed below shows a message handler written in Visual Basic. The code is fairly straightforward. All it does is accept a message and either respond to it or pass it on to another handler. Don't worry about the specifics here. This handler will be discussed in depth later in the chapter.

```
Public Function WindowProc(ByVal hw As Long, _
    ByVal uMsg As Long, _
    ByVal wParam As Long, _
    ByVal lParam As Long) As Long

    'Intercept appropriate messages...
    Select Case uMsg
        Case WM_MOUSEMOVE
            'Eat the message
            Debug.Print "WM_MOUSEMOVE"
        Case Else
            'Pass un-intercepted messages
            'on to the original handler
```

```
            WindowProc = CallWindowProc(lpPrevWndProc, _
                hw, _
                uMsg, _
                wParam, _
                lParam)
    End Select
End Function
```

You can think of a message as a command. When you send a message to a window, you are telling it to do something. When a window receives a message, it has the option to respond to, or ignore, the message. How the window behaves depends on its design. As you go through this chapter you will see how messages are sent and received. At the end of the chapter is a list of the more common messages you can use in your applications. The list is by no means all-inclusive. It would take a lot of paper to adequately describe all of the messages available to you, so only the most common and useful ones have been included here.

Sending Messages

Much of your programming efforts will involve sending messages to controls and windows. In fact, most of the functionality you can achieve through Visual Basic properties can be achieved using windows messages.

The two most common methods of sending messages are using the SendMessage and PostMessage APIs, discussed below. You will use SendMessage often, as you will see throughout this chapter.

SendMessage

Description

The SendMessage API is used to send messages to window controls that can be addressed with a handle.

VB Declaration

```
Private Declare Function SendMessage Lib "user32" _
    Alias "SendMessageA" _
    (ByVal hwnd As Long, _
```

```
    ByVal wMsg As Long, _
    ByVal wParam As Long, _
    lParam As Any) As Long
```

Parameters

Parameter	Description
hwnd	Handle to the window you are sending the message to.
wMsg	The message you are sending.
wParam	Use of wParam depends on the message you are sending.
lParam	Use of lParam depends on the message you are sending.

Notes

The SendMessage API waits for the message to be processed by its target before returning control to your application.

Example

The following example shows how you can use the WM_SETTEXT message to set the caption of a Visual Basic form. Note that all these messages, WM_SETTEXT and so on, can be found with the API Viewer.

```
Private Sub Command1_Click()
    Dim rc As Long
    Dim cap As String

    cap = "Sent Text" & Chr$(0)

    rc = SendMessage(hwnd, WM_SETTEXT, 0, ByVal cap)
End Sub
```

In the above example, the WM_SETTEXT message requires that the lParam argument be set to a buffer containing the text you wish to set. You can replace the handle with another value depending on what you want to set. For example, you could use the value Command1.hWnd to set the caption of a command button named Command1.

The following example uses the WM_CLOSE message to tell the Visual Basic form to close itself. You can send this message to another window if you have its handle.

```
Private Sub Command2_Click()
    Dim rc As Long

    rc = SendMessage(hwnd, WM_CLOSE, 0, 0)
End Sub
```

PostMessage

Description

The PostMessage API is an alternative to the SendMessage API. It differs from SendMessage in that it does not wait for the message to be processed before returning control to your application.

VB Declaration

```
Private Declare Function PostMessage Lib "user32" _
    Alias "PostMessageA" _
    (ByVal hwnd As Long, _
    ByVal wMsg As Long, _
    ByVal wParam As Long, _
    ByVal lParam As Long) As Long
```

Parameters

Parameter	Description
hwnd	Handle to the window you are sending the message to.
wMsg	The message you are sending.
wParam	Use of wParam depends on the message you are sending.
lParam	Use of lParam depends on the message you are sending.

Notes

Unlike the SendMessage API, PostMessage returns control immediately to your application rather than waiting for the message to be processed by its target.

Example

This example shows how you can use the PostMessage API to send keystrokes to a window. This algorithm was used in a word expander to send keystrokes to Microsoft Word and other editors, such as Notepad and Wordpad. If you are adventurous enough, you could write your own SendKeys utility.

```
Private Sub Command1_Click()
    Dim i As Integer
    Dim rc As Long
    Dim buff As String

    buff = "This text was sent through messages."

    For i = 1 To Len(buff)
        rc = PostMessage(txtText.hwnd, _
            WM_CHAR, _
            Asc(Mid$(buff, i, 1)), _
            0)
    Next
End Sub
```

In this example, the WM_CHAR message expects the wParam argument to be set to the ASCII value of the character to be sent. You will learn more about windows messages later in this chapter.

Subclassing Windows

As you have seen, sending messages using the SendMessage API is easy. All you need to do is select the message you wish to send and pass the appropriate arguments. Sending messages can add significant functionality to controls that were left out for one reason or another.

Responding to messages is fairly easy in Visual Basic. Most forms and controls have event handlers that actually intercept the most common windows messages for you. But now you're in the big leagues and you want more power. You need to start intercepting and responding to other messages.

You can add your own message handler in Visual Basic using a technique known as *subclassing*. Subclassing is the process of hooking into a window's message handler and trapping selected messages within your own message handler. You can hook another window's message handler using the SetWindowLong API, which allows you to change the address table for a window. Doing so allows you to replace a window's address with your own. The result is that something will be redirected to the address you pass to the API. The code to hook into another window is shown below:

```
Public Function Hook(hwnd As Long) As Long
    'Set the global hwWnd variable
    ghWnd = hwnd

    'Set WindowProc to intercept window messages sent
    'to ghWnd
    lpPrevWndProc = SetWindowLong(ghWnd, _
        GWL_WNDPROC, _
        AddressOf WindowProc)

    'Set return code
    Hook = 0
End Function
```

The first thing done here was to take the handle to the window and set a global variable. This will allow you to access this handle from other functions you will need. So you might ask why the example didn't use a property to store the handle. Simply put, a message handler must be placed in a standard module for it to work. As a result, all of the subclassing code in this chapter will reside in a single module.

The next step is to store the address of the existing message processor for ghWnd. This is returned from SetWindowLong and stored in lpPrevWndProc. We will need this later to unhook from the handler.

The arguments for SetWindowLong are simple. The first argument is the handle of the window you want to modify. The second argument is the offset of the address you want to modify. The GWL_WNDPROC constant tells the API that you want to change the address of the message handler for the window. The final argument is the new address. The AddressOf keyword allows you to obtain the address of a procedure in Visual Basic so it can be passed to an API. Using the

`AddressOf WindowProc` argument, you are passing the address of your own message handler to the window. The result is that all of the target window's messages will pass through your message handler!

Whenever you subclass a window you must properly unhook it when you are done, or you will most likely experience unpredictable behavior in your system. You can reverse the hook by calling `SetWindowLong` with the handle you originally retained when you established the hook. Use the code below to unhook your message handler:

```
Public Function Unhook() As Long
    Dim rc As Long

    'Set the message handler back to the original
    rc = SetWindowLong(ghWnd, GWL_WNDPROC, _
            lpPrevWndProc)

    'Return the result code
    Unhook = rc
End Function
```

This `Unhook` function is straightforward. You simply pass back the address you obtained in `lpPrevWndProc`. This will set the address of `GWL_WNDPROC` back to its original address.

The message handling code is actually quite simple, as you will see. The function is structured to receive the arguments in the same manner and order that `SendMessage` dispatches them. You have the same four arguments: the window's handle, the message, and two additional arguments.

To make your message handler work, all you need to do is add the appropriate messages in the `Select Case` handler and call your code.

```
Public Function WindowProc(ByVal hw As Long, _
    ByVal uMsg As Long, _
    ByVal wParam As Long, _
    ByVal lParam As Long) As Long

    'Intercept appropriate messages...
    Select Case uMsg
        Case WM_MOUSEMOVE
            'Eat the message
            Debug.Print "WM_MOUSEMOVE"
```

```
        Case Else
            'Pass un-intercepted messages
            'on to the original handler
            WindowProc = CallWindowProc(lpPrevWndProc, _
                hw, _
                uMsg, _
                wParam, _
                lParam)
    End Select
End Function
```

When the target window receives a message, it gets passed to the address specified by GWL_WNDPROC. Since you replaced this address, the message gets passed to your handler, WindowProc. Since you are responding to messages, the first thing you want to do is check the message argument, uMsg. This is done in the Select Case block above. You can add a Case statement for each message you wish to trap. Once you have a message trapped, you can examine the values stored in wParam and lParam. What you do with these values will depend on which message you are processing. You can look up the meaning of these arguments at the end of this chapter.

Since all messages are now being routed through your program, you need a way to pass back the unused ones so the target window can continue about its business. Your job when subclassing a window is to achieve your functionality while being as unobtrusive as possible. If you don't intercept a message, you should pass it back to the target window. Since you retained the address of the target's message handler, you can call the CallWindowProc API and pass the message back to the target's message handler.

TIP   The complete source code for the subclassing module is located on the Sybex Web site at www.sybex.com.

Message Categories

There are hundreds, if not thousands, of messages used throughout Windows. Most Windows controls have a set of messages they can receive and respond to. Fortunately, these messages are easily identifiable based on their prefix. For example, general windows messages are prefixed with the letters WM and an underscore.

Table 3.1 shows many of the categories of messages and their respective prefixes.

TABLE 3.1: Message Categories

Prefix	Category
BM_	Button message.
BN_	Button notification message.
CB_	Combo box message.
CBN_	Combo box notification message.
CDM_	Common dialog message.
DRV_	Driver message.
EM_	Edit control message.
EN_	Edit control notification message.
IMC_	Input method editor message.
IMN_	Input method editor notification message.
LB_	List box message.
LBN_	List box notification message.
MIM_	MIDI input message.
MOM_	MIDI output message.
SB_	Status bar message.
SBM_	Scroll bar message.
WM_	General windows message.

Because there are so many messages available, it would require a complete book just to cover them adequately. As a result, not all of the messages are covered here. Instead, the more common and useful messages you are likely to encounter while working with Visual Basic will be addressed.

Combo Box Messages

Before looking at combo box messages it is important to understand the makeup of a combo box control. A combo box is actually two controls combined. One control is an edit box. This is where you type directly into the combo box control. The second component is a list box control. You can see these components in Figure 3.3.

FIGURE 3.3:

Combo box controls

Various messages deal with each individual subcomponent.

Most of the functionality provided by the following messages is already built into the intrinsic Visual Basic combo box control.

CB_ADDSTRING

Description

The CB_ADDSTRING message is used to add a string to a combo box. This is the same as Visual Basic's AddItem method.

Parameters

Parameter	Description
wParam	Unused. Set to 0.
lParam	Address to the string to be added.

Example

```
Dim buff As String
Dim rc as Long

buff = "Item 1"

rc = SendMessage(cboItems.hWnd, _
        CB_ADDSTRING, 0, ByVal buff)
```

CB_DELETESTRING

Description

The CB_DELETESTRING message is used to delete an item from a combo box. This is similar to the RemoveItem method.

Parameters

Parameter	Description
wParam	Index of the item to delete.
lParam	Unused. Set to 0.

Example

```
Dim rc as Long

rc = SendMessage(cboItems.hWnd, _
        CB_DELETESTRING, 3, 0)
```

CB_DIR

Description

The CB_DIR message allows you to quickly add a list of files to the combo's list box.

Parameters

Parameter	Description
wParam	File attributes mask.
lParam	The path and filespec, such as *.* or *.txt, that you wish to include in the list portion of the combo box.

Notes

You can restrict or expand the list of files to include by setting wParam to the appropriate attributes. For example, you could set wParam to DDL_HIDDEN to add all the hidden files in the directory. The following is a list of attributes you can use:

```
DDL_ARCHIVE
DDL_DIRECTORY
DDL_DRIVES
DDL_EXCLUSIVE
DDL_HIDDEN
DDL_READONLY
DDL_READWRITE
DDL_SYSTEM
```

Example

The following code shows how you can add the list of drives on your system to a combo box:

```
Dim rc As Long
Dim path As String

path = App.path

rc = SendMessage(cboCombo.hwnd, _
     CB_DIR, _
     DDL_DRIVES, _
     ByVal path)
```

CB_FINDSTRING

Description

The CB_FINDSTRING message adds significant power to a combo box. Sending this message causes the list box portion of a combo box to find an item that begins with the text specified in `lParam`. If the command is successful, `SendMessage` returns the index position of the match within the list.

Parameters

Parameter	Description
wParam	The index before the first item you want to search. If you want to search the entire list, set this to –1.
lParam	Buffer to the string to search for.

Example

```
Dim buf As String

buf = Trim$(txtItems.Text)

cboItems.ListIndex = SendMessage(cboItems.hwnd, _
        CB_FINDSTRING, -1, ByVal buf)
```

CB_FINDSTRINGEXACT

Description

The `CB_FINDSTRINGEXACT` message finds a list item that exactly matches the text specified in `lParam`.

Parameters

Parameter	Description
wParam	The index before the first item you want to search. If you want to search the entire list, set this to –1.
lParam	Buffer to the string to search for.

Example

```
Dim buf As String

buf = Trim$(txtItems.Text)
```

```
cboItems.ListIndex = SendMessage(cboItems.hwnd, _
        CB_FINDSTRINGEXACT, -1, ByVal buf)
```

CB_GETCOUNT

Description

The CB_GETCOUNT message allows you to retrieve the number of items in the combo's list box. This is the same as retrieving the combo's ListCount property.

Parameters

Parameter	Description
wParam	Unused. Set to 0.
lParam	Unused. Set to 0.

Example

```
Dim rc As Long

rc = SendMessage(cboCombo.hwnd, _
        CB_GETCOUNT, 0, 0)
```

CB_GETCURSEL

Description

Sending the CB_GETCURSEL message returns the index of the current selection within the list box portion of the combo box. This is the equivalent of Visual Basic's ListIndex property.

Parameters

Parameter	Description
wParam	Unused. Set to 0.
lParam	Unused. Set to 0.

Example

```
Dim rc As Long

rc = SendMessage(cboCombo.hwnd, _
        CB_GETCURSEL, 0, 0)
```

CB_GETDROPPEDSTATE

Description

Send the CB_GETDROPPEDSTATE message to a combo box to determine if the list box is dropped down or not. If the list box is opened, then SendMessage returns True. Otherwise, it returns False.

Parameters

Parameter	Description
wParam	Unused. Set to 0.
lParam	Unused. Set to 0.

Example

```
Dim rc As Long

rc = SendMessage(cboCombo.hwnd, _
        CB_GETDROPPEDSTATE, 0, 0)
```

CB_GETEDITSEL

Description

The CB_GETEDITSEL message is used to return the starting and ending positions of the selection within the edit portion of a combo box control. If this message call is successful, then the wParam argument returns the equivalent of Visual Basic's .SelStart property. Visual Basic's .SelLength property is the equivalent of the formula lParam–wParam.

Parameters

Parameter	Description
wParam	Returns the starting position of the selection.
lParam	Returns the ending position of the selection.

Example

```
Dim rc As Long
Dim startPos As Long
Dim endPos As Long

rc = SendMessage(cboCombo.hwnd, _
        CB_GETEDITSEL, startPos, endPos)
```

CB_GETEXTENDEDUI

Description

Send the CB_GETEXTENDEDUI message to determine if a combo box control has an extended user interface. If it does, then SendMessage returns True.

Parameters

Parameter	Description
wParam	Unused. Set to 0.
lParam	Unused. Set to 0.

Example

```
Dim rc As Long

rc = SendMessage(cboCombo.hwnd, _
        CB_GETEXTENDEDUI, 0, 0)
```

CB_GETLBTEXT

Description

The CB_GETLBTEXT message returns the text of a list item in the list box portion of a combo box control.

Parameters

Parameter	Description
wParam	The index to retrieve.
lParam	Pointer to a buffer to return the listitem text.

Example

In this example, the second item in the combo box is returned. Keep in mind that combo boxes start with a 0 index.

```
Dim rc As Long
Dim buff As String * 255
Dim index As Long

index = 1
rc = SendMessage(cboCombo.hwnd, _
        CB_GETLBTEXT, index, ByVal buff)
```

CB_GETLBTEXTLEN

Description

The CB_GETLBTEXTLEN message returns the length of a list item in the list box portion of a combo box control. If the call is successful, SendMessage returns the length of the text in bytes.

Parameters

Parameter	Description
wParam	The index of the item you wish to examine.
lParam	Unused. Set to 0.

Example

In this example, the length of the second item in the combo box is returned.

```
Dim rc As Long
Dim index As Long

index = 1
rc = SendMessage(cboCombo.hwnd, _
        CB_GETLBTEXTLEN, index, 0)
```

CB_LIMITTEXT

Description

The CB_LIMITTEXT message is sent to set the maximum length of the text within the editable portion of the combo box.

Parameters

Parameter	Description
wParam	The maximum length of the text allowed in the edit box.
lParam	Unused. Set to 0.

Example

If you wanted to restrict a combo to five characters, you would call SendMessage with CB_LIMITTEXT, as shown below:

```
Private Sub cmdLimitText_Click()
    Dim rc As Long

    rc = SendMessage(cboCombo.hwnd, _
        CB_LIMITTEXT, 5, 0)
End Sub
```

CB_RESETCONTENT

Description

The CB_RESETCONTENT message is used to clear the combo of all items, including typed text. This is the equivalent of the .Clear method of the combo box control.

Parameters

Parameter	Description
wParam	Unused. Set to 0.
lParam	Unused. Set to 0.

Example

```
Dim rc as Long

rc = SendMessage(cboCombo.hWnd, _
        CB_RESETCONTENT, 0, 0)
```

CB_SELECTSTRING

Description

The CB_SELECTSTRING message is the same as the CB_FINDSTRING message, but when a match is found it is copied into the edit control portion of the combo box control.

Parameters

Parameter	Description
wParam	Starting index. Use –1 to search the entire list.
lParam	Pointer to the string to search for.

Example

This example will search the entire list for the word HELLO. Notice that the string to be searched must have a null character appended.

```
Dim rc As Long
Dim findString As String

findString = "HELLO" & Chr$(0)
rc = SendMessage(cboCombo.hwnd, _
        CB_SELECTSTRING, -1, ByVal findString)
```

CB_SETCURSEL

Description

Send the CB_SETCURSEL message to select an item in the list portion of the combo box control. This is the same as setting the .ListIndex property.

Parameters

Parameter	Description
wParam	Index of the item to select.
lParam	Unused. Set to 0.

Example

This example points to the second item in the list. To retrieve that item name, send the result of this code to CB_GETLBTEXT.

```
Dim rc As Long

rc = SendMessage(cboCombo.hwnd, _
        CB_SETCURSEL, 1, 0)
```

CB_SETEXTENDEDUI

Description

The CB_SETEXTENDEDUI message sets the extended user interface on a combo box that has a style of Dropdown or DropdownList.

Parameters

Parameter	Description
wParam	Set to True to make the combo box use the extended interface.
lParam	Unused. Set to 0.

Example

This example allows the drop-down combo box to be opened by using the down arrow. If a 0 is passed as the wParam parameter it turns off the extended user interface, which means the down arrow is no longer used for opening the drop-down combo box.

```
Dim rc As Long

rc = SendMessage(cboCombo.hwnd, _
        CB_SETEXTENDEDUI, 1, 0)
```

CB_SHOWDROPDOWN

Description

The CB_SHOWDROPDOWN message shows or hides the list box portion of a combo box control.

Parameters

Parameter	Description
wParam	True to show the list, False to hide it.
lParam	Unused. Set to 0.

Example

Sending this message is easy, as you can see:

```
Private Sub cmdOpen_Click()
    Dim rc As Long
```

```
rc = SendMessage(cboNames.hWnd, _
        CB_SHOWDROPDOWN, _
        True, 0)
End Sub
```

Calling this procedure repeatedly acts like a toggle, alternatively opening and closing the combo box.

Edit Control Messages

Visual Basic's text box control is a subclassed version of the windows edit control. As a result, you can use most edit control messages on the text box control in your Visual Basic applications.

Most of the functionality provided by the following messages is already built into the intrinsic Visual Basic text box control.

EM_CANUNDO

Description

Send the EM_CANUNDO message to determine if an edit control can undo an operation, such as pasting data from the clipboard. SendMessage will return True if the edit control supports EM_CANUNDO.

Parameters

Parameter	Description
wParam	Unused. Set to 0.
lParam	Unused. Set to 0.

Example

```
Dim rc As Long

rc = SendMessage(txtText.hwnd, _
        EM_CANUNDO, 0, 0)
```

EM_EMPTYUNDOBUFFER

Description

Send the EM_EMPTYUNDOBUFFER message to an edit control to clear the undo buffer for the control.

Parameters

Parameter	Description
wParam	Unused. Set to 0.
lParam	Unused. Set to 0.

Example

```
SendMessage(txtText.hwnd, _
            EM_EMPTYUNDOBUFFER, 0, 0)
```

EM_GETFIRSTVISIBLELINE

Description

The EM_GETFIRSTVISIBLELINE message returns the index of the first visible line of a text box that has its .MultiLine property set to True.

Parameters

Parameter	Description
wParam	Unused. Set to 0.
lParam	Unused. Set to 0.

Example

```
Dim rc As Long

rc = SendMessage(txtText.hwnd, _
        EM_GETFIRSTVISIBLELINE, 0, 0)
```

EM_GETHANDLE

Description

The EM_GETHANDLE message returns the handle to the memory containing the text within a multi-line edit control.

Parameters

Parameter	Description
wParam	Unused. Set to 0.
lParam	Unused. Set to 0.

Example

```
Dim rc As Long

rc = SendMessage(txtText.hwnd, _
        EM_GETHANDLE, 0, 0)
```

EM_GETLINE

Description

The EM_GETLINE message copies a line of text from an edit control to a user-defined buffer.

Parameters

Parameter	Description
wParam	Index to the line you want to copy. It is ignored if the edit control is a single-line control.
lParam	Address of the buffer to store the line of text.

Example

This example returns the second line of a multi-line text box. The buffer to hold the line needs to be filled with spaces. Also remember that in a multi-line text box, the first line is referenced from a 0 starting point.

```
Dim rc As Long
Dim buff As String

buff = Space$(20)
rc = SendMessage(txtText.hwnd, _
        EM_GETLINE, 1, ByVal buff )
```

EM_GETLINECOUNT

Description

The EM_GETLINECOUNT message returns the number of lines in a multi-line edit control.

Parameters

Parameter	Description
wParam	Unused. Set to 0.
lParam	Unused. Set to 0.

Example

```
Dim rc As Long
    rc = SendMessage(txtBuffer.hwnd, _
        EM_GETLINECOUNT, 0, 0)
```

EM_GETMODIFY

Description

Send the EM_GETMODIFY message to determine if the contents of an edit control have been modified. SendMessage returns True if the text has been modified.

Parameters

Parameter	Description
wParam	Unused. Set to 0.
lParam	Unused. Set to 0.

Example

```
Dim dirtyflag As Long
dirtyflag = SendMessage(txtBuffer.hwnd, _
            EM_GETMODIFY, 0, 0)
```

EM_GETPASSWORDCHAR

Description

Sending the EM_GETPASSWORDCHAR message makes SendMessage return the password character defined for an edit control.

Parameters

Parameter	Description
wParam	Unused. Set to 0.
lParam	Unused. Set to 0.

Example

This example returns the character code that was used to encrypt the password. By default, this is the asterisk (*) character, which is a 42 value.

```
Dim rc As Long

rc = SendMessage(txtBuffer.hwnd, _
     EM_GETPASSWORDCHAR, 0, 0)
```

EM_GETSEL

Description

Sending the EM_GETSEL message to an edit control returns the starting and ending positions of the selection within the edit control.

Parameters

Parameter	Description
wParam	Starting position of the text you wish to retrieve.
lParam	Ending position of the text you wish to retrieve.

Example

```
Dim rc As Long
Dim startpos As Long
Dim endpos As Long

rc = SendMessage(txtText.hwnd, _
        EM_GETSEL, startpos, endpos)
```

EM_LIMITTEXT

Description

You can limit the amount of text an edit control will allow by sending the EM_LIMITTEXT message to the edit control.

Parameters

Parameter	Description
wParam	Maximum length allowed in the edit control.
lParam	Unused. Set to 0.

Example

```
Dim rc As Long

rc = SendMessage(txtBuffer.hWnd, _
        EM_LIMITTEXT, 5, 0)
```

EM_LINELENGTH

Description

Sending the EM_LINELENGTH message to an edit control returns the length in bytes of the line specified in wParam.

Parameters

Parameter	Description
wParam	Index of the line you wish to work with.
lParam	Unused. Set to 0.

Example

```
Dim rc As Long

rc = SendMessage(txtBuffer.hWnd, _
        EM_LINELENGTH, 1, 0)
```

EM_LINESCROLL

Description

Use the EM_LINESCROLL message to scroll a multi-line edit box horizontally or vertically. SendMessage will return True on success, or False if the edit control is not multi-line.

Parameters

Parameter	Description
wParam	Number of characters to scroll horizontally.
lParam	Number of characters to scroll vertically.

Example

This example will scroll the multi-line textbox up five rows and over five columns.

```
Dim rc As Long

rc = SendMessage(txtBuffer.hWnd, _
        EM_LINESCROLL, 5, 5 )
```

EM_REPLACESEL

Description

Use the EM_REPLACESEL message to replace the selected text with the contents of a buffer.

Parameters

Parameter	Description
wParam	Boolean value to determine if the action can be undone.
lParam	Pointer to a buffer containing the text that will replace the selection.

Example

```
Dim rc As Long
Dim buff As String

buff = "Newtext" & Chr$(0)
rc = SendMessage(txtText.hwnd, _
        EM_REPLACESEL, True, ByVal buff)
```

EM_SETHANDLE

Description

Send the EM_SETHANDLE message to a multi-line edit control to set the handle of the edit control buffer to a buffer you allocate in memory.

Parameters

Parameter	Description
wParam	Handle to the memory you allocated for the edit control to use.
lParam	Unused. Set to 0.

Example

```
Dim rc As Long
Dim newbuffer As Long

rc = SendMessage(txtText.hwnd, _
        EM_SETHANDLE, newbuffer, 0)
```

EM_SETMODIFY

Description

The EM_SETMODIFY message sets or clears the modification bit, often called the dirty flag, of an edit control.

Parameters

Parameter	Description
wParam	Boolean value used to set the modification bit.
lParam	Unused. Set to 0.

Example

```
SendMessage(txtText.hwnd, _
        EM_SETMODIFY, 1 , 0)
```

EM_SETPASSWORDCHAR

Description

The EM_SETPASSWORDCHAR message sets the character used to cover up text when an edit control is set to password mode. This is the same as setting the .PasswordChar property of a text box control.

Parameters

Parameter	Description
wParam	ASCII value of the character to be used as the password mask.
lParam	Unused. Set to 0.

Example

This example sets the password character to an exclamation point.

```
Dim rc As Long

rc = SendMessage(txtText.hwnd, _
        EM_SETPASSWORDCHAR, 33, 0)
```

EM_SETREADONLY

Description

Send the EM_SETREADONLY message to an edit control to make it read-only. This is the same as setting the .Locked property of a text box to True.

Parameters

Parameter	Description
wParam	Boolean value that says to set or clear the read-only style bit of the edit control.
lParam	Unused. Set to 0.

Example

```
SendMessage txtEditor.hWnd, _
             EM_SETREADONLY, True, 0
```

EM_SETSEL

Description

Send the EM_SETSEL message to highlight the text that lies between the values passed between wParam and lParam.

Parameters

Parameter	Description
wParam	Starting position of the selection.
lParam	Ending position of the selection.

Example

This example shows how to highlight eight characters of text starting at the 10th byte in the edit control.

```
SendMessage txtEditor.hWnd, _
             EM_SETSEL, 10, 17
```

Windows Messages

Under Windows, applications wait for the operating system to send the application a message. These messages are then acted on by your program. There is a plethora of windows messages that can be sent by Windows to your application. While there are numerous messages, not all have to be handled by the application. Any messages that are not directly handled by your application are passed back to windows to process it.

WM_CHAR

Description

The WM_CHAR message is sent to a control when a key is pressed on the keyboard. Use this message to simulate keystrokes, much like the SendKeys command in Visual Basic. For more information on sending keystrokes, refer to Chapter 10, *Working with the Keyboard and Mouse.*

Parameters

Parameter	Description
wParam	ASCII value for the key you wish to send.
lParam	Extended information about the key pressed.

Example

This example sends the letter A to the text box.

```
Dim rc As Long

rc = SendMessage(txtText.hwnd, _
      WM_CHAR, 65, 1)
```

WM_CHILDACTIVATE

Description

The WM_CHILDACTIVATE message is sent to an MDI child window when it receives the focus and when it is moved or resized.

Parameters

Parameter	Description
wParam	Unused. Set to 0.
lParam	Unused. Set to 0.

Example

```
Dim rc As Long

rc = SendMessage(hwnd, _
        WM_CHILDACTIVATE, 0, 0)
```

WM_CLEAR

Description

The WM_CLEAR message is sent to an edit control to instruct it to clear the current selection.

Parameters

Parameter	Description
wParam	Unused. Set to 0.
lParam	Unused. Set to 0.

Example

```
Dim rc As Long

rc = SendMessage(txtText.hwnd, _
        WM_CLEAR, 0, 0)
```

WM_CLOSE

Description

The WM_CLOSE message is sent to instruct a window to close. This message is particularly useful when you want to tell a window to close that is outside your application. It is also useful when you want to detect when your application has been instructed to close.

Parameters

Parameter	Description
wParam	Unused. Set to 0.
lParam	Unused. Set to 0.

Example

```
Dim rc As Long

rc = SendMessage(hwnd, _
        WM_CLOSE, 0, 0)
```

WM_COPY

Description

The WM_COPY message is sent to an edit or combo box control to cause the control to copy its contents to the clipboard. The same functionality can be achieved by calling the Clipboard.SetData method in Visual Basic.

Parameters

Parameter	Description
wParam	Unused. Set to 0.
lParam	Unused. Set to 0.

Example

```
Dim rc As Long

rc = SendMessage(txtText.hwnd, _
        WM_COPY, 0, 0)
```

WM_CUT

Description

The WM_CUT message is sent to a control that supports clipboard operations to cause the control to cut its contents to the clipboard. The same functionality can be achieved by calling the Clipboard.SetData method and clearing the data from the control.

Parameters

Parameter	Description
wParam	Unused. Set to 0.
lParam	Unused. Set to 0.

Example

```
Dim rc As Long

rc = SendMessage(txtText.hwnd, _
        WM_CUT, 0, 0)
```

WM_DESTROY

Description

A window receives the WM_DESTROY message after its form has been removed, but before the window is removed from memory.

Parameters

Parameter	Description
wParam	Unused. Set to 0.
lParam	Unused. Set to 0.

Example

```
Dim rc As Long

rc = SendMessage(hwnd, _
      WM_DESTROY, 0, 0)
```

WM_GETTEXT

Description

The WM_GETTEXT message tells an edit control to copy the selected text into a buffer.

Parameters

Parameter	Description
wParam	The number of bytes to copy.
lParam	Address of the buffer that will receive the text.

Example

This example copies the first nine characters from the text box into the variable buff. The 10th character is the null character.

```
Dim rc As Long
Dim buff As String

Buff = Space$(20)
rc = SendMessage(txtText.hwnd, _
      WM_GETTEXT, 10, ByVal buff)
```

WM_KEYDOWN

Description

The WM_KEYDOWN message is posted to a window when a non-system key is pressed. You can send this message using the PostMessage API.

Parameters

Parameter	Description
wParam	Virtual key code of the key pressed on the keyboard. This will not always be the ASCII value of the key.
lParam	Additional key data.

Example

```
Dim rc As Long

rc = SendMessage(txtText.hwnd, _
     WM_KEYDOWN, 65, 1)
```

WM_KEYUP

Description

The WM_KEYUP message is received when a key is released on the keyboard. This message is handled through Visual Basic's KeyUp event.

Parameters

Parameter	Description
wParam	Virtual key code.
lParam	Additional key data.

Example

```
Dim rc As Long

rc = SendMessage(txtText.hwnd, _
     WM_KEYUP, 65, 1)
```

WM_MDICASCADE

Description

The WM_MDICASCADE message instructs MDI child windows to arrange themselves in a cascading format within the MDI parent window.

Parameters

Parameter	Description
wParam	The only supported flag is MDITILE_SKIPDISABLED.
lParam	Unused. Set to 0.

Example

This example instructs the mdiWindow application to cascade its child windows.

```
Dim rc As Long

rc = SendMessage(mdiWindow.hwnd, _
        WM_MDICASCADE, MDITILE_SKIPDISABLED, 0)
```

WM_MDIICONARRANGE

Description

The WM_MDIICONARRANGE message instructs MDI child windows to arrange themselves as icons within the MDI parent window.

Parameters

Parameter	Description
wParam	Unused. Set to 0.
lParam	Unused. Set to 0.

Example

This example causes the MDI application to rearrange all of its minimized child windows.

```
Dim rc As Long

rc = SendMessage(mdiWindow.hwnd, _
        WM_MDIICONARRANGE, 0, 0)
```

WM_MDIMAXIMIZE

Description

The WM_MDIMAXIMIZE message instructs an MDI child window to maximize itself.

Parameters

Parameter	Description
wParam	Handle of the child window to maximize.
lParam	Unused. Set to 0.

Example

This example causes the MDI application to maximize this particular child window.

```
Dim rc As Long

rc = SendMessage(mdiWindow.hwnd, _
        WM_MDIMAXIMIZE, mdiChild.hwnd, 0)
```

WM_MDIRESTORE

Description

The WM_MDIRESTORE message instructs an MDI child window to restore itself to its previous state.

Parameters

Parameter	Description
wParam	Handle to the MDI child window to restore.
lParam	Unused. Set to 0.

Example

This example causes the MDI application to restore this particular child window.

```
Dim rc As Long

rc = SendMessage(mdiWindow.hwnd, _
        WM_MDIRESTORE, mdiChild.hwnd, 0)
```

WM_MDITILE

Description

The WM_MDITILE message instructs an MDI parent window to arrange its MDI child windows in a tile format.

Parameters

Parameter	Description
wParam	Tiling flags. Specifying MDITILE_HORIZONTAL will tile the child windows horizontally. Specifying MDITILE_VERTICAL will tile the child windows vertically. MDITILE_SKIPDISABLED can be specified if you don't want to tile disabled child windows.
lParam	Unused. Set to 0.

Example

This example causes the MDI application to tile all of its child windows.

```
Dim rc As Long

rc = SendMessage(mdiWindow.hwnd, _
        WM_MDITILE, MDITILE_HORIZONTAL, 0)
```

WM_MOUSEMOVE

Description

The WM_MOUSEMOVE message is posted to a window when the mouse moves over the window. Visual Basic handles this message through the MouseMove event.

Parameters

Parameter	Description
wParam	Can be one of the following: MK_CONTROL, MK_LBUTTON, MK_MBUTTON, MK_RBUTTON, MK_SHIFT, MK_XBUTTON1, or MK_XBUTTON2.
lParam	Horizontal and vertical position.

Example

This sample code sends a message to the application, pointed to by hwnd, that the left mouse button was pressed at the location of y = 100, x = 300.

```
Dim rc As Long

rc = SendMessage(hwnd, _
        WM_MOUSEMOVE, MK_LBUTTON, 1000300)
```

WM_PASTE

Description

The WM_PASTE message is sent to a control that supports cut and paste functions. Sending this message is the equivalent of calling the Clipboard.GetData method in Visual Basic.

Parameters

Parameter	Description
wParam	Unused. Set to 0.
lParam	Unused. Set to 0.

Example

This example pastes the information from the clipboard into the text box.

```
Dim rc As Long

rc = SendMessage(txtText.hwnd, _
        WM_PASTE, 0, 0)
```

WM_QUIT

Description

The WM_QUIT message is sent to a window to request that it be destroyed.

Parameters

Parameter	Description
wParam	The exit code.
lParam	Unused.

Example

```
Dim rc As Long

rc = SendMessage(hwnd, _
        WM_QUIT, 0, 0)
```

WM_SETTEXT

Description

The WM_SETTEXT message sets the text of the destination window.

Parameters

Parameter	Description
wParam	Unused. Set to 0.
lParam	Address of the buffer containing the text.

Example

This example shows how to set the caption of the default form. By changing the handle in SendMessage, you can set the caption on a button and the text within a text box control.

```
Dim buff As String

buff = "This was sent through a message!"

SendMessage hwnd, WM_SETTEXT, 0, ByVal buff
```

WM_UNDO

Description

The WM_UNDO message is sent to undo the last operation in an edit box. This is useful when you are writing your own text editors that require undo functionality.

Parameters

Parameter	Description
wParam	Unused. Set to 0.
lParam	Unused. Set to 0.

Example

```
Private Sub mnuEditUndo_Click()
    SendMessage txtBuffer.hwnd, WM_UNDO, 0, 0
End Sub
```

WM_USER

Description

The WM_USER message is not so much a message as it is a base constant to which an offset is added to define a new message. For example, the WM_CHOOSEFONT _SETFLAGS message is defined by adding 102 to WM_USER, as shown:

```
WM_CHOOSEFONT_SETFLAGS = (WM_USER + 102)
```

But Wait, There's More!

As you can see, there are a number of messages you can use in your applications. You can use them as notifications to your application through subclassing, and send them to other controls and applications using the `SendMessage` and `PostMesage` APIs. If you want to know more about these messages, as well as others, go to the Microsoft Developers Network at `http://msdn.microsoft.com`.

Memory Management

When working with the Windows API it is important that you understand the various forms of memory and how they work. Without a good grasp of how memory works, it will be difficult to work with the more advanced APIs.

Understanding how memory is allocated and accessed is especially important when you work with the Windows API because you are actually making two different languages work together. The way they do this is by properly communicating what memory locations are used and how they are used.

As you read in Chapter 1, strings are passed to APIs by reference. That is, their memory address is passed so the API can have direct access to the same memory location that Visual Basic is using. If either Visual Basic or the API misinterpret or misuse the memory, the API call can crash.

Memory Defined

In Windows there are basically two types of memory: random access memory, also known as RAM, and virtual memory. These two types of memory work together to enable you to boot the system, run applications, surf the Internet, and everything else you do.

RAM is like a workspace. Consider for a moment the physical desktop you work on, not the Windows desktop. When you work on a project, you take the paperwork out of a folder in a drawer and place it on your desktop. When you are done with the task you put it back in its folder in the drawer.

If you are a busy person, you will often take out more than one thing to work on. Since you are a programmer you probably pull out your CDs, notepad, pencils, programming books, and a 12-pack of soda. I'm sure your desktop gets pretty full. So what do you do next?

If you're like me, you revert to putting the books on the floor, place the soda within arm's reach, and scatter your papers all over the desk where nobody can find them but you.

Since I put my books on the floor, I can easily grab one and bring it up to my desktop and read it. When I'm done I put it back. Basically speaking, I have virtually unlimited workspace.

Virtual memory works in the same manner. As you load up more and more applications or open large documents, you consume memory. Windows itself eats up a considerable amount. In fact, if it weren't for virtual memory, Windows 95 couldn't run on a 486 with 8 MB of RAM. It's slow, but it does work.

Windows swaps memory much like you swap books. In fact, RAM acts much like a cache for your most recently used applications and data. As you use something it gets pulled into RAM so you can work with it quickly. If something else is open, but you're not using it at the moment, Windows will take a snapshot of its memory footprint and write it to disk, and then free the memory for something else. When you need it again, Windows will load the program and data back into RAM and possibly write something else to the hard disk. This process is called swapping. The file that Windows swaps data into is called a swap file and is actually a form of virtual memory.

When Windows boots, it knows that it actually has more memory available to it than the physical RAM installed on the motherboard. As a result, Windows anticipates using virtual memory in addition to RAM.

Memory Models

There are two types of memory models: segmented and flat. Back in the days when 32-bit operating systems were non-existent, computers generally came with small quantities of RAM. My Commodore Vic-20 actually had a whopping 4 KB of RAM! This small amount of RAM made it easy for 8-bit hardware to access all of the memory contiguously. In essence, early computers used a flat memory model.

As software demands grew, so did memory requirements. Unfortunately, as memory was added, processors with wider busses were not readily available. As a result, software developers had to devise memory-addressing techniques to access memory beyond the computer's normal limits. Enter the segmented memory model.

The Segmented Memory Model

The early IBM PCs came with 256 KB of RAM. At the time nobody ever thought it would get used up. When it did, computers were updated progressively as applications demanded. Soon enough there was so much memory that the computer couldn't address all of it cleanly.

To get around this, systems were designed to use a segment address and an off-set address. This allowed the system to address much more memory than the original system design. By using a segment and offset, programmers could finally do more with the computer, but it was more difficult to write code that could work in that manner. Figure 4.1 shows how the segmented memory model works.

FIGURE 4.1:

The segmented memory model

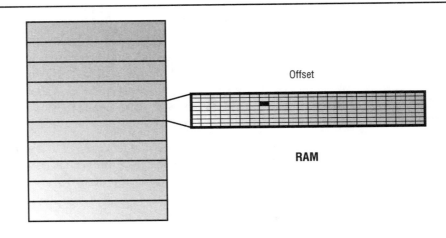

The Flat Memory Model

With the advent of the 32-bit operating system, the limitations of computer memory were blown off the map. Since it is mathematically possible to count into the trillions in 32-bit binary, programmers could directly access memory without having to fiddle with segments and offsets.

The result of the 32-bit operating system is the flat memory model, as shown in Figure 4.2. As you can see, there are no segments or blocks of memory to worry about. Using the flat memory model you can basically access any portion of memory without having to jump through hoops to do it. In addition, memory chunks can be larger.

Remember the 64 KB limit for controls in Visual Basic 3? They disappeared with the 32-bit version of Visual Basic 4. Versions 5 and 6 are purely 32-bit development environments, so they don't have the same memory restrictions from the days of old.

FIGURE 4.2:

The flat memory model

RAM

Working with Memory

In Visual Basic you are shielded from much of the memory management required to make a program tick. Assembler didn't have memory management. C was not much better and that is the language the API was developed with. C++ got a little better with memory management, but Visual Basic is a breeze.

In the Windows environment you can easily allocate memory. However, since Windows also swaps memory around behind the scenes you need to lock it and keep a handle to it. And like your mom always told you as a kid, you need to clean up after yourself. This is especially important when dealing with computers. Nobody likes an application that takes memory and holds onto it after the program dies.

Windows provides several APIs that allow you to allocate and lock memory for use with other APIs. These APIs are described below.

GlobalAlloc

Description

The GlobalAlloc API is used to allocate a chunk of memory from the global heap.

C Prototype

```
HGLOBAL GlobalAlloc(UINT uFlags,
    DWORD dwBytes);
```

VB Declaration

```
Private Declare Function GlobalAlloc Lib "kernel32" _
    (ByVal wFlags As Long, _
    ByVal dwBytes As Long) As Long
```

Parameters

Parameter	Description
wFlags	Flags that can be combined to specify the type of memory allocation.
dwBytes	The number of bytes to allocate.
Returns	On success, the API returns a handle to the allocated memory. Otherwise it returns 0.

Notes

You can use any of the following constants in the wFlags property when allocating memory. Use GMEM_FIXED if you want to allocate a fixed block of memory. Use GMEM_MOVEABLE when you want to allocate a moveable block of memory. If you want to initialize the memory with zeros, specify GMEM_ZEROINIT in the wFlags argument.

Example

```
Dim hMem as Long

hMem = GlobalAlloc(GMEM_ZEROINIT, 255)
```

GlobalReAlloc

Description

The GlobalReAlloc API re-allocates a previously allocated chunk of memory. You can call this API to increase the chunk of memory you previously allocated with GlobalAlloc.

C Prototype

```
HGLOBAL GlobalReAlloc(HGLOBAL hMem,
    DWORD dwBytes,
    UINT uFlags);
```

VB Declaration

```
Private Declare Function GlobalReAlloc _
    Lib "kernel32" _
    Alias "GlobalReAlloc" _
    (ByVal hMem As Long, _
    ByVal dwBytes As Long, _
    ByVal wFlags As Long) As Long
```

Parameters

Parameter	Description
hMem	Handle to the memory that was previously allocated using GlobalAlloc.
dwBytes	The number of bytes to allocate.
wFlags	Flags that can be combined to specify the type of memory allocation. Refer to the Notes under GlobalAlloc for more information.
Returns	Returns the handle to the allocated memory on success, or 0 on failure.

Example

```
Dim hMem as Long

hMem = GlobalAlloc(GMEM_ZEROINIT, 255)
.
.
.
hMem = GlobalReAlloc(hMem, 512, GMEM_ZEROINIT)
```

GlobalLock

Description

The GlobalLock API is used to lock memory allocated with GlobalAlloc. The memory must be locked before it can be used. Otherwise, Windows may move the memory around and your handle to it will become invalid. If this API call is successful, it will return a handle to the locked memory and increase the lock count of the memory by 1.

C Prototype

```
LPVOID GlobalLock(HGLOBAL hMem);
```

VB Declaration

```
Private Declare Function GlobalLock Lib "kernel32" _
    (ByVal hMem As Long) As Long
```

Parameters

Parameter	Description
hMem	Handle of the memory to lock.
Returns	Returns a handle to the locked memory.

Example

```
Dim hMem as Long
Dim hLock as Long

hMem = GlobalAlloc(GMEM_ZEROINIT, 255)
If hMem <> 0 Then
    hLock = GlobalLock(hMem)
    .
    .
    .
```

GlobalFree

Description

When you are done with your chunk of memory, release it with the GlobalFree API. This also decreases the lock count by 1.

C Prototype

```
HGLOBAL GlobalFree(HGLOBAL hMem);
```

VB Declaration

```
Private Declare Function GlobalFree Lib "kernel32" _
    (ByVal hMem As Long) As Long
```

Parameters

Parameter	Description
hMem	Handle to the allocated memory you want to free.
Returns	Returns 0 on success, or the handle to the allocated memory on failure.

Example

```
Dim hMem as Long

hMem = GlobalAlloc(GMEM_ZEROINIT, 255)
If hMem <> 0 Then
    .
    .
    .
    GlobalFree hMem
End If
```

GlobalUnlock

Description

When you are done working with locked memory you must unlock it with the GlobalUnlock API.

C Prototype

```
BOOL GlobalUnlock(HGLOBAL hMem);
```

VB Declaration

```
Private Declare Function GlobalUnlock Lib "kernel32" _
    (ByVal hMem As Long) As Long
```

Parameters

Parameter	Description
hMem	Handle to the locked memory.
Returns	Returns True on success, False on failure.

Example

```
Dim hMem as Long
Dim hLock as Long

hMem = GlobalAlloc(GMEM_ZEROINIT, 255)
If hMem <> 0 Then
    hLock = GlobalLock(hMem)
    If hLock<>0 Then
        .
        .
        .
        GlobalUnlock hLock
    End If

    GlobalFree hMem
End If
```

CopyMemory

Description

The CopyMemory API allows you to copy data from one memory location to another.

C Prototype

```
VOID CopyMemory (PVOID Destination,
    CONST VOID *Source,
    DWORD Length);
```

VB Declaration

```
Private Declare Sub CopyMemory Lib "kernel32" _
    Alias "RtlMoveMemory" _
    (Destination As Any, _
    Source As Any, _
    ByVal Length As Long)
```

Parameters

Parameter	Description
Destination	Address of the destination memory block.
Source	Address of the source memory block.
Length	The size, in bytes, of the block to copy.
Returns	None

Example

```
Dim Destination As Long
Dim Source As Long

CopyMemory Destination, Source, 4
```

ZeroMemory

Description

The ZeroMemory API fills a chunk of memory with zeros. This is useful when initializing a newly created buffer.

C Prototype

```
VOID ZeroMemory(PVOID Destination,
    DWORD Length);
```

VB Declaration

```
Private Declare Sub ZeroMemory Lib "KERNEL32" _
    Alias "RtlMoveMemory" _
    (dest As Any, _
    ByVal numBytes As Long)
```

Parameters

Parameter	Description
dest	Address of the buffer to fill.
numBytes	Number of bytes to fill.
Returns	None

Example

The following example shows how to use the APIs to allocate and lock global memory, and then unlock and release it:

```
Dim hMem As Long
Dim hLockedMem As Long
Dim rc As Long

'Allocate some memory
hMem = GlobalAlloc(GMEM_MOVEABLE Or GMEM_ZEROINIT, 512)
If hMem <> 0 Then
    'Lock the memory
    hLockedMem = GlobalLock(hMem)

    'Do something...

    'Always unlock the memory
    rc = GlobalUnlock(hLockedMem)

    'Release the memory
    rc = GlobalFree(hMem)
End If
```

Virtual Memory

Virtual memory is disk space that is read from and written to when RAM is full. Virtual memory gives the illusion of unlimited memory by linking a small chunk of RAM with a large chunk of memory stored on a disk device, as shown in Figure 4.3. As the RAM gets full, other inactive applications and/or data get swapped to the swap file on the hard drive to make room in RAM. Since RAM is significantly faster than virtual memory, it makes sense to keep the active applications in RAM so the user gets the perception of speed.

FIGURE 4.3:

Virtual memory

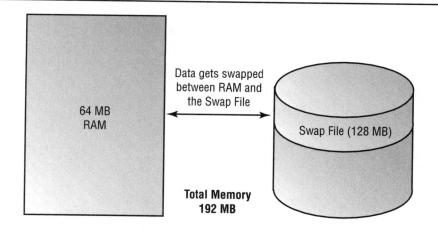

By using virtual data you actually make room for more applications and data than you normally could with RAM alone. In fact, your actual memory capacity becomes the sum of your RAM plus the size of your swap file.

NOTE   In Windows NT, the swap file is also known as a *paging file*.

Although you will probably never need to use them, there are several APIs that allow you to work with the virtual memory in Windows. These APIs are described below.

VirtualAlloc

Description

The VirtualAlloc API allocates a chunk of virtual memory.

C Prototype

```
LPVOID VirtualAlloc(LPVOID lpAddress,
    DWORD dwSize,
    DWORD flAllocationType,
    DWORD flProtect);
```

VB Declaration

```
Private Declare Function VirtualAlloc Lib "kernel32" _
    Alias "VirtualAlloc" _
    (lpAddress As Any, _
    ByVal dwSize As Long, _
    ByVal flAllocationType As Long, _
    ByVal flProtect As Long) As Long
```

Parameters

Parameter	Description
lpAddress	Set to 0 to let the system set the starting address of the allocated memory.
dwSize	The amount of memory to allocate.
flAllocationType	The type of allocation to perform. Can be a combination of the following: MEM_COMMIT, MEM_RESERVE, MEM_TOP_DOWN, MEM_PHYSICAL, MEM_RESET, or MEM_WRITE_WATCH.
flProtect	The memory protection mode to use if MEM_COMMIT is selected in flAllocationType. Can be any of the following: PAGE_READONLY, PAGE_READWRITE, PAGE_EXECUTE, PAGE_EXECUTE_READ, PAGE_EXECUTE_READWRITE, PAGE_GUARD, PAGE_NOACCESS, or PAGE_NOCACHE.

Returns   On success, this API returns the address of the first byte of allocated memory. If it fails, the API returns 0.

VirtualLock

Description

The VirtualLock API is used to lock a chunk of virtual memory in RAM and prevent it from being swapped to the swap file.

C Prototype

```
BOOL VirtualLock(LPVOID lpAddress,
    DWORD dwSize);
```

VB Declaration

```
Private Declare Function VirtualLock Lib "kernel32" _
    Alias "VirtualLock" _
    (lpAddress As Any, _
    ByVal dwSize As Long) As Long
```

Parameters

Parameter	Description
lpAddress	The address in memory to lock.
dwSize	Size of memory to lock.
Returns	Returns True on success, False on failure.

VirtualUnlock

Description

The VirtualUnlock API unlocks a chunk of allocated virtual memory.

C Prototype

```
BOOL VirtualUnlock(LPVOID lpAddress,
    DWORD dwSize);
```

VB Declaration

```
Private Declare Function VirtualUnlock Lib "kernel32" _
    Alias "VirtualUnlock" _
    (lpAddress As Any, _
    ByVal dwSize As Long) As Long
```

Parameters

Parameter	Description
lpAddress	Address of locked memory.
dwSize	Size of memory to be unlocked.
Returns	Returns True on success, False on failure.

VirtualFree

Description

The VirtualFree API releases a chunk of allocated virtual memory.

C Prototype

```
BOOL VirtualFree(LPVOID lpAddress,
    DWORD dwSize,
    DWORD dwFreeType);
```

VB Declaration

```
Private Declare Function VirtualFree Lib "kernel32" _
    Alias "VirtualFree" _
    (lpAddress As Any, _
    ByVal dwSize As Long, _
    ByVal dwFreeType As Long) As Long
```

Parameters

Parameter	Description
lpAddress	Address of the memory to be released.
dwSize	The amount of memory to be released.

dwFreeType   Use MEM_DECOMMIT to free the memory but keep it
                               reserved. Use MEM_RELEASE to completely free and
                               release the memory.

Returns   Returns True on success, False on failure.

The Stack

The stack is an area of memory used to temporarily hold data and the addresses
of variables between function calls. As shown in Figure 4.4, the stack works in a
last-in, first-out manner, much like a stack of dishes. When data is pushed onto
the stack, everything currently in the stack is shifted downward. When the data is
popped off of the stack, everything else shifts up.

FIGURE 4.4:

The stack

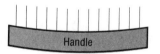
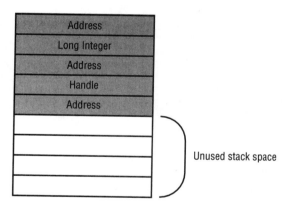

In some circumstances you can completely fill up the stack until it cannot hold
any more data. When this happens you will get a Stack Overflow error. The most
common cause of a stack overflow is a recursive function that repeatedly calls
itself and pushes data on the stack without pulling it off. If you receive a stack
overflow error message you should first look for any recursive code.

The Heap

The heap is a chunk of memory reserved for an application to store variables whose number and size cannot be determined until run time. Visual Basic uses the heap to store information about the controls and data within your application. It is unlikely that you will work with the heap directly, so the APIs are not covered here.

Moving On

There are many things you will do with the APIs that require some form of memory management. You will see several examples as you progress through the book. You will find yourself working with memory, especially when you work with large buffers like those used for bitmapped data and data structures. You will get some experience with these in the latter chapters of the book.

Now that you have had an adequate dose of API theory, let's get into the practical application of the Windows API.

CHAPTER

FIVE

5

Obtaining System Information

- General Windows APIs

- Hardware Settings

- Building the Object Library

Visual Basic comes with a plethora of controls and ActiveX objects that make your programming job easier, but Visual Basic does not include objects that retrieve information about your computer system. For example, how would you determine what processor your computer uses or how much memory your computer has? The SysInfo control allows you to determine the version and platform of Windows, but lacks additional functionality that is extremely useful.

This chapter covers the APIs that yield important information about your system. This information can be useful when you write applications that require specific hardware configurations, such as multimedia kiosks or network administration tools. In addition, it is important to know what environment your application runs on because many APIs are different between Windows 9x and Windows NT/2000.

While working through this chapter, you will not only learn the APIs, but will develop memory, processor, and operating system classes. Then you will create a system information viewer, shown in Figure 5.1, to demonstrate how the APIs and classes function.

FIGURE 5.1:

System information viewer

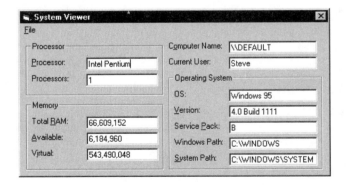

General Windows APIs

Perhaps the most common system-related APIs are those that describe Windows and its environment. Using the API you can retrieve important and common information, such as the Windows platform, version, build number, and current service pack, as well as the paths to the Windows and System directories. It is important for the Visual Basic programmer to understand how to retrieve these values, as they are commonly used to install applications and determine if certain applications can even run on particular platforms.

It's often necessary to retrieve the name of the folder where Windows is installed. This is especially useful if you have Windows 9x and Windows NT installed on the same machine in a dual-boot configuration. You may want to install an application on one platform, but keep it separated from the other. Or perhaps you want to maintain separate configurations of your application for each platform.

The key to achieving this functionality is to avoid hard coding. The major disadvantage to hard coding is that your application makes assumptions about the system it's installed on. For example, suppose your application needs to store an initialization file in the Windows folder. If you hard code this location to be C:\Windows, your application will break when it gets installed on a computer where the user installed Windows to C:\Win95 or C:\WinNT. You can avoid this problem by using the GetWindowsDirectory API to let Windows tell you where it lives.

In addition to retrieving the Windows directory, you will often need to retrieve the Windows\System directory. This is the folder where most of your DLLs and other Windows applets reside.

TIP   Determining the location of your Windows folder and its System folder is especially important when writing setup applications or platform-specific applications.

GetWindowsDirectory

Description

The GetWindowsDirectory API is used to retrieve the name of the directory in which Windows 9x or Windows NT is installed.

C Prototype

```
UINT GetWindowsDirectory(
    LPTSTR lpBuffer,
    UINT uSize);
```

VB Declaration

```
Private Declare Function GetWindowsDirectory _
    Lib "kernel32" _
    Alias "GetWindowsDirectoryA" _
    (ByVal lpBuffer As String,
    ByVal nSize As Long) As Long
```

Parameters

Parameter	Description
lpBuffer	Buffer string used to store the result.
nSize	Long integer containing the maximum size of the buffer.
Returns	On success, the length of the path stored in lpBuffer, otherwise 0.

Example

Before calling the API you need to create a buffer large enough to hold the complete path to the Windows directory. Then pass this buffer and the size of the buffer as arguments to the function. If the function is successful, lpBuffer will contain the path to your Windows folder, and nSize will be set to the length of the path in bytes. Consider the following code:

```
Public Function WindowsPath() As String
    Dim rc As Long
    Dim lpBuffer As String
    Dim nSize As Long

    nSize = 255
    lpBuffer = Space$(nSize)
    rc = GetWindowsDirectory(lpBuffer, nSize)

    If rc <> 0 Then
        WindowsPath = Left$(lpBuffer, rc)
    Else
        WindowsPath = ""
    End If
End Function
```

As you can see, nSize is set to 255, which is how many bytes of memory Visual Basic will allocate for lpBuffer. The actual memory allocation is achieved using the Space$() function. Once these variables are set, they are passed by reference so the function can write directly to the memory space allocated by Visual Basic. If the function call is successful, it will return the length of the full path to the Windows directory.

GetSystemDirectory

Description

The GetSystemDirectory API returns the name of the Windows \System or \System32 folder.

C Prototype

```
UINT GetSystemDirectory(
    LPTSTR lpBuffer,
    UINT uSize);
```

VB Declaration

```
Private Declare Function GetSystemDirectory _
    Lib "kernel32" _
    Alias "GetSystemDirectoryA"
    (ByVal lpBuffer As String, _
    ByVal nSize As Long) As Long
```

Parameters

Parameter	Description
lpBuffer	Buffer string used to store the result.
nSize	Long integer containing the size of the buffer.
Returns	On success, the length of the path stored in lpBuffer, otherwise 0.

Example

The GetSystemDirectory function works in the same manner as its GetWindows-Directory counterpart; simply allocate an adequately sized buffer and call the function appropriately, as shown in the code below:

```
Public Function SystemPath() As String
    Dim rc As Long
    Dim lpBuffer As String
    Dim nSize As Long

    nSize = 255
    lpBuffer = Space$(nSize)
    rc = GetSystemDirectory(lpBuffer, nSize)

    If rc <> 0 Then
        SystemPath = Left$(lpBuffer, rc)
    Else
        SystemPath = ""
    End If
End Function
```

GetVersionEx

Description

The GetVersionEx API retrieves information about the Windows platform and version.

C Prototype

```
BOOL GetVersionEx(
    LPOSVERSIONINFO lpVersionInformation);
```

VB Declaration

```
Private Declare Function GetVersionEx _
    Lib "kernel32" _
    Alias "GetVersionExA" _
    (lpVersionInformation As OSVERSIONINFO) As Long
```

Parameters

Parameter	Description
lpVersionInformation	An OSVERSIONINFO structure that will be populated with the data. Refer to the Notes below.
Returns	Returns True on success, False on error.

Example

```
Dim osVer As OSVERSIONINFO
Dim rc As Long

osVer.dwOSVersionInfoSize = Len(osVer)

rc = GetVersionEx(osVer)
```

Notes

Before passing this structure to the function, you must set the dwOSVersionInfo-Size member to the size of the structure. This is best achieved using the Len() function:

```
lpVersionInformation.dwOSVersionInfoSize = _
    Len(lpVersionInformation)
```

The OSVERSIONINFO structure is listed below:

```
Private Type OSVERSIONINFO
    dwOSVersionInfoSize As Long
    dwMajorVersion As Long
    dwMinorVersion As Long
    dwBuildNumber As Long
    dwPlatformId As Long
    szCSDVersion As String * 128
End Type
```

As already noted, dwOSVersionInfoSize contains the size of the structure. dwMajorVersion, dwMinorVersion, and dwBuildNumber contain the components that make up the Windows version. The dwPlatformID member contains a Long value that represents the Windows platform; i.e., Windows 95 or Windows NT. Finally, szCSDVersion contains the Corrective Service Disk (CSD), or service pack number.

GetComputerName

Description

The GetComputerName API retrieves the name of the computer. This is the name you see in the Network Neighborhood.

C Prototype

```
BOOL GetComputerName(LPTSTR lpBuffer,
    LPDWORD nSize);
```

VB Declaration

```
Private Declare Function GetComputerName _
    Lib "kernel32" _
    Alias "GetComputerNameA" _
    (ByVal lpBuffer As String, _
    nSize As Long) As Long
```

Parameters

Parameter	Description
lpBuffer	Buffer string used to store the result.
nSize	Long integer containing the size of the buffer.
Returns	Returns True on success, False on error.

Example

```
Dim rc As Long
Dim strCN As String
Dim nSize As Long

nSize = 255
strCN = Space$(nSize)

rc = GetComputerName(strCN, nSize)
```

Notes

Allocate an adequately sized buffer before calling this API.

GetUserName

Description

Use the GetUserName API to get the name of the user logged into Windows.

C Prototype

```
BOOL GetUserName(LPTSTR lpBuffer,
    LPDWORD nSize);
```

VB Declaration

```
Private Declare Function GetUserName _
    Lib "advapi32.dll" _
    Alias "GetUserNameA" _
    (ByVal lpBuffer As String, _
    nSize As Long) As Long
```

Parameters

Parameter	Description
lpBuffer	Buffer string used to store the result.
nSize	Long integer containing the size of the buffer.
Returns	Returns True on success, False on error.

Example

```
Dim rc As Long
Dim strUN As String
Dim nSize As Long

nSize = 255
strUN = Space$(nSize)

rc = GetUserName(strUN, nSize)
```

Notes

Allocate an adequately sized buffer before calling this API.

ExitWindowsEx

Description

The ExitWindowsEx API allows you to log off, shutdown, or reboot your computer.

C Prototype

```
BOOL ExitWindowsEx(
    UINT uFlags,
    DWORD dwReserved);
```

VB Declaration

```
Private Declare Function ExitWindowsEx _
    Lib "user32" _
    (ByVal uFlags As Long, _
    ByVal dwReserved As Long) As Long
```

Parameters

Parameter	Description
uFlags	Any of the following appropriate constants: EWX_LOGOFF, EWX_SHUTDOWN, EWX_REBOOT, EWX_FORCE, EWX_POWEROFF, and EWX_FORCE-IFHUNG.
dwReserved	Set this value to 0.
Returns	Returns True on success, False on error.

Example

```
rc=ExitWindowsEx(EWX_LOGOFF, 0)
```

Notes

The easiest task to accomplish with this function is to log off the system. If you are using Windows NT, you need to give your process token shutdown privileges to shut down or reboot the system. For more information, refer to the example later in this chapter.

Hardware Settings

In addition to obtaining information about Windows, it's useful to obtain the basic information about your hardware configuration, including memory and processor type. Perhaps you have developed a graphics application that requires a great deal of memory. Using the memory-related APIs, such as GlobalMemory-Status, would help make your application aware of its environment. If the user's system does not have enough memory to run your application, you can display a dialog, rather than let the user continue while the computer screeches to a halt as memory gets used.

In addition, mathematical and scientific applications tend to be processor-intensive. It would be useful if your application knew whether the hardware it runs on could handle the intensive processing.

The next two APIs, GlobalMemoryStatus and GetSystemInfo, will allow you to retrieve the appropriate memory and processor information.

GlobalMemoryStatus

Description

The GlobalMemoryStatus API returns information pertaining to your system's memory configuration.

C Prototype

```
void GlobalMemoryStatus(LPMEMORYSTATUS lpBuffer);
```

VB Declaration

```
Private Declare Sub GlobalMemoryStatus _
    Lib "kernel32" _
    (lpBuffer As MEMORYSTATUS)
```

Parameters

Parameter	Description
lpBuffer	A pointer to a MEMORYSTATUS structure that will be filled with memory information.
Returns	None

Example

```
Dim memstatus As MEMORYSTATUS

GlobalMemoryStatus memstatus
```

Notes

There are no special requirements when using this function. Simply declare a variable of the MEMORYSTATUS data type and pass it to GlobalMemoryStatus. The MEMORYSTATUS structure is detailed below:

```
Private Type MEMORYSTATUS
    dwLength As Long
    dwMemoryLoad As Long
    dwTotalPhys As Long
    dwAvailPhys As Long
    dwTotalPageFile As Long
    dwAvailPageFile As Long
    dwTotalVirtual As Long
    dwAvailVirtual As Long
End Type
```

The most important member is dwTotalPhys, which returns the amount of physical RAM installed. In addition, the dwAvailPhys member yields the amount of physical RAM available at the time of the function call.

GetSystemInfo

Description

The GetSystemInfo API returns information about the system, particularly information about your processor(s).

C Prototype

```
VOID GetSystemInfo(
    LPSYSTEM_INFO lpSystemInfo);
```

VB Declaration

```
Private Declare Sub GetSystemInfo _
    Lib "kernel32" _
    (lpSystemInfo As SYSTEM_INFO)
```

Parameters

Parameter	Description
lpSystemInfo	A pointer to a SYSTEM_INFO structure that will be filled with memory information. Refer to the Notes below.
Returns	None

Example

```
Dim SystemStatus As SYSTEM_INFO

GetSystemInfo SystemStatus
```

Notes

You can retrieve processor information from the dwNumberOfProcessors and dwProcessorType members of the SYSTEM_INFO structure, as shown below:

```
Private Type SYSTEM_INFO
    dwOemID As Long
    dwPageSize As Long
    lpMinimumApplicationAddress As Long
    lpMaximumApplicationAddress As Long
    dwActiveProcessorMask As Long
    dwNumberOfProcessors As Long
    dwProcessorType As Long
    dwAllocationGranularity As Long
    dwReserved As Long
End Type
```

As you can probably gather, dwNumberOfProcessors returns a Long integer representing the number of processors installed in the system. This will generally be 1 unless you are working with server-class computer systems.

Perhaps the more descriptive member is dwProcessorType, which returns a Long integer representing the processor type. Fortunately, these values can easily be mapped to the following constants:

```
Private Const PROCESSOR_INTEL_386 = 386
Private Const PROCESSOR_INTEL_486 = 486
Private Const PROCESSOR_INTEL_PENTIUM = 586
Private Const PROCESSOR_MIPS_R4000 = 4000
Private Const PROCESSOR_ALPHA_21064 = 21064
```

Building the Object Library

Now that you have seen the various system-related APIs, you can encapsulate them into classes so you can reuse them in your projects.

Let's start by examining the system class sample code in this chapter, which will provide information about Windows.

The following code is used to obtain system information before the class is accessed by the user. The reason for this is that the data will not change, and you don't want to waste precious CPU cycles by calling these routines over and over when you only want to obtain one value. Instead, obtain the values now, and store them in `Private` variables that can be read when the user accesses a particular property. Listing 5.1, and the listings that follow, pulls the various system APIs together into an application.

LISTING 5.1   Retrieving System Information

```
Private Sub Class_Initialize()
  Dim osvi As OSVERSIONINFO

  'Get Windows information
  osvi.dwOSVersionInfoSize = Len(osvi)
  If GetVersionEx(osvi) <> 0 Then
      If osvi.dwPlatformId = _
          VER_PLATFORM_WIN32_WINDOWS Then
              mOS = "Windows 95"
      End If

      If osvi.dwPlatformId = VER_PLATFORM_WIN32_NT Then
          mOS = "Windows NT"
      End If

      mVersion = Trim$(CStr(osvi.dwMajorVersion)) & _
          "." & Trim$(CStr(osvi.dwMinorVersion))
      mBuild = Trim$(CStr(osvi.dwBuildNumber _
          And &HFFFF&))
      mCSD = Trim$(CStr(osvi.szCSDVersion))
  Else
      mOS = ""
      mVersion = ""
      mBuild = ""
```

```
      mCSD = ""
   End If

   'Get the Windows Information
   GetWindowsInfo

   'Get the UserID and Computer Name
   GetNetworkInfo
End Sub
```

The code to retrieve the system information is executed in the `Initialize` event. For the sake of code clarity, Windows and network information is collected in the `GetWindowsInfo` and `GetNetworkInfo` procedure calls, as shown below:

```
Private Sub GetWindowsInfo()
   Dim rc As Long
   Dim lpBuffer As String
   Dim nSize As Long

   'Create a buffer large ennough to hold
   'the Windows directory
   nSize = 255
   lpBuffer = Space$(nSize)

   'Call the API
   rc = GetWindowsDirectory(lpBuffer, nSize)

   If rc <> 0 Then
       'Return the Windows directory
       mWindowsPath = Left$(lpBuffer, _
           InStr(lpBuffer, Chr$(0)) - 1)
   Else
       mWindowsPath = ""
   End If

   'Reset the buffer
   lpBuffer = Space$(nSize)

   'Call the API
   rc = GetSystemDirectory(lpBuffer, nSize)

   If rc <> 0 Then
```

```
            'Return the System directory
            mWindowsSystemPath = Left$(lpBuffer, _
                InStr(lpBuffer, Chr$(0)) - 1)
      Else
            mWindowsSystemPath = ""
      End If
End Sub
```

The GetNetworkInfo API retrieves the username and the name of the workstation. These values are handy to have if you require any form of user management or tracking. As you can see from the code below, these API calls are simple:

```
Private Sub GetNetworkInfo()
  Dim rc As Long
  Dim lpBuffer As String
  Dim nSize As Long

  'Create a buffer large ennough to hold
  'the computer name
  nSize = 255
  lpBuffer = Space$(nSize)

  'Call the API
  rc = GetComputerName(lpBuffer, nSize)

  If rc <> 0 Then
    'Return the computer name
    mComputerName = Left$(lpBuffer, _
        InStr(lpBuffer, Chr$(0)) - 1)
  Else
      mComputerName = ""
  End If
  'Fill the buffer with spaces
   nSize = 255
  lpBuffer = Space$(nSize)

  'Call the API
  rc = GetUserName(lpBuffer, nSize)
  If rc <> 0 Then
    'Return the user name
    mUserName = Left$(lpBuffer, _
        InStr(lpBuffer, Chr$(0)) - 1)
  Else
```

```
        mUserName = ""
    End If
End Sub
```

Since this class is designed to handle much of the system functionality in your operating system, it makes sense to add some code to allow the user to programmatically log off, shut down, and reboot. To accomplish this you need to give the object the shutdown privilege. Do this by obtaining the object's process token, assigning it the shutdown privilege, and recording the privilege to the token. The following code demonstrates how this is done:

```
Private Sub AllowTokenShutdown()
  Dim hProcessHandle As Long
  Dim hTokenHandle As Long
  Dim tmpLuid As LUID
  Dim tkp As TOKEN_PRIVILEGES
  Dim tkpNewButIgnored As TOKEN_PRIVILEGES
  Dim lBuffer As Long

 'Get the handle to the current process
  hProcessHandle = GetCurrentProcess()

 'Get the process token
  OpenProcessToken hProcessHandle, _
    (TOKEN_ADJUST_PRIVILEGES Or TOKEN_QUERY), _
    hTokenHandle

 'Get the LUID for shutdown privilege
  LookupPrivilegeValue "", "SeShutdownPrivilege", _ tmpLuid
  With tkp
     .PrivilegeCount = 1
     .TheLuid = tmpLuid
     .Attributes = SE_PRIVILEGE_ENABLED
  End With

 'Enable shutdown access for this token
  AdjustTokenPrivileges hTokenHandle, _
     False, _
     tkp, _
     Len(tkpNewButIgnored), _
     tkpNewButIgnored, _
     lBuffer
End Sub
```

The first step is to get the handle for the current process. Once you have this, you can open the process token using the `OpenProcessToken` API. After you have a valid process token, give it the shutdown privilege by setting the `.Attributes` member of the TOKEN_PRIVILEGES structure to SE_PRIVILEGE_ENABLED. Then modify the token's privileges by passing the structure to the `AdjustToken-Privileges` API. Now you're ready to shut down.

You can see the calls to this function in the **Reboot** and **Shutdown** methods listed below:

```
Public Sub Logoff()
  Dim rc As Long

  'Call the API
  rc = ExitWindowsEx(EWX_LOGOFF, 0&)
End Sub

Public Sub Reboot()
  Dim rc As Long

  'Give this process token access to shutdown
  AllowTokenShutdown

  'Call the API
  rc = ExitWindowsEx(EWX_REBOOT, 0&)
End Sub

Public Sub Shutdown()
  Dim rc As Long

  'Give this process token access to shutdown
  AllowTokenShutdown

  'Call the API
  rc = ExitWindowsEx(EWX_SHUTDOWN, 0&)
End Sub
```

Now that you have seen how the system class works, you can include it in your projects and retrieve system information without having to rewrite the code for the APIs.

Let's look at the memory class, which allows you to retrieve system memory information from your applications. The code for the class is in Listing 5.2.

LISTING 5.2   The Memory Class

```
Private Sub Class_Initialize()
  Dim lpmstMemStat As MEMORYSTATUS

  'Call the API and populate the MEMORYSTATUS structure
  GlobalMemoryStatus lpmstMemStat

  'Copy the values from the structure to the properties
  mMemory = lpmstMemStat.dwTotalPhys
  mAvailableMemory = lpmstMemStat.dwAvailPhys
  mVirtualMemory = lpmstMemStat.dwTotalPageFile
End Sub
```

The last class to examine is the processor class, shown in Listing 5.3.

LISTING 5.3   The Processor Class

```
Private Sub Class_Initialize()
  Dim lpSystemInfo As SYSTEM_INFO

  'Call the API to fill the structure
  GetSystemInfo lpSystemInfo

  'Determine the number of precessors
  mProcessors = lpSystemInfo.dwNumberOfProcessors

  'Get the processor type
  Select Case lpSystemInfo.dwProcessorType
      Case PROCESSOR_INTEL_386
          mProcessor = "Intel 386"
      Case PROCESSOR_INTEL_486
          mProcessor = "Intel 486"
      Case PROCESSOR_INTEL_PENTIUM
          mProcessor = "Intel Pentium"
      Case PROCESSOR_MIPS_R4000
          mProcessor = "MIPS R4000"
      Case PROCESSOR_ALPHA_21064
```

```
                mProcessor = "Alpha 21064"
          Case Else
                mProcessor = "586"
      End Select
    End Sub
```

Now that you have seen the three classes, you can see how they are used by the system viewer applet, shown in Listing 5.4 below. As you progress through this book you can continue to add functionality to the applet if you wish.

TIP   If the code seems like too much to type in, you can download the code from the Sybex Web site at `http://www.sybex.com`!

LISTING 5.4   **The System Viewer Applet**

```
Option Explicit

Private s As clsSystem
Private m As clsMemory
Private p As clsProcessor

Private Sub Form_Load()
    Set s = New clsSystem
    Set p = New clsProcessor
    Set m = New clsMemory

    With s
        txtComputerName.Text = "\\" & .ComputerName
        txtCurrentUser.Text = .UserName
    End With

    With m
        'Populate the memory fields
        txtTotalRAM.Text = Format$(.Memory, "###,###")
        txtRAMAvail.Text = Format$(.AvailableMemory, _
"###,###")
        txtTotalVirtual.Text = Format$(.VirtualMemory, _
"###,###")
    End With
```

```
With p
    'populate the processor fields
    txtProcessor.Text = .Processor
    txtProcessors.Text = .Processors
End With

With s
    'Populate the OS fields
    txtOS.Text = .OperatingSystem
    txtVersion.Text = .Version & " Build " _
            & .Build
    txtCSD.Text = .ServicePack
    txtWinPath.Text = .WindowsPath
    txtSysPath.Text = .WindowsSystemPath
End With
End Sub
```

There is a lot more system information you can retrieve from the Windows API. You can get information about your display resolution, color depth, system time, time zone and locale, peripherals, and much more. To cover all the possibilities would require a completely separate book on the subject. However, as you progress through this book, you will pick up more code and techniques that will help you create and expand your class library.

CHAPTER

SIX

6

Dialog APIs

- Message Boxes

- Common Dialogs

- Network Dialogs

Dialogs are a simple, but commonly overlooked, area of an application. However, they are critical interface components that help contribute to the user's overall experience. They allow the program to interact with the user and allow the user to specify actions.

Visual Basic provides three categories of dialogs for you to use. These include the message box, input box, and common dialog control. The message box allows you to raise the standard dialogs you see when a confirmation is required from the user, as well as various informational dialogs, such as error messages and confirmations. The input box is used to elicit input from the user. Finally, the common dialog control gives you access to some of the standard Windows selection dialogs, including the open, save, color selection, font selection, and printer selection dialogs.

Unfortunately, the functionality of these dialogs can be limited depending on your requirements, and some dialogs such as a directory selection dialog are simply omitted. Fortunately the Windows API allows you to call these dialogs directly, as well as some obvious ones not intrinsic to Visual Basic.

Message Boxes

Message boxes are the staple of the Windows interface. Almost every Windows application displays a message box at some time. Message boxes are commonly used to display information and then request acceptance or acknowledgment of that information, as shown in Figure 6.1. This is often accomplished by displaying a status message of some sort. Other times the message box can be configured to display an error message.

FIGURE 6.1:

Message box

The Visual Basic `MsgBox()` function actually wraps the `MessageBox` API. You don't need to use this API; in fact, it would just be unnecessary work. However, we will show the API so you can see how Visual Basic wraps the Windows API in many ways.

MessageBox

Description

The MessageBox API displays a message box similar to Visual Basic's MsgBox() command.

C Prototype

```
int MessageBox(HWND hWnd,
    LPCTSTR lpText,
    LPCTSTR lpCaption,
    UINT uType);
```

VB Declaration

```
Private Declare Function MessageBox Lib "user32" _
    Alias "MessageBoxA" _
    (ByVal hWnd As Long, _
    ByVal lpText As String, _
    ByVal lpCaption As String, _
    ByVal wType As Long) As Long
```

Parameters

Parameter	Description
hWnd	Handle to the dialog's owner.
lpText	The text you wish to display in the body of the dialog.
lpCaption	The caption of the message box.
wType	The dialog definition. You can use a combination of the same arguments you use in the standard MsgBox function, such as vbYesNo and vbInformation.
Returns	Returns the value of the button that was clicked.

Example

```
Dim rc As Long

rc = MessageBox(hWnd, _
        "Text Title", _
        "Caption", _
        vbYesNo)
```

MessageBoxEx

Description

The MessageBoxEx API displays a message box, but allows the buttons to be displayed in different languages, depending on the value passed via the wLanguage-ID argument, and the locales installed on your system. For example, you cannot specify to use Chinese if you have the localized English version of Windows installed.

C Prototype

```
int MessageBoxEx(HWND hWnd,
    LPCTSTR lpText,
    LPCTSTR lpCaption,
    UINT uType,
    WORD wLanguageId);
```

VB Declaration

```
Private Declare Function MessageBoxEx Lib "user32" _
    Alias "MessageBoxExA" _
    (ByVal hWnd As Long, _
    ByVal lpText As String, _
    ByVal lpCaption As String, _
    ByVal uType As Long, _
    ByVal wLanguageId As Long) As Long
```

Parameters

Parameter	Description
hWnd	Handle to the dialog's owner.
lpText	The text you wish to display in the body of the dialog.

lpCaption	The caption of the message box.
uType	The dialog definition. You can use a combination of the same arguments you use in the standard MsgBox function, such as vbYesNo and vbInformation.
wLanguageId	The language ID used in the dialog. This value depends on the locales installed on your system. The constants begin with the LANG_ prefix.
Returns	Returns the number of the button clicked. These values are the same as those used in Visual Basic, such as vbYes, vbNo, and vbCancel.

Notes

The main reason to use this API is to specify an alternate language. Do this by passing the appropriate value in the wLanguageId parameter.

Example

The following example makes the button text appear in Spanish:

```
.
.
.
wLanguageID = LANG_SPANISH

rc = MessageBoxEx(hWnd, _
       Message, _
       Caption, _
       vbYesNo + vbCritical, _
       wLanguageID)
.
.
.
```

MessageBoxIndirect

Description

The MessageBoxIndirect API allows you to display a message box with more features.

C Prototype

```
int MessageBoxIndirect(LPMSGBOXPARAMS lpMsgBoxParams);
```

VB Declaration

```
Private Declare Function MessageBoxIndirect Lib "user32" _
    Alias "MessageBoxIndirectA" _
    (lpMsgBoxParams As MSGBOXPARAMS) As Long
```

Parameters

Parameter	Description
lpMsgBoxParams	Pointer to a MSGBOXPARAMS structure. Refer to the Notes below.
Returns	Returns the number of the button clicked to acknowledge the message box.

Notes

The MSGBOXPARAMS structure contains members that allow you to specify the caption, text, icon, and other features of the message box you wish to display. The structure's declaration is shown below:

```
Type MSGBOXPARAMS
    cbSize As Long
    hwndOwner As Long
    hInstance As Long
    lpszText As String
    lpszCaption As String
    dwStyle As Long
    lpszIcon As String
    dwContextHelpId As Long
    lpfnMsgBoxCallback As Long
    dwLanguageId As Long
End Type
```

Each member is described below:

Member	Description
cbSize	The size of the structure.
hwndOwner	Handle to the window that owns this dialog.

`hInstance`	The instance of this application. You can set this to `App.hInstance`.
`lpszText`	The text that appears in the body of the dialog.
`lpszCaption`	The caption of the dialog.
`dwStyle`	The dialog definition. You can use a combination of the same arguments you use in the standard `MsgBox` function, such as `vbYesNo` and `vbInformation`.
`lpszIcon`	The icon to display on the dialog.
`dwContextHelpId`	The context ID for an online Help system.
`lpfnMsgBoxCallback`	The address of a callback function that processes messages directed at the dialog.
`DwLanguageId`	The language ID used in the dialog.

Example

Here is an example of how to call this function. Note that not all the fields of the MSGBOXPARAMS need to be filled in.

```
Dim rc As Long
Dim msg As MSGBOXPARAMS

msg.cbSize = Len(msg)
msg.hwndOwner = hWnd
msg.hInstance = App.hInstance
msg.lpszText = "Text"
msg.lpszCaption = "Caption"
msg.dwStyle = vbYesNo
```

Common Dialogs

Visual Basic's common dialog control provides a few of the most common dialogs you will require in your programming efforts. Included are dialogs to open and save files, pick colors, select fonts and printers, and display the online Help system. However, Microsoft left out a few other common dialogs, such as the directory picker, and the network connection and disconnection dialogs.

All of these dialogs can be created and accessed via the Windows API. In addition, they don't require the overhead of ComCtl32.OCX!

Selecting Files

Selecting files is achieved by calling the GetOpenFileName API. Calling this API brings up the Open dialog box, as shown in Figure 6.2. There are a number of configuration options you can set to allow it to filter on specific files, enable multiple selections, and many other things. Let's look at the API and then a sample function.

FIGURE 6.2:

The File Open dialog

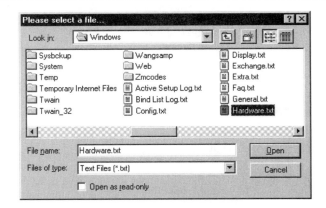

GetOpenFileName

Description

The GetOpenFileName API displays the file selection dialog you normally see when selecting Open from the File menu.

C Prototype

```
BOOL GetOpenFileName(LPOPENFILENAME lpofn);
```

VB Declaration

```
Private Declare Function GetOpenFileName Lib _
    "comdlg32.dll" _
```

```
Alias "GetOpenFileNameA" _
(lpOpenFilename As OPENFILENAME) As Long
```

Parameters

Parameter	Description
lpOpenFilename	Pointer to an OPENFILENAME structure. Refer to the Notes below for more information.
Returns	Returns True on success, False on failure.

Notes

As you can see from the declaration below, the OPENFILENAME structure contains quite a few members. Many of these members are obvious, and there are a few you will probably never require.

```
Private Type OPENFILENAME
    lStructSize As Long
    hwndOwner As Long
    hInstance As Long
    lpstrFilter As String
    lpstrCustomFilter As String
    nMaxCustFilter As Long
    nFilterIndex As Long
    lpstrFile As String
    nMaxFile As Long
    lpstrFileTitle As String
    nMaxFileTitle As Long
    lpstrInitialDir As String
    lpstrTitle As String
    flags As Long
    nFileOffset As Integer
    nFileExtension As Integer
    lpstrDefExt As String
    lCustData As Long
    lpfnHook As Long
    lpTemplateName As String
End Type
```

Each member is described below:

Member	Description
lStructSize	Size of the structure. Set this to the value returned from Len(x).
hwndOwner	Handle to the owner of this dialog.
hInstance	Instance of the application. Use App.hInstance.
lpstrFilter	The filter of the file types displayed in the Files of Type field. This string must be terminated with two null characters.
lpstrCustomFilter	This parameter is a pointer to a buffer used to preserve the filter pattern chosen by the user.
nMaxCustFilter	The size in bytes of the buffer in lpstrCustom-Filter.
nFilterIndex	The index of the filter you wish to set as the default.
lpstrFile	The fully qualified path name of the file used to initialize the dialog. If you use this member, it must be preceded with a null character.
nMaxFile	The size in bytes of the buffer used for lpstrFile.
lpstrFileTitle	Pointer to the buffer that receives the path and filename selected by the user.
nMaxFileTitle	Maximum length of the buffer specified in lpstrFileTitle.
lpstrInitialDir	A string containing the initial directory. If this value is null, then the current directory is used. On Windows 2000 and Windows 98, if this value is null and the current directory contains files that match the specified file filter, the current directory is used. If no files match, the user's personal file directory of the current user is used.
lpstrTitle	Caption of the dialog.

flags	A set of options used to configure the dialog. The flags are constants that begin with OFN_. For more information on flags you can set, refer to the API quick reference at the end of this book.
nFileOffset	Specifies the number of bytes to the first character in the filename. This allows you to extract the filename from the path. Since the number is zero-based, subtract one from the value returned in this member.
nFileExtension	Specifies the number of bytes to the first character of the file extension. Since the number is zero-based, subtract one from the value returned in this member.
lpstrDefExt	Default extension of the file. Used when called by GetSaveFileName.
lCustData	Custom data passed to the message handler specified in the lpfnHook member.
lpfnHook	The address of the hook procedure. To enable a message hook, set the OFN_ENABLEHOOK flag in addition to any other flags.
lpTemplateName	Pointer to a string that names the template dialog included in the resource specified by the hInstance member.

Example

The following example shows how to call the GetOpenFileName API in Visual Basic:

```
Dim rc As Long
Dim pOpenfilename As OPENFILENAME
Const MAX_BUFFER_LENGTH = 256

With pOpenfilename
    .hwndOwner = hWnd
    .hInstance = App.hInstance
    .lpstrTitle = "Open"
    .lpstrInitialDir = App.Path
    .lpstrFilter = "All Files" & Chr$(0) & "*.*" & Chr$(0)
    .nFilterIndex = 1
```

```
        .lpstrFile = String(MAX_BUFFER_LENGTH, 0)
        .nMaxFile = MAX_BUFFER_LENGTH - 1
        .lpstrFileTitle = .lpstrFile
        .nMaxFileTitle = MAX_BUFFER_LENGTH - 1
        .lStructSize = Len(pOpenfilename)
    End With

    rc = GetOpenFileName(pOpenfilename)

    If rc Then
        'A file selected
        FileOpen = Left$(pOpenfilename.lpstrFile, _
                   pOpenfilename.nMaxFile)
    Else
        'The cancel button was pressed
        FileOpen = ""
    End If
```

This example is fairly straightforward. Before calling the API, the appropriate members of the OPENFILE structure are filled in. Once the structure is filled in, the GetOpenFileName API is called. If the call is successful, the API returns a non-zero value and the fully qualified path to the selected file is returned in the lpstrFile member. The length of the value returned is stored in nMaxFile.

Selecting a Filename to Save

The opposite of retrieving a filename is setting one in the file Save dialog shown in Figure 6.3. You can accomplish this by calling the GetSaveFileName API.

FIGURE 6.3:

The File Save dialog

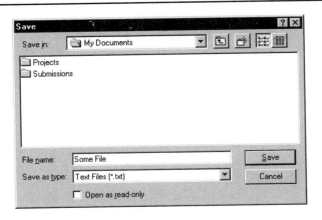

Calling this API is identical to calling GetOpenFileName with the exception of setting the .lpstrDefExt member variable in the OPENFILENAME structure.

GetSaveFileName

Description

The GetSaveFileName API displays the file selection dialog you normally see when selecting Save from the File menu.

C Prototype

```
BOOL GetSaveFileName(LPOPENFILENAME lpofn);
```

VB Declaration

```
Private Declare Function GetSaveFileName _
    Lib "comdlg32.dll" _
    Alias "GetSaveFileNameA" _
    (lpOpenFilename As OPENFILENAME) As Long
```

Parameters

Parameter	Description
lpOpenFilename	Pointer to an OPENFILENAME structure. Refer to the Notes under the GetOpenFileName API in the previous section.

Example

```
Dim rc As Long
Dim pOpenfilename As OPENFILENAME
Const MAX_BUFFER_LENGTH = 256

With pOpenfilename
    .hwndOwner = hWnd
    .hInstance = App.hInstance
    .lpstrTitle = "Save"
    .lpstrInitialDir = App.Path
    .lpstrFilter = "All Files" & Chr$(0) & "*.*" & Chr$(0)
    .nFilterIndex = FilterIndex
```

```
      .lpstrDefExt = ".txt"
      .lpstrFile = String(MAX_BUFFER_LENGTH, 0)
      .nMaxFile = MAX_BUFFER_LENGTH - 1
      .lpstrFileTitle = .lpstrFile
      .nMaxFileTitle = MAX_BUFFER_LENGTH
      .lStructSize = Len(pOpenfilename)
  End With

  rc = GetSaveFileName(pOpenfilename)

  If rc Then
      'A file selected
      FileSave = Left$(pOpenfilename.lpstrFile, _
              pOpenfilename.nMaxFile)
  Else
      'The cancel button was pressed
      FileSave = ""
  End If
```

Selecting a Folder

For some reason Microsoft left out the directory selection dialog (Figure 6.4) from the Common Dialog control. In fact, the API is not even declared in the API Viewer. How many times have you placed a Directory control on a form to emulate the Windows directory picker? Well, now you can use the API to achieve the same functionality found in Windows.

FIGURE 6.4:

The Directory Selection dialog

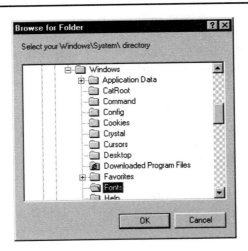

SHBrowseForFolder

Description

The SHBrowseForFolder API allows you to browse for many types of folders, such as file folders, printers, and networks.

C Prototype

```
WINSHELLAPI LPITEMIDLIST WINAPI SHBrowseForFolder(LPBROWSEINFO lpbi);
```

VB Declaration

```
Private Declare Function SHBrowseForFolder _
    Lib "shell32.dll" _
    Alias "SHBrowseForFolderA" _
    (lpBrowseInfo As BROWSEINFO) As Long
```

Parameters

Parameter	Description
lpBrowseInfo	Pointer to a BROWSEINFO structure. Refer to the Notes below for a description of this structure and its members.
Returns	On success, this API returns an identifier list for the selected namespace.

Notes

This function uses a single parameter made up of the following structure:

```
Private Type BROWSEINFO
    hOwner As Long
    pidlRoot As Long
    pszDisplayName As String
    lpszTitle As String
    ulFlags As Long
    lpfn As Long
    lParam As Long
    iImage As Long
End Type
```

Each member is described below:

Member	Description
hOwner	Handle to the window that called this dialog.
pidlRoot	Identifier list pointing to the top-most folder you wish to browse from.
pszDisplayName	Buffer used to hold the display name of the folder selected by the user.
lpszTitle	The caption of the browse dialog.
ulFlags	The flags to determine what to browse for.
lpfn	The address of a callback function the dialog calls when an event occurs. You can set this to null.
lParam	A value passed to the callback function if one is specified.
iImage	A buffer to hold the index to the image of the selected folder.

The most interesting member of this structure is ulFlags. By setting this member appropriately you can narrow the scope of folders you are allowed to browse. You can set this member to one of the following values:

Value	Result
BIF_RETURNONLYFSDIRS (&H1)	Allows you to browse for file system folders only.
BIF_DONTGOBELOWDOMAIN (&H2)	Using this value forces the user to stay within the domain level of the Network Neighborhood.
BIF_STATUSTEXT (&H4)	Displays a status bar on the selection dialog.
BIF_RETURNFSANCESTORS (&H8)	Returns file system ancestors only.
BIF_BROWSEFORCOMPUTER (&H1000)	Allows you to browse for a computer.
BIF_BROWSEFORPRINTER (&H2000)	Allows you to browse the Printers folder.

Before you can use the folder name from the SHBrowseForFolder API, you
need to extract it from the identifier list returned by the API call. Do this with the
SHGetPathFromIDList API. You will see how these APIs work together to enable
you to successfully browse for a folder.

Example

Since this function relies on the SHGetPathFromIDList in order to use the folder
name, refer to the example following the SHGetPathFromIDList API.

SHGetPathFromIDList

Description

The SHGetPathFromIDList API converts an item identifier list to a file system path.

C Prototype

```
WINSHELLAPI BOOL WINAPI SHGetPathFromIDList(   LPCITEMIDLIST pidl,
    LPSTR pszPath);
```

VB Declaration

```
Private Declare Function SHGetPathFromIDList _
    Lib "shell32.dll" _
    Alias "SHGetPathFromIDListA" _
    (ByVal pidl As Long, _
    ByVal pszPath As String) As Long
```

Parameters

Parameter	Description
pidl	Identifier list returned from the SHBrowseFor-Folder API.
pszPath	The path extracted from the identifier list.
Returns	Returns True if the API call is successful, otherwise it returns False.

Example

The following example incorporates both of the previous APIs to allow the user to select a folder:

```
Public Function GetFolder(Optional Title As String, _
        Optional hWnd) As String

    Dim bi As BROWSEINFO
    Dim pidl As Long
    Dim folder As String

    folder = String$(255, Chr$(0))

    With bi
        If IsNumeric(hWnd) Then .hOwner = hWnd
        .ulFlags = BIF_RETURNONLYFSDIRS
        .pidlRoot = 0
        If Title <> "" Then
            .lpszTitle = Title & Chr$(0)
        Else
            .lpszTitle = "Select a Folder" & Chr$(0)
        End If
    End With

    pidl = SHBrowseForFolder(bi)

    If SHGetPathFromIDList(ByVal pidl, ByVal folder) Then
        GetFolder = Left(folder, InStr(folder, _
                Chr$(0)) - 1)
    Else
        GetFolder = ""
    End If

End Function
```

Browsing for a folder is similar to the other API calls in this chapter. First, dimension bi as a BROWSEINFO structure and pidl as a Long integer. Then allocate a buffer large enough to return the full path selected in the dialog using the String$ function.

The next step is to populate the BROWSEINFO structure before passing it to the SHBrowseForFolder API. In the example above, the ulFlags member is set to

BIF_RETURNONLYFSDIRS so the function only returns file system folders. You can modify the function, as necessary, to browse for other things.

After the other relevant members are filled in, SHBrowseForFolder is called. If the API call is successful, it returns the identifier list (pidl) that represents the selected folder.

Once you have a valid identifier list, call SHGetPathFromIDList, which will return a null-terminated string containing the path to the selected folder. Then the identifier list is released with a call to the CoTaskMemFree API.

Color Selection

The color selection dialog shown in Figure 6.5 is yet another dialog encapsulated in the Common Dialog control. In fact, this control basically wraps the Choose-Color API, as described below.

FIGURE 6.5:

The Color Selection dialog

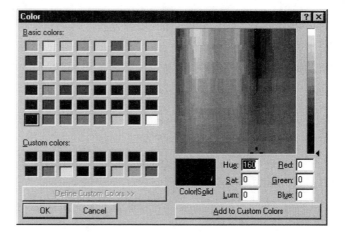

ChooseColor

Decription

The ChooseColor API displays the color selection dialog.

C Prototype

```
BOOL ChooseColor(LPCHOOSECOLOR lpcc);
```

VB Declaration

```
Private Declare Function ChooseColor Lib "comdlg32.dll" _
    Alias "ChooseColorA" _
    (lpChooseColor As udtCHOOSECOLOR) As Long
```

Parameters

Parameter	Description
lpChooseColor	Pointer to a CHOOSECOLOR structure. Refer to the Notes below for more information.
Returns	Returns True if the user selects a color. Otherwise the API returns False.

Notes

The CHOOSECOLOR structure contains member variables you can set to initialize and customize the color selection dialog.

```
Private Type udtCHOOSECOLOR
    lStructSize As Long
    hwndOwner As Long
    hInstance As Long
    rgbResult As Long
    lpCustColors As String
    flags As Long
    lCustData As Long
    lpfnHook As Long
    lpTemplateName As String
End Type
```

Each member is described below:

Member	Description
lStructSize	Size of the structure.
hwndOwner	Handle to the window that called this dialog.
hInstance	Instance of the application that called this dialog.

`rgbResult`	Used to return the value of the color selected by the user.
`lpCustColors`	Pointer to an array of custom color entries for the dialog box.
`flags`	Flags you can use to initialize and customize the color selection dialog. The flags are specified with the prefix CC_.
`lCustData`	Application-defined message that is sent to a custom message handler for this dialog.
`lpfnHook`	Address of a custom message hook.
`lpTemplateName`	Name of the template this dialog is based on.

Example

```
Public Function GetColor() As Long
    Dim rc As Long
    Dim pChooseColor As udtCHOOSECOLOR
    Dim CustomColors() As Byte

    'Initailize the UDT for the color dialog
    With pChooseColor
        .hwndOwner = 0
        .hInstance = App.hInstance
        .lpCustColors = StrConv(CustomColors, vbUnicode)
        .flags = 0
        .lStructSize = Len(pChooseColor)
    End With

    'Call the API
    rc = ChooseColor(pChooseColor)

    'Return the RGB value of the color
    If rc Then
        GetColor = pChooseColor.rgbResult
    End If
End Function
```

The lpCustColors member requires a bit of attention. You will notice that CustomColors() is defined as an ANSI byte array. This is an array that holds the values of the custom colors defined in the dialog. Even if you don't require custom colors you must still set this member. Use the StrConv() function to convert the array to Unicode.

Once the structure is configured properly, call the ChooseColor API. If the call is successful, the API returns True. Assuming the API call is successful, the selected color is returned as a Long integer via the rgbResult member. You can pass this value directly into color properties, such as BackColor and ForeColor.

Font Selection

The font selection dialog, shown in Figure 6.6, is by far the most difficult to work with, but it offers many features. You can raise the dialog by calling the Choose-Font API, as described below.

FIGURE 6.6:

The Font Selection dialog

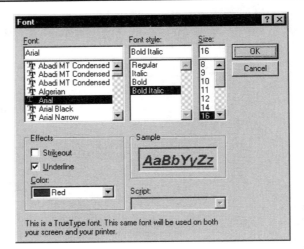

ChooseFont

Description

The ChooseFont API displays the font selection dialog and returns font properties set by the user.

C Prototype

```
BOOL ChooseFont(LPCHOOSEFONT lpcf);
```

VB Declaration

```
Private Declare Function ChooseFont Lib "comdlg32.dll" _
    Alias "ChooseFontA" _
    (lpChooseFont As udtCHOOSEFONT) As Long
```

Parameters

Parameter	Description
lpChooseFont	Pointer to a CHOOSEFONT structure. Refer to the Notes below for more information.
Returns	If a font is selected, the API returns True. Otherwise it returns False.

Notes

The CHOOSEFONT structure is one of the more complicated structures in this chapter. As you can see, it too has many members.

```
Type udtCHOOSEFONT
    lStructSize As Long
    hwndOwner As Long
    hdc As Long
    lpLogFont As Long
    iPointSize As Long
    flags As Long
    rgbColors As Long
    lCustData As Long
    lpfnHook As Long
    lpTemplateName As String
    hInstance As Long
    lpszStyle As String
    nFontType As Integer
    MISSING_ALIGNMENT As Integer
    nSizeMin As Long
    nSizeMax As Long
End Type
```

Each member is described below:

Member	Description
lStructSize	The size of the structure.
hwndOwner	Handle to the window that called this dialog.
hdc	The device context of the printer whose fonts will be listed in this dialog.
lpLogFont	Pointer to a LOGFONT structure described below.
iPointSize	The size of the selected font in 1/10 of a point. For example, to select a font size of 36, set this member to 360.
flags	Flags you can set to initialize and customize the font selection dialog.
rgbColors	Value of the color of the font.
lCustData	Application-defined message passed to the custom message handler specified in the lpfnHook member.
lpfnHook	Address of a custom message handler for this dialog.
lpTemplateName	Name of the template this dialog is based on. This can be null.
hInstance	Instance handle. Set this to App.hInstance.
lpszStyle	Address of the buffer that contains the style data for this dialog.
nFontType	The type of font used in the dialog.
MISSING_ALIGNMENT	Reserved. Do not use.
nSizeMin	Minimum font size displayed in the font selection dialog.
nSizeMax	Maximum font size displayed in the font selection dialog.

```
Private Type udtLOGFONT
    lfHeight As Long
    lfWidth As Long
    lfEscapement As Long
    lfOrientation As Long
    lfWeight As Long
    lfItalic As Byte
    lfUnderline As Byte
    lfStrikeOut As Byte
    lfCharSet As Byte
    lfOutPrecision As Byte
    lfClipPrecision As Byte
    lfQuality As Byte
    lfPitchAndFamily As Byte
    lfFaceName As String * LF_FACESIZE
End Type
```

Each member is described below:

Member	Description
lfHeight	The height of the font in logical units.
lfWidth	The width of the font in logical units.
lfEscapement	This is the angle, in 10ths of a degree that the text is drawn.
lfOrientation	Set to the same value as lfEscapement.
lfWeight	The weight of the font. This can be a value between 100 and 900. The higher the value, the darker the font.
lfItalic	If set to True, the font is italic.
lfUnderline	If set to True, the font is underlined.
lfStrikeOut	If set to True, the font is overstriked.
lfCharSet	The character set in which the font belongs.
lfOutPrecision	Used by the graphics device interface to determine the precision of the font.
lfClipPrecision	This specifies how precise the clipping region is defined when a character is too wide for its clipping region.

lfQuality	The display quality of the font. Can be set to DEFAULT_QUALITY, DRAFT_QUALITY, or PROOF_QUALITY.
lfPitchAndFamily	Specifies the pitch and family of this font. The Pitch can be DEFAULT_PITCH, FIXED_PITCH, or VARIABLE_PITCH and is set in the two low-order bytes. The font Family is loaded in bits 4 through 7 and can be FF_DECORATIVE, FF_DONTCARE, FF_MODERM, FF_ROMAN, FF_SCRIPT, or FF_SWISS.
lfFaceName	Buffer containing the name of the type face. This string is LF_FACESIZE bytes long.

Example

```
Public Function GetFont(Optional FontName As String, _
      Optional Size As Integer, _
      Optional Bold As Boolean, _
      Optional Italic As Boolean, _
      Optional Underline As Boolean, _
      Optional Strikeout As Boolean, _
      Optional Color As Long, _
      Optional hWnd) As Long

   Dim rc As Long
   Dim pChooseFont As udtCHOOSEFONT
   Dim pLogFont As udtLOGFONT

   'Initailize the buffer
   With pLogFont
       .lfFaceName = FontName & Chr$(0)
       .lfItalic = Italic
       .lfUnderline = Underline
       .lfStrikeOut = Strikeout
   End With

   'Initialize the structure
   With pChooseFont
       .hInstance = App.hInstance
       If IsNumeric(hWnd) Then .hwndOwner = hWnd
       .flags = CF_BOTH + CF_INITTOLOGFONTSTRUCT + _
           CF_EFFECTS + CF_NOSCRIPTSEL
```

```
            If IsNumeric(Size) Then .iPointSize = -(Size * 10)
            If Bold Then .nFontType = .nFontType + _
                    BOLD_FONTTYPE
            If Italic Then .nFontType = .nFontType + _
                    ITALIC_FONTTYPE
            If IsNumeric(Color) Then .rgbColors = Color
            .lStructSize = Len(pChooseFont)
            .lpLogFont = VarPtr(pLogFont)
        End With

        'Call the API
        rc = ChooseFont(pChooseFont)

        If rc Then
            'Success!
            FontName = StrConv(pLogFont.lfFaceName, vbUnicode)
            FontName = Left$(FontName, InStr(FontName, _
                    vbNullChar) - 1)

            'Return it's properties
            With pChooseFont
                Size = .iPointSize / 10
                Bold = (.nFontType And BOLD_FONTTYPE)
                Italic = (.nFontType And ITALIC_FONTTYPE)
                Underline = (pLogFont.lfUnderline)
                Strikeout = (pLogFont.lfStrikeOut)
            End With

            'Return the font name
            GetFont = rc
        Else
            'The user clicked cancel
            GetFont = 0
        End If
End Function
```

This example deserves some explanation. It is much like the other dialog APIs in that you populate a structure, pass it to the API, and extract its values. However, the structure members are the key to correctly making this API call.

You will notice that the LOGFONT structure was initialized first. You do not have to use this structure, but it exposes more of the dialog's functionality. First, set the name of the font and append a null-terminating character to the end. Then set the lpItalic, lfUnderline, and lfStrikeOut members appropriately. In this example, these properties are set based on the arguments passed to the GetFont() function.

Once the appropriate members are set, start populating the members of the CHOOSEFONT structure. Perhaps the most important member here is the flags member. There are many bit masks you can choose from that begin with CF_ in the API Viewer.

The following list shows some of the bit masks you can use to change the options on the dialog:

flag	result
CF_BOTH	This flag is a combination of the CF_SCREEN-FONTS and CF_PRINTERFONTS flags.
CF_FIXEDPITCHONLY	This flag causes the dialog to display on the fixed-pitch fonts.
CF_NOSIZESEL	Setting this flag disables the font size selection on the dialog.
CF_NOSTYLESEL	Setting this flag disables the style selection on the dialog.
CF_PRINTERFONTS	This flag causes the dialog to list printer fonts in the fonts list.
CF_SCALABLEONLY	This flag makes the dialog list scalable fonts only.
CF_SCREENFONTS	This flag makes the dialog list screen fonts.
CF_SHOWHELP	This flag shows the Help button on the dialog.

By setting the CF_BOTH bit mask, both screen and printer fonts are listed in the dialog. If you want to use the LOGFONT structure to customize the dialog, you must set the CF_INITTOLOGFONTSTRUCT bit mask, as shown in the example.

The CF_EFFECTS bit mask allows you to display the underline, strikeout, and font color fields. The CF_NOSCRIPTSEL flag disables the script selection field in the dialog.

Once the appropriate members are set in the CHOOSEFONT structure, call the ChooseFont API. If the call is successful, the API will return a non-zero (True) value. Then you can extract the font properties from the CHOOSEFONT and LOG-FONT structures, as needed.

Network Dialogs

The obvious dialogs that were left out of the Common Dialog control are the network connection and disconnection dialogs. The connection dialogs shown in Figures 6.7 and 6.8 allow the user to connect a drive or port to a network resource, such as a shared folder or printer.

FIGURE 6.7:

Connect network
(Windows 9x)

FIGURE 6.8:

Connect network
(Windows NT)

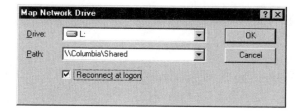

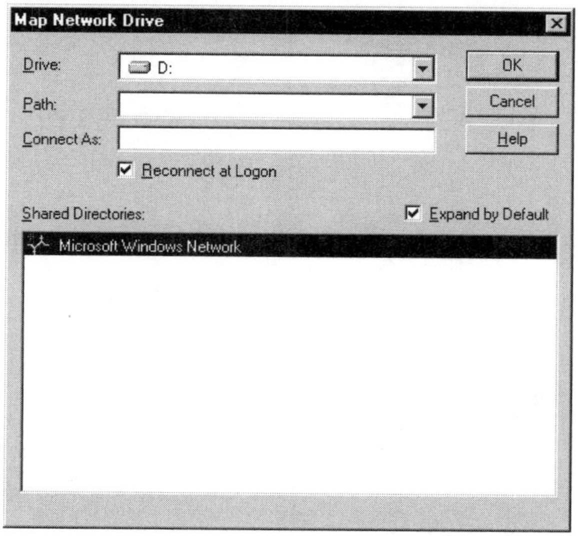

Because of the difference in security models between Windows 9x and Windows NT, the connection dialogs appear different, but will achieve the same results. However, the NT version allows you to specify the username to use during the connection process.

WNetConnectionDialog

Description

The WNetConnectionDialog API displays a dialog that allows you to connect to a network resource, such as a file share or a printer.

C Prototype

```
DWORD WNetConnectionDialog(HWND hwnd,
    DWORD dwType);
```

VB Declaration

```
Private Declare Function WNetConnectionDialog _
    Lib "mpr.dll" _
    (ByVal hWnd As Long, _
    ByVal dwType As Long) As Long
```

Parameters

Parameter	Description
hWnd	Handle to the dialog's owner.
dwType	Type of resource to connect to. Can be either RESOURCETYPE_DISK or RESOURCETYPE_PRINT.
Returns	Returns NO_ERRORS if successful, otherwise an error code.

Example

```
Public Function Connect(Mode As ConnectionType, _
        Optional hWnd As Long) As Long
    Dim rc As Long
```

```
    If IsNumeric(hWnd) Then
        rc = WNetConnectionDialog(hWnd, Mode)
    Else
        rc = WNetConnectionDialog(0, Mode)
    End If
End Function
```

As you can see this API is easy to call, but is so useful it's hard to imagine why it wasn't included in the Common Dialog control. You can set the hWnd argument so the dialog will be destroyed appropriately should your application be terminated, but the more important argument is dwType. Set this appropriately so you can specify if the user is connecting to a shared folder or a shared printer.

In addition to the connection dialogs, the Windows API also provides disconnection dialogs, as shown in Figure 6.9.

FIGURE 6.9:

Disconnect network

WNetDisconnectDialog

Description

The WNetDisconnectDialog API displays the disconnection dialog for a network resource.

C Prototype

```
DWORD WNetDisconnectDialog(HWND hwnd,
    DWORD dwType);
```

VB Declaration

```
Private Declare Function WNetDisconnectDialog _
    Lib "mpr.dll" _
```

```
(ByVal hwnd As Long, _
ByVal dwType As Long) As Long
```

Parameters

Parameter	Description
Hwnd	Handle to the dialog's owner.
dwType	Type of resource to connect to. Can be either RESOURCETYPE_DISK or RESOURCETYPE_PRINT.
Returns	Returns NO_ERRORS if successful, otherwise an error code.

Example

```
Public Function Disconnect(Mode As ConnectionType, _
        Optional hWnd As Long) As Long
    Dim rc As Long

    If IsNumeric(hWnd) Then
        rc = WNetDisconnectDialog(hWnd, Mode)
    Else
        rc = WNetDisconnectDialog(0, Mode)
    End If
End Function
```

Again, this API call is simple. You only need to be concerned with the resource type you wish to work with.

Now that you can use the API to raise almost any Windows dialog, you can wrap these APIs in functions contained in a class module. Since some of these dialogs are tricky to use, containing them in a reusable class object makes sense and will save you development time in the future.

CHAPTER

SEVEN

7

File Operations

- General File Operations

- Obtaining File Properties

- Working with Directories

The most basic file operations consist of creating and/or opening files, reading or writing data, and closing the files.

The Windows API allows you to perform all of these functions, but with a bit more power and flexibility than Visual Basic's intrinsic file operations functions. For example, using the API you can show the progress dialogs that are built into Windows, move entire directory trees, and even use the Recycle Bin. Although some of the same functionality can be achieved using Visual Basic's intrinsic file operation command, their corresponding APIs are described in this chapter.

General File Operations

As you go through this chapter you will see some of the code that makes the application in Figure 7.1 tick. This sample application allows you to browse files and see and manipulate file properties. Everything is driven from a reusable file class that can be downloaded from the Sybex Web site at www.sybex.com.

FIGURE 7.1:

Accessing file properties

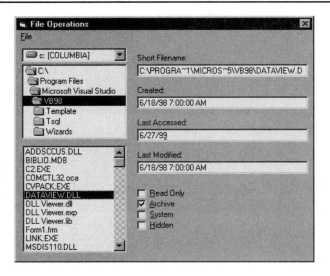

By the end of this chapter you will know enough about file APIs to build your own file class that allows you to perform more tasks than Visual Basic can do alone.

CreateFile

Description

The CreateFile API is used to create and open files, such as directories, pipes, mailslots, and flat files.

C Prototype

```
HANDLE CreateFile(LPCTSTR lpFileName,
    DWORD dwDesiredAccess,
    DWORD dwShareMode,
    LPSECURITY_ATTRIBUTES lpSecurityAttributes,
    DWORD dwCreationDisposition,
    DWORD dwFlagsAndAttributes,
    HANDLE hTemplateFile);
```

VB Declaration

```
Private Declare Function CreateFile Lib "kernel32" _
    Alias "CreateFileA" _
    (ByVal lpFileName As String, _
    ByVal dwDesiredAccess As Long, _
    ByVal dwShareMode As Long, _
    lpSecurityAttributes As SECURITY_ATTRIBUTES, _
    ByVal dwCreationDisposition As Long, _
    ByVal dwFlagsAndAttributes As Long, _
    ByVal hTemplateFile As Long) As Long
```

Parameters

Parameter	Description
lpFilename	The name of the file to be created.
dwDesiredAccess	The desired access mode for the file.
dwSharedMode	Specifies the file-sharing mode the file will use when it's created. This can be set to one of the following: FILE_SHARE_DELETE, FILE_SHARE_READ, or FILE_SHARE_WRITE.

lpSecurityAttributes	A SECURITY_ATTRIBUTES structure specifying the security descriptor of the directory. The SECURITY_ATTRIBUTES structure is described in detail under the API.
dwCreationDisposition	The mode in which the directory was created. Refer to the Notes below.
dwFlagsAndAttributes	There are numerous flags that can be used for this variable, in fact, too many to list here. These are the main ones: FILE_ATTRIBUTE-_ARCHIVE, FILE_ATTRIBUTE_SYSTEM, FILE-_ATTRIBUTE_NORMAL, FILE_ATTRIBUTE-_READONLY, and FILE_ATTRIBUTE_HIDDEN.
HTemplateFile	Handle to another file to be used as a template for this one.
Returns	File handle to the newly created file. Otherwise, an INVALID_HANDLE_VALUE is returned. For additional error information, call the Get-LastError function.

Notes

The dwCreationDisposition member describes the mode in which the file is opened. For example, specifying CREATE_NEW makes CreateFile create a new file if the file doesn't already exist. CREATE_ALWAYS causes CreateFile to create a new file and overwrite an existing file if it does exist. Specifying OPEN_EXISTING opens a file if it already exists. OPEN_ALWAYS opens the file if it exists. If it doesn't exist, then a new file is created.

Example

```
Dim rc As Long
Dim lpsec As SECURITY_ATTRIBUTES

lpsec.nLength = Len(lpsec)
lpsec.bInheritHandle = True

rc = CreateFile("junk.txt", GENERIC_WRITE, _
    FILE_SHARE_READ, _
    lpsec, _
```

```
    CREATE_NEW, _
    FILE_ATTRIBUTE_NORMAL, _
    GENERIC_READ)
```

OpenFile

Description

The OpenFile API opens, creates, or deletes a file.

C Prototype

```
HFILE OpenFile(LPCSTR lpFileName,
    LPOFSTRUCT lpReOpenBuff,
    UINT uStyle);
```

VB Declaration

```
Private Declare Function OpenFile Lib "kernel32" _
    (ByVal lpFileName As String, _
    lpReOpenBuff As OFSTRUCT, _
    ByVal wStyle As Long) As Long
```

Parameters

Parameter	Description
lpFilename	Name of the file to be opened.
lpReOpenBuff	Pointer to an OFSTRUCT structure. Refer to the Notes below.
wStyle	The mode to open the file. Here are a few of these styles: OF_CREATE, OF_DELETE, OF_EXIST, OF_READ, OF_READWRITE, and OF_WRITE.
Returns	Returns the file handle to the opened file. Otherwise, returns HFILE_ERROR. For additional error information, call the GetLastError function.

Notes

You must pass the OFSTRUCT structure to the function. This structure holds information about the file being opened.

```
Private Type OFSTRUCT
    cBytes As Byte
    fFixedDisk As Byte
    nErrCode As Integer
    Reserved1 As Integer
    Reserved2 As Integer
    szPathName(OFS_MAXPATHNAME) As Byte
End Type
```

Each member is described below:

Member	Description
cBytes	The length of the structure.
fFixedDisk	Set this to a number other than 0 to specify a file on a hard drive.
nErrCode	Returns the error code if the API call fails.
Reserved1	Reserved. Set to 0.
Reserved2	Reserved. Set to 0.
szPathName	Byte array containing the path and filename.

Example

```
Dim rc As Long
Dim lpopen As OFSTRUCT

lpopen.cBytes = Len(lpopen)
lpopen.fFixedDisk = 1

rc = OpenFile("junk.txt", _
    lpopen, _
    OF_READ)
```

lClose

Description

The lClose API closes a file that was opened with CreateFile or OpenFile.

C Prototype

```
HFILE _lclose(HFILE hFile);
```

VB Declaration

```
Private Declare Function lclose Lib "kernel32" _
    Alias "_lclose" _
    (ByVal hFile As Long) As Long
```

Parameters

Parameter	Description
hfile	Handle to the file you wish to close.
Returns	Zero if successful. Otherwise, returns HFILE-_ERROR. For additional error information, call the GetLastError function.

Example

```
Dim rc As Long
Dim rc1 as long
Dim lpopen As OFSTRUCT

lpopen.cBytes = Len(lpopen)
lpopen.fFixedDisk = 1

rc = OpenFile("junk.txt", _
    lpopen, _
    OF_READ)

rc1 = lclose(rc)
```

CopyFile

Description

The CopyFile API copies an existing file to a new file. This is the same as Visual Basic's FileCopy command, except it allows you to abort if the destination file already exists.

C Prototype

```
BOOL CopyFile(LPCTSTR lpExistingFileName,
    LPCTSTR lpNewFileName,
    BOOL bFailIfExists);
```

VB Declaration

```
Private Declare Function CopyFile Lib "kernel32" _
    Alias "CopyFileA" _
    (ByVal lpExistingFileName As String, _
    ByVal lpNewFileName As String, _
    ByVal bFailIfExists As Long) As Long
```

Parameters

Parameter	Description
lpExistingFilename	Name of the file to be copied.
lpNewFilename	Name of the destination file.
bFailIfExists	Set to True if you do not want to overwrite an existing file.
Returns	A non-zero value is returned if this call is successful. If the value is zero, then an error occurred. For additional error information, call the GetLastError function.

Example

```
Public Function Copy(NewFilename As String, _
        Overwrite As Boolean) As Long

    Dim rc As Long

    'Call the API
    rc = CopyFile(ByVal mFilename, _
            ByVal NewFilename, _
            Not Overwrite)

    'Return result
    If rc <> 0 Then
        Copy = 0
```

```
      Else
          Copy = -1
      End If
End Function
```

DeleteFile

Description

The DeleteFile API allows you to delete a file from a disk. This API returns
True if the call is successful.

C Prototype

```
BOOL DeleteFile(LPCTSTR lpFileName);
```

VB Declaration

```
Private Declare Function DeleteFile Lib "kernel32" _
    Alias "DeleteFileA" _
    (ByVal lpFileName As String) As Long
```

Parameters

Parameter	Description
lpFilename	The name of the file to delete.
Returns	A non-zero value is returned if this call is successful. If the value is zero, then an error occurred. For additional error information, call the GetLastError function.

Example

This example shows how to use the DeleteFile API to delete a file off the hard
drive. You will notice it calls a function called Recycle. This function allows you
to send a file to the Recycle Bin if AllowUndo is set to True. The code for the Recycle Bin function is covered in Chapter 9.

```
Public Function Delete(Optional AllowUndo As Boolean) _
        As Long

    Dim rc As Long
```

```
                      If AllowUndo Then
                          'Send the file to the recycle bin...
                          Delete = Recycle(True)
                      Else
                          'Permanently delete the file
                          rc = DeleteFile(ByVal mFilename)

                          'Return result
                          If rc Then
                              Delete = 0
                          Else
                              Delete = -1
                          End If
                      End If
                  End Function
```

Obtaining File Properties

In addition to creating, opening, and closing files, it is useful to have the ability to access various properties of a file. Unfortunately, Visual Basic doesn't allow you to do this without the Windows API.

This section will demonstrate how to retrieve a file's short filename, its attributes, as well as its date and time stamps. The examples in this section are based on the clsFile class that is available for download from the Sybex Web site at www.sybex.com.

GetShortPathName

Description

The GetShortPathName API retrieves the short path and filename of a Long filename passed to it.

C Prototype

```
DWORD GetShortPathName(LPCTSTR lpszLongPath,
    LPTSTR lpszShortPath,
    DWORD cchBuffer);
```

VB Declaration

```
Private Declare Function GetShortPathName Lib "kernel32" _
    Alias "GetShortPathNameA" _
    (ByVal lpszLongPath As String, _
    ByVal lpszShortPath As String, _
    ByVal cchBuffer As Long) As Long
```

Parameters

Parameter	Description
lpszLongPath	The Long path and filename.
lpszShortPath	Buffer that returns the Short path and filename if the API call is successful.
cchBuffer	The size of the buffer.
Returns	Length of lpszShortPath. If zero is returned, this function fails. For additional error information, call the GetLastError function.

Example

The following example shows how to pass a Long filename to the GetShortPath-Name API to retrieve the file's Short filename:

```
Public Property Get ShortFilename() As String
    Dim rc As String
    Dim lpBuff As String
    Dim cbBuff As Long

    'Allocate a buffer
    lpBuff = String$(255, Chr$(0))
    cbBuff = Len(lpBuff)

    'Call the API
    rc = GetShortPathName(ByVal mFilename, _
            ByVal lpBuff, cbBuff)

    If rc Then
        ShortFilename = Left$(lpBuff, cbBuff)
    Else
        ShortFilename = ""
```

```
      End If
   End Property
```

This example is fairly straightforward. First, an adequate buffer is allocated to hold the Short path, then the API is called. If the call is successful, the API returns True and the Short path and filename are stored in lpBuff. cbBuff contains the number of bytes contained in lpBuff. The extra null characters are extracted by using the Left$() function.

GetFileAttributes

Description

The GetFileAttributes API retrieves the attributes of a file, such as the archive, hidden, read-only, and system attributes.

C Prototype

```
DWORD GetFileAttributes(LPCTSTR lpFileName);
```

VB Declaration

```
Private Declare Function GetFileAttributes Lib "kernel32" _
   Alias "GetFileAttributesA" _
   (ByVal lpFileName As String) As Long
```

Parameters

Parameter	Description
lpFilename	The name of the file whose attributes you wish to retrieve.
Returns	Returns the attribute of the file or directory. Otherwise a –1 is returned. For additional error information, call the GetLastError function.

Example

Using this API is quite simple, as you can see from the sample code:

```
'Get the file attributes
rc = GetFileAttributes(mFilename)
```

```
If rc <> 1 Then
    mReadOnly = rc And FILE_ATTRIBUTE_READONLY
    mArchive = rc And FILE_ATTRIBUTE_ARCHIVE
    mSystem = rc And FILE_ATTRIBUTE_SYSTEM
    mHidden = rc And FILE_ATTRIBUTE_HIDDEN
    mCompressed = rc And FILE_ATTRIBUTE_COMPRESSED
End If
```

If the API call is successful, a file attributes mask is returned. If the call is unsuccessful, the API returns 1. To determine the file's attributes, test the mask by using And with the attribute mask you wish to check for.

SetFileAttributes

Description

The SetFileAttributes API sets the attributes of a file, such as read-only, archive, system, and hidden.

C Prototype

```
BOOL SetFileAttributes(LPCTSTR lpFileName,
    DWORD dwFileAttributes);
```

VB Declaration

```
Private Declare Function SetFileAttributes _
    Lib "kernel32" Alias _
    "SetFileAttributesA" _
    (ByVal lpFileName As String, _
    ByVal dwFileAttributes As Long) As Long
```

Parameters

Parameter	Description
lpFilename	The name of the file whose attributes you wish to set.
dwFileAttributes	A Long integer composed of the file attributes mask.

Returns If successful, a non-zero value is returned. If zero is returned, an error has occurred. For additional error information, call the GetLastError function.

Example

Setting a file's attributes is very similar to retrieving them. All you need to do is build an attribute mask by Oring the attribute with a mask, as shown in the sample code below:

```
Private Sub SetAttributes()
    Dim rc As Long
    Dim fa As Long

    If mReadOnly Then fa = fa Or FILE_ATTRIBUTE_READONLY
    If mArchive Then fa = fa Or FILE_ATTRIBUTE_ARCHIVE
    If mSystem Then fa = fa Or FILE_ATTRIBUTE_SYSTEM
    If mHidden Then fa = fa Or FILE_ATTRIBUTE_HIDDEN
If mCompressed Then _
        fa = fa Or FILE_ATTRIBUTE_COMPRESSED

    rc = SetFileAttributes(mFilename, fa)
End Sub
```

Once you build up your attribute mask, pass it to the SetFileAttributes API.

GetFileTime

Description

The GetFileTime API retrieves a file's date and time stamps for the creation time, last access time, and modification time.

C Prototype

```
BOOL GetFileTime(HANDLE hFile,
    LPFILETIME lpCreationTime,
    LPFILETIME lpLastAccessTime,
    LPFILETIME lpLastWriteTime);
```

VB Declaration

```
Private Declare Function GetFileTime Lib "kernel32" _
    (ByVal hFile As Long, _
    lpCreationTime As FILETIME, _
    lpLastAccessTime As FILETIME, _
    lpLastWriteTime As FILETIME) As Long
```

Parameters

Parameter	Description
hFile	Handle to the file whose date and time stamps you wish to access.
lpCreationTime	Returns a FILETIME structure containing the date and time the file was created.
lpLastAccessTime	Returns a FILETIME structure containing the date and time the file was last accessed.
lpLastWriteTime	Returns a FILETIME structure containing the date and time the file was last modified.
Returns	If successful, a non-zero value is returned. If zero is returned, an error has occurred. For additional error information, call the GetLastError function.

Notes

Here is the FILETIME structure that will get filled in with this function call.

```
Private Type FILETIME
    dwLowDateTime As Long
    dwHighDateTime As Long
End Type
```

Use the FileTimeToSystemTime function to convert this FILETIME structure to a file date and time, which are easily displayed.

Example

Refer to the example under FileTimeToSystemTime.

FileTimeToSystemTime

Description

The FileTimeToSystemTime API converts the data contained in a FILETIME structure to a more usable SYSTEMTIME structure.

C Prototype

```
BOOL FileTimeToSystemTime(CONST FILETIME *lpFileTime,
    LPSYSTEMTIME lpSystemTime);
```

VB Declaration

```
Private Declare Function FileTimeToSystemTime _
    Lib "kernel32" _
    (lpFileTime As FILETIME, _
    lpSystemTime As SYSTEMTIME) As Long
```

Parameters

Parameter	Description
lpFileTime	The FILETIME structure to be converted.
lpSystemTime	The SYSTEMTIME structure to be populated with the date and time information. Refer to the Notes below.
Returns	If successful, a non-zero value is returned. If zero is returned, an error has occurred. For additional error information, call the GetLastError function.

Notes

The SYSTEMTIME structure is much more user-friendly than its FILETIME counterpart.

```
Private Type SYSTEMTIME
    wYear As Integer
    wMonth As Integer
    wDayOfWeek As Integer
    wDay As Integer
    wHour As Integer
```

```
        wMinute As Integer
        wSecond As Integer
        wMilliseconds As Integer
    End Type
```

Each member is described below:

Member	Description
wYear	The year component of the date.
wMonth	The month component of the date.
wDayOfWeek	The day of the week.
wDay	The day component of the date.
wHour	The hour component of the time.
wMinute	The minute component of the time.
wSecond	The second component of the time.
wMilliseconds	The millisecond component of the time.

Example

Retrieving the file's time stamps is a little bit trickier than you might think. At first glance the GetFileTime API looks like all you need to do is get the time stamps, but that is not the case. Take a look at the code below:

```
Private Function GetFileTimes()
    Dim rc As Long
    Dim lpCreationTime As FILETIME
    Dim lpLastAccessTime As FILETIME
    Dim lpLastWriteTime As FILETIME
    Dim hFile As Long
    Dim lpBuff As OFSTRUCT
    Dim lpsCT As SYSTEMTIME
    Dim lpsLAT As SYSTEMTIME
    Dim lpsLWT As SYSTEMTIME

    'Get a handle to the file
    hFile = OpenFile(ByVal mFilename, lpBuff, OF_READ)
    If hFile <> 0 Then
        'Get the file dates
        rc = GetFileTime(hFile, _
```

```
                lpCreationTime, _
                lpLastAccessTime, _
                lpLastWriteTime)

        If rc <> 0 Then
            'Convert the creation time to
            'VB date/time format
            rc = FileTimeToSystemTime(lpCreationTime, _
                    lpsCT)
            If rc <> 0 Then
                With lpsCT
                    mCreated = CStr(.wMonth) & "/" & _
                            CStr(.wDay) & "/" & _
                            CStr(.wYear) & " " & _
                            CStr(.wHour) & ":" & _
                            CStr(.wMinute) & ":" & _
                            CStr(.wSecond)
                End With
            End If


            'Convert the last-access time to
            'VB date/time format
            rc = FileTimeToSystemTime(lpLastAccessTime, _
                    lpsLAT)
            If rc <> 0 Then
                With lpsLAT
                    mLastAccessed = CStr(.wMonth) & "/" & _
                            CStr(.wDay) & "/" & _
                            CStr(.wYear)
                End With
            End If


            'Convert the last-write time to
            'VB date/time format
            rc = FileTimeToSystemTime(lpLastWriteTime, _
                    lpsLWT)

            If rc <> 0 Then
                With lpsLWT
                    mLastModified = CStr(.wMonth) & "/" & _
                            CStr(.wDay) & "/" & _
                            CStr(.wYear) & " " & _
                            CStr(.wHour) & ":" & _
```

```
                                    CStr(.wMinute) & ":" & _
                                    CStr(.wSecond)
                    End With
                End If
            End If

            'Close the file
            rc = lclose(hFile)
        End If
    End Function
```

Before you can get the date and time stamps from a file you must first open it using the `OpenFile` API. Since the file will not be written to, open it with the `OF_READ` flag. This opens the file in read-only mode.

Once you obtain a handle to the open file pass it to the `GetFileTime` API. If the API call is successful, it will return a number other than 0, and the `FILETIME` structures will be filled with the file's time stamp data. However, this data is not usable in its returned state.

To get usable date and time data from the `FILETIME` structure you need to convert it to a `SYSTEMTIME` structure using the `FileTimeToSystemTime` API. If this API call is successful the return code will be a number other than 0, and the `SYSTEMTIME` structures will be populated. Now the data is usable.

In this example, you want to return the date and time stamps using Visual Basic's `Date` format. To do this, you must append each piece of the date and time together and convert it to a date. Do this by using the `Year()`, `Month()`, `Day()`, `Hour()`, `Minute()`, and `Second()` functions.

SetFileTime

Description

The `SetFileTime` API sets the date and time stamps for a file.

C Prototype

```
BOOL SetFileTime(HANDLE hFile,
    CONST FILETIME *lpCreationTime,
    CONST FILETIME *lpLastAccessTime,
    CONST FILETIME *lpLastWriteTime);
```

VB Declaration

```
Private Declare Function SetFileTime Lib "kernel32" _
    (ByVal hFile As Long, _
    lpCreationTime As FILETIME, _
    lpLastAccessTime As FILETIME, _
    lpLastWriteTime As FILETIME) As Long
```

Parameters

Parameter	Description
lpCreationTime	A FILETIME structure containing the date and time the file was created.
lpLastAccessTime	A FILETIME structure containing the date and time the file was last accessed.
lpLastWriteTime	A FILETIME structure containing the date and time the file was last modified.
Returns	If successful, a non-zero value is returned. If zero is returned, an error has occurred. For additional error information, call the GetLastError function.

Example

Refer to the example under SystemTimeToFileTime.

SystemTimeToFileTime

Description

The SystemTimeToFileTime API converts a SYSTEMTIME structure to a FILETIME structure, which can be passed to the SetFileTime API.

C Prototype

```
BOOL SystemTimeToFileTime(CONST SYSTEMTIME *lpSystemTime,
    LPFILETIME lpFileTime);
```

VB Declaration

```
Private Declare Function SystemTimeToFileTime _
    Lib "kernel32" _
    (lpSystemTime As SYSTEMTIME, _
    lpFileTime As FILETIME) As Long
```

Parameters

Parameter	Description
lpSystemTime	A SYSTEMTIME structure containing the date and time you wish to convert to a FILETIME structure.
lpFileTime	The FILETIME structure to be populated by the API.
Returns	If successful, a non-zero value is returned. If zero is returned, an error has occurred. For additional error information, call the GetLastError function.

Example

```
Private Function SetFileTimes()
    Dim rc As Long
    Dim lpCreationTime As FILETIME
    Dim lpLastAccessTime As FILETIME
    Dim lpLastWriteTime As FILETIME
    Dim hFile As Long
    Dim lpBuff As OFSTRUCT
    Dim lpsCT As SYSTEMTIME
    Dim lpsLAT As SYSTEMTIME
    Dim lpsLWT As SYSTEMTIME

    'Get a handle to the file
    hFile = OpenFile(ByVal mFilename, lpBuff, OF_WRITE)
    If hFile <> 0 Then
        'Convert creation date/time
        With lpsCT
            .wMonth = Month(mCreated)
            .wDay = Day(mCreated)
            .wYear = Year(mCreated)
            .wHour = Hour(mCreated)
```

```
                .wMinute = Minute(mCreated)
                .wSecond = Second(mCreated)
            End With
            rc = SystemTimeToFileTime(lpsCT, lpCreationTime)

            'Convert creation date/time
            With lpsLAT
                .wMonth = Month(mLastAccessed)
                .wDay = Day(mLastAccessed)
                .wYear = Year(mLastAccessed)
            End With
            rc = SystemTimeToFileTime(lpsLAT, lpLastAccessTime)

            'Convert creation date/time
            With lpsLWT
                .wMonth = Month(mLastModified)
                .wDay = Day(mLastModified)
                .wYear = Year(mLastModified)
                .wHour = Hour(mLastModified)
                .wMinute = Minute(mLastModified)
                .wSecond = Second(mLastModified)
            End With
            rc = SystemTimeToFileTime(lpsLWT, lpLastWriteTime)

            'Save the new file dates & times
            rc = SetFileTime(hFile, _
                    lpCreationTime, _
                    lpLastAccessTime, _
                    lpLastWriteTime)

            'Close the file
            rc = lclose(hFile)
        End If
    End Function
```

Working with Directories

Although Visual Basic provides easy-to-use directory functions, the Windows API allows you to perform more flexible and powerful operations on directories.

Under Windows NT you can use the Windows API to create directories with security attributes applied to them. You can use other directories as templates for new directories.

In addition to your basic directory functionality, you can even copy or move entire directory trees with a single API call. You no longer need to write recursive Visual Basic code to achieve the same functionality.

CreateDirectory

Description

The CreateDirectory API creates a directory on a drive, with optional security.

C Prototype

```
BOOL CreateDirectory(LPCTSTR lpPathName,
    LPSECURITY_ATTRIBUTES lpSecurityAttributes);
```

VB Declaration

```
Private Declare Function CreateDirectory Lib "kernel32" _
    Alias "CreateDirectoryA" _
    (ByVal lpPathName As String, _
    lpSecurityAttributes As SECURITY_ATTRIBUTES) As Long
```

Parameters

Parameter	Description
lpPathName	The path to the directory you wish to create.
lpSecurityAttributes	A SECURITY_ATTRIBUTES structure containing the security options you want to apply to the directory being created. Refer to the Notes below for more information.
Returns	If successful, a non-zero value is returned. If zero is returned, an error has occurred. For additional error information, call the Get-LastError function.

Notes

The SECURITY_ATTRIBUTES structure is used to pass a security descriptor to the directory.

```
Private Type SECURITY_ATTRIBUTES
    nLength As Long
    lpSecurityDescriptor As Long
    bInheritHandle As Long
End Type
```

Each member is described below:

Member	Description
nLength	The size of this structure.
lpSecurityDescriptor	The security descriptor for this file. You can set this to 0 to specify the security descriptor for the current process.
bInheritHandle	If set to True, the handle to this structure can be inherited by other processes.

Example

```
Public Function Create(Path As String) As Long
    Dim rc As Long
    Dim lpSA As SECURITY_ATTRIBUTES

    'We're not concerned with security
    'attributes for this example
    With lpSA
        .bInheritHandle = False
        .lpSecurityDescriptor = 0
        .nLength = Len(lpSA)
    End With

    'Call the API
    rc = CreateDirectory(ByVal Path, lpSA)

    'Return result
    If rc <> 0 Then
        Create = 0
```

```
       Else
            Create = -1
       End If
End Function
```

CreateDirectoryEx

Description

The CreateDirectoryEx API works the same way as the CreateDirectory API, except it allows you to specify a directory as a template for the one being created.

C Prototype

```
BOOL CreateDirectoryEx(LPCTSTR lpTemplateDirectory,
    LPCTSTR lpNewDirectory,
    LPSECURITY_ATTRIBUTES lpSecurityAttributes);
```

VB Declaration

```
Private Declare Function CreateDirectoryEx Lib "kernel32" _
    Alias "CreateDirectoryExA" _
    (ByVal lpTemplateDirectory As String, _
    ByVal lpNewDirectory As String, _
    lpSecurityAttributes As SECURITY_ATTRIBUTES) As Long
```

Parameters

Parameter	Description
lpTemplateDirectory	The name of the directory that this directory will be based on.
lpNewDirectory	The name of the directory to be created.
lpSecurityAttributes	A SECURITY_ATTRIBUTES structure specifying the security descriptor for the directory being created. Refer to the Notes in the previous section for details about this structure.
Returns	If successful, a non-zero value is returned. If zero is returned, an error has occurred. For additional error information, call the Get-LastError function.

RemoveDirectory

Description

The RemoveDirectory API removes an empty directory from the drive.

C Prototype

```
BOOL RemoveDirectory(LPCTSTR lpPathName);
```

VB Declaration

```
Private Declare Function RemoveDirectory Lib "kernel32" _
    Alias "RemoveDirectoryA" _
    (ByVal lpPathName As String) As Long
```

Parameters

Parameter	Description
lpPathName	The name of the directory to be deleted.
Returns	If successful, a non-zero value is returned. If zero is returned, an error has occurred. For additional error information, call the GetLastError function.

Example

```
Public Function Delete(Path As String) As Boolean
    Delete = RemoveDirectory(ByVal Path)
End Function
```

MoveFile

Description

The MoveFile API moves or renames a file or directory and all of its contents. The API returns True if the call is successful.

C Prototype

```
BOOL MoveFile(LPCTSTR lpExistingFileName,
    LPCTSTR);
```

VB Declaration

```
Private Declare Function MoveFile Lib "kernel32" _
    Alias "MoveFileA" _
    (ByVal lpExistingFileName As String, _
    ByVal lpNewFileName As String) As Long
```

Parameters

Parameter	Description
lpExistingFilename	The name of the source to be moved.
lpNewFilename	The name of the destination.
Returns	If successful, a non-zero value is returned. If zero is returned, an error has occurred. For additional error information, call the GetLastError function.

Example

The following example uses the MoveFile API to rename a directory:

```
Public Function Rename(OldPath As String, _
       NewPath As String) As Boolean
    Rename = MoveFile(ByVal OldPath, ByVal NewPath)
End Function
```

SHFileOperation

Description

The SHFileOperation API allows you to perform most file operations, such as copy, move, rename, and delete. This API is a bit more powerful that the previous APIs, as it allows you to show a dialog, and works with nested folders without requiring any recursive coding.

C Prototype

```
WINSHELLAPI int WINAPI SHFileOperation(
    LPSHFILEOPSTRUCT lpFileOp);
```

VB Declaration

```
Private Declare Function SHFileOperation _
    Lib "shell32.dll" _
    (lpFileOp As SHFILEOPSTRUCT) As Long
```

Parameters

Parameter	Description
lpFileOp	A SHFILEOPSTRUCT structure used to instruct the API what to do.
Returns	If successful, zero is returned.

Notes

The SHFILEOPSTRUCT structure is used to pass the appropriate command and parameters to the SHFileOperation API.

```
Private Type SHFILEOPSTRUCT
    hwnd As Long
    wFunc As Long
    pFrom As String
    pTo As String
    fFlags As Integer
    fAnyOperationsAborted As Long
    hNameMappings As Long
    lpszProgressTitle As
End Type
```

Each member is described below:

Member	Description
hwnd	Handle to the window that called this API.
wFunc	The operation to be performed by SHFile-Operation. This can be one of the following: FO_COPY, FO_DELETE, FO_MOVE, or FO_RENAME.
pFrom	The source file or directory of the operation. Multiple files can be separated by individual null characters. This member must be terminated by two nulls.

pTo	The destination file or directory of the operation. Multiple files can be separated by individual null characters. This member must be terminated by two nulls.
fFlags	A flag mask used to customize the behavior of the operation being carried out.
fAnyOperationsAborted	Returns a Boolean value indicating if any file operation was aborted.
hNameMappings	Handle to an SHNAMEMAPPING structure if the user specifies FOF_WANTMAPPINGHANDLE in the fFlags member. You will rarely require this in Visual Basic.
lpszProgressTitle	The title to display on the progress dialog if the FOF_SIMPLEPROGRESS flag is specified in the fFlags member.

The fFlags member can be set to any combination of the following flags:

flag	results
FOF_ALLOWUNDO	Allows an operation to be undone.
FOF_FILESONLY	Set this flag if you pass a file filter instead of a file or directory name.
FOF_MULTIDESTFILES	The pTo member specifies multiple individual files.
FOF_NOCONFIRMATION	Disables the confirmation dialog.
FOF_NOCONFIRMMKDIR	Disables the dialog displayed when a new folder is about to be created. This is the same as clicking the Yes to All button.
FOF_RENAMEONCOLLISION	Renames files if matching files already exist.
FOF_SILENT	All dialogs are suppressed.
FOF_SIMPLEPROGRESS	Displays the simple progress bar, which doesn't show filenames.
FOF_WANTMAPPINGHANDLE	Used to store names of files that were renamed if FOF_RENAMEONCOLLISION is specified.

Example

This example shows how to use SHFileOperation to copy an entire tree structure, much like the XCOPY command in DOS.

```
Public Function XCopy(Source As String, _
        Destination As String, _
        Optional Silent As Boolean) As Long

    Dim rc As Long
    Dim lpFileOp As SHFILEOPSTRUCT

    With lpFileOp
        .hwnd = 0
        .pFrom = Source & Chr$(0) & Chr$(0)
        .pTo = Destination & Chr$(0) & Chr$(0)
        .wFunc = FO_COPY
        If Silent Then
            .fFlags = .fFlags + _
                    FOF_SILENT + _
                    FOF_NOCONFIRMATION + _
                    FOF_NOCONFIRMMKDIR
        End If
    End With

    'Call the API
    rc = SHFileOperation(lpFileOp)
End Function
```

The trick to using this API is correctly populating the SHFILEOPSTRUCT structure. You can specify the command to perform, as well as several powerful and flexible options. For example, when a user calls this function with Silent set to False, the user will see the standard file copy progress dialog you normally see when moving files in Explorer.

Note that the pFrom and pTo members must be terminated with two null characters. This allows you to pass multiple files in each member using single nulls as delimiters.

CHAPTER
EIGHT

8

Working with Forms and Windows

- Making a Form Float

- Moving a Form Without a Caption

- Flashing the Form's Caption

- Accessing Other Windows

Sometimes you may want your application to appear as a form that requires a response from the user. The reminders in Microsoft Outlook will gracefully interrupt you while you work. They pop up out of nowhere and stay there until you acknowledge them. You can make your application rise above the others using the `BringWindowToTop` API. This API is good for making your form or application appear, but sometimes you don't want it to go away.

Making a Form Float

It is sometimes beneficial to make your application float above all others. Clocks and toolbars are good examples of forms that float. You may have occasion to require this functionality in your application. Using the `SetWindowPos` API you can do just that.

A window is layered on the screen based on the its z-order. The z-order is actually the position of the window along the z-axis. Going back to geometry, there are basically three dimensions, or axes. The x-axis determines an object's horizontal position relative to a reference point. The y-axis determines the objects vertical position relative to a reference point. And the z-axis determines an object's distance from the reference point.

Windows uses the same three axes to position windows. You are already familiar with the `.Left` and `.Top` properties to position a form on the screen. The following APIs work by changing the window's z-order, or placement along the z-axis, as shown in Figure 8.1.

FIGURE 8.1:

How windows use the z-order

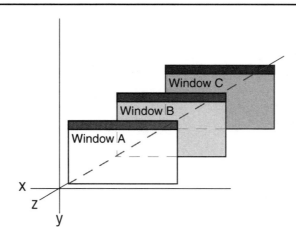

BringWindowToTop

Description

The BringWindowToTop API brings the specified window to the top of the z-order.

C Prototype

```
BOOL BringWindowToTop(HWND hWnd);
```

VB Declaration

```
Private Declare Function BringWindowToTop Lib "user32" _
    Alias "BringWindowToTop" _
    (ByVal hwnd As Long) As Long
```

Parameters

Parameter	Description
HWnd	Handle to the window to bring to the top.
Returns	If successful, a non-zero value is returned. If zero is returned, an error has occurred. For additional error information, call the GetLastError function.

Example

```
Dim rc As Long

rc = BringWindowToTop(hwnd)
```

SetWindowPos

Description

The SetWindowPos API is used to change the size, position, and z-order of a window.

C Prototype

```
BOOL SetWindowPos(HWND hWnd,
    HWND hWndInsertAfter,
```

```
int X,
int Y,
int cx,
int cy,
UINT uFlags);
```

VB Declaration

```
Private Declare Function SetWindowPos Lib "user32" _
    (ByVal hwnd As Long, _
    ByVal hWndInsertAfter As Long, _
    ByVal X As Long, _
    ByVal Y As Long, _
    ByVal cx As Long, _
    ByVal cy As Long, _
    ByVal wFlags As Long) As Long
```

Parameters

Parameter	Description
hWnd	Handle to the window to position.
hWndInsertAfter	A constant specifying the window's position in the z-order relative to other windows.
X	The leftmost position of the window.
Y	The topmost position of the window.
cx	The rightmost position of the window.
cy	The lowest portion of the window.
wFlags	Optional display flags. Refer to the Notes below.
Returns	If successful, a non-zero value is returned. If zero is returned, an error has occurred. For additional error information, call the GetLastError function.

Notes

There are many flags you can set. The ones you are most likely to use in Visual Basic are listed below.

Flag	Description
SWP_HIDEWINDOW	Hides the window.
SWP_NOACTIVATE	Prevents the form's Activate() event from firing after the form has been moved or resized.
SWP_NOMOVE	Prevents the window from moving horizontally or vertically.
SWP_NOREDRAW	Prevents the window from redrawing itself.
SWP_NOREPOSITION	Prevents the window's owner from changing its z-order.
SWP_NOSIZE	Prevents the window from resizing.
SWP_NOZORDER	Retains the current z-order. Use this flag if you want to reposition or resize the form, but don't want to change its z-order.
SWP_SHOWWINDOW	Shows the window.

Example

```
Private Sub Form_Resize()
    Dim rc As Long

    If WindowState <> vbMinimized Then
        rc = SetWindowPos(hwnd, HWND_TOPMOST, _
                0, 0, 0, 0, SWP_NOMOVE Or SWP_NOSIZE)
    End If
End Sub
```

In this example, the window is brought to the top and made to float. The user cannot resize it. This is accomplished by setting the hWndInsertAfter parameter to HWND_TOPMOST, which makes the window float. To prevent the form from moving or resizing, the SWP_NOMOVE and SWP_NOSIZE flags are passed.

Notice that this code is in the form's Resize() event. This ensures that the form will stay on top. When a window is minimized or maximized it loses its permanent position within the z-order. In other words, it will stop floating. By placing it in the Resize() event, the form will always stay on top, even after it is minimized.

Moving a Form Without a Caption

Sometimes it is useful to have a form without a caption. For example, many graphical equalizers and mixer applets that ship with your multimedia hardware do not utilize a caption. Instead, they sport a more natural remote control or stereo component interface. While this looks cool, the major drawback to this feature is that you cannot ordinarily move a window around without a caption.

However, there is hope if you want to make a cool interface that the user can position at will. Using the SendMessage and ReleaseCapture APIs you can move any form without a caption. In fact, you can use any Visual Basic control that has a handle (.hWnd) property as an anchor to drag your form around.

Let's look at the two APIs and see how to use them.

ReleaseCapture

Description

The ReleaseCapture API is used to release the mouse input to a window.

C Prototype

```
BOOL ReleaseCapture(VOID)
```

VB Declaration

```
Private Declare Function ReleaseCapture Lib "user32" _
    Alias "ReleaseCapture" () As Long
```

Parameters

Parameter	Description
None	No parameter is needed to call this function.
Returns	If successful, a non-zero value is returned. If zero is returned, an error has occurred and a call to GetLastError can be made to retrieve extended error information.

Example

This example allows you to move a form around by dragging the form. The form may or may not have a caption, but the form background acts as the anchor.

```
Private Sub Form_MouseDown(Button As Integer, _
        Shift As Integer, _
        X As Single, _
        Y As Single)

    Dim rc As Long

    'Release the mouse capture
    ReleaseCapture

    'Send the mousemove to the hidden caption
    rc = SendMessage(hwnd, _
            WM_SYSCOMMAND, _
            MOUSE_MOVE, 0)
End Sub
```

The first API, `ReleaseCapture`, removes the mouse capture from the form. This prevents the `MouseDown` event from being called recursively, which could place your program in an endless loop.

Once the mouse has been released, simulate a mouse-down message on the window's title bar by sending the `WM_SYSCOMMAND` message with the `MOUSE_MOVE` parameter. The result is a simulated drag event on the form's caption, which causes the form to move.

If you wanted to use another control as an anchor, place this code within the control's `MouseDown` event and change the `hWnd` property to the handle of the control that serves as the anchor.

Flashing the Form's Caption

The Windows 95 user interface guidelines suggest flashing a form's title bar to grab the user's attention. You may have noticed this effect when your printer runs out of paper and the reminder message appears on your screen.

By flashing the title bar, a user receives a visual cue that something requires attention. As a matter of fact the application's button on the Task Bar will also flash, so even if the application or window is hidden you still receive a notification from the Task Bar.

Use this technique if your application ever requires the immediate attention of the user. You can do this using the FlashWindow API.

FlashWindow

Description

The FlashWindow API is used to alternately change the appearance of a window's title bar. By calling this API repeatedly, you can make the title bar flash to grab the user's attention.

C Prototype

```
BOOL FlashWindow(HWND hWnd,
    BOOL bInvert);
```

VB Declaration

```
Private Declare Function FlashWindow Lib "user32" _
    Alias "FlashWindow" _
    (ByVal hwnd As Long, _
    ByVal bInvert As Long) As Long
```

Parameters

Parameter	Description
hwnd	Handle to the window to flash.
bInvert	Boolean value used to toggle the inverted state of the title bar. Set this to True and call this API repeatedly.
Returns	A zero indicates that the window was not active prior to making this call. A non-zero indicates that the window was active before this call.

Example

```
Private Sub tmrTimer_Timer()
    Dim rc As Long

    rc = FlashWindow(hwnd, True)
End Sub
```

Accessing Other Windows

There will be times when you need to access other applications. For example, you may need to take control of another application.

I once wrote a word expander, much like the auto-complete feature in Microsoft Word. In order to send words and keystrokes to the other application I had to determine its handle. This required a number of APIs that did everything from determining the application with the focus to obtaining the handle of the destination window that received the expanded text.

While this is only one example of how you may communicate with external applications, there are many other reasons to do so. The APIs described in this section will help get you on your way!

DestroyWindow

Description

The DestroyWindow API is used to destroy another window and remove it from memory.

C Prototype

```
BOOL DestroyWindow(HWND hWnd);
```

VB Declaration

```
Private Declare Function DestroyWindow Lib "user32" _
    Alias "DestroyWindow" _
    (ByVal hwnd As Long) As Long
```

Parameters

Parameter	Description
hwnd	The handle to the window to destroy.
Returns	If successful, a non-zero value is returned. If zero is returned, an error has occurred and a call to GetLastError can be made to retrieve extended error information.

Example

```
Dim rc As Long

rc = DestroyWindow( hwnd)
```

EnumWindows

Description

The EnumWindows API is used to enumerate all top-level windows.

C Prototype

```
BOOL EnumWindows(WNDENUMPROC lpEnumFunc,
    LPARAM lParam);
```

VB Declaration

```
Private Declare Function EnumWindows Lib "user32" _
    (ByVal lpEnumFunc As Long, _
    ByVal lParam As Long) As Long
```

Parameters

Parameter	Description
lpEnumFunc	Address of a callback function used to enumerate the windows.
LParam	An application-defined value used to pass to the callback function specified in the lpEnumFunc parameter.

| Returns | If successful, a non-zero value is returned. If zero is returned, an error has occurred and a call to `GetLastError` can be made to retrieve extended error information. |

Example

There are two parts to this example. The first part calls the API and the second part is the required callback function.

```
Public Function ListWindows() As Long
    Dim rc As Long
    Dim lParam As Long

    'Were not concerned with a custom message
    'at this time
    lParam = 0

    'Call the API
    ListWindows = EnumWindows(AddressOf EnumWindowsProc, lParam)
End Function
```

As always, the callback function must reside in a standard basic module, not a class or form.

```
Public Function EnumWindowsProc(ByVal hwnd As Long, _
        ByVal lParam As Long) As Boolean

    Dim w As clsWindows

    Set w = New clsWindows
        Debug.Print w.WindowTitle(hwnd)
    Set w = Nothing

    EnumWindowsProc = True
End Function
```

Within the `EnumWindowsProc` function, note that the two parameters are hWnd and lParam. Both of these must be passed by value since their values are of concern, and not their addresses. Also, the function must return a Boolean value. You must return `True` to enumerate more windows, or `False` to stop enumerating.

Within the callback function you can do whatever you like. More often than not, however, you will want to return or check the window's caption, and then respond accordingly. In this example, the callback simply calls a method in the clsWindows class, which returns the window's caption.

GetDesktopWindow

Description

The GetDesktopWindow API is used to retrieve the handle to the desktop window. This is the parent window to all other windows in the system.

C Prototype

```
HWND GetDesktopWindow(VOID)
```

VB Declaration

```
Private Declare Function GetDesktopWindow Lib "user32" _
    Alias "GetDesktopWindow" () As Long
```

Parameters

Parameter	Description
None	
Returns	The desktop window handle is returned.

Example

```
hwndDesktop = GetDesktopWindow()
```

FindWindow

Description

The FindWindow API finds the first window with the same class name and/or the same window title as those specified in this API's arguments.

C Prototype

```
HWND FindWindow(LPCTSTR lpClassName,
    LPCTSTR lpWindowName);
```

VB Declaration

```
Private Declare Function FindWindow Lib "user32" _
    Alias "FindWindowA" _
    (ByVal lpClassName As String, _
    ByVal lpWindowName As String) As Long
```

Parameters

Parameter	Description
LpClassName	A string containing the class name of the window to find.
LpWindowName	A string containing the caption of the window to find.
Returns	If successful, a handle to the window is returned, otherwise a Null value indicates an error. Use the GetLastError function to retrieve any extended error information.

Notes

Some useful class names are listed below:

Class Name	Application
MSPaintApp	Paint
Notepad	Notepad
OpusApp	Microsoft Word
ProgMan	Program Manager
SciCalc	Calculator
ThunderMain	Visual Basic
WordPadClass	WordPad

Of course there are many other window classes. You can pass a handle to the GetClassName API to determine a window's class name.

Example

```
Public Function Find(Caption As String, _
        Optional ClassName As String) As Long

    If IsNull(ClassName) Then ClassName = ""

    Find = FindWindow(ClassName, Caption)
End Function
```

GetForegroundWindow

Description

The GetForegroundWindow API retrieves the handle of the foreground window, or the window with the focus.

C Prototype

```
HWND GetForegroundWindow(VOID)
```

VB Declaration

```
Private Declare Function GetForegroundWindow _
    Lib "user32" _
    Alias "GetForegroundWindow" () As Long
```

Parameters

Parameter	Description
None	
Returns	The foreground window handle is returned. If Null is returned, this could indicate that the window is losing activation.

Example

```
hwndForeground = GetForegroundWindow()
```

GetNextWindow

Description

The GetNextWindow API gets the handle of the next window in the z-order.

C Prototype

```
HWND GetNextWindow(HWND hWnd,
    UINT wCmd);
```

VB Declaration

```
Private Declare Function GetNextWindow Lib "user32" _
    Alias "GetWindow" _
    (ByVal hwnd As Long, _
    ByVal wFlag As Long) As Long
```

Parameters

Parameter	Description
hwnd	Handle to the current window.
wFlag	The direction to move through the z-order. This can be either GW_HWNDNEXT or GW_HWNDPREV.
Returns	The next or previous window handle is returned. If Null is returned, there is no next or previous window.

Example

This code returns the window handle of the next available window.

```
hwndWindow = GetNextWindow(hwnd, GW_HWNDNEXT)
```

GetWindowText

Description

The GetWindowText API is used to retrieve the text within the title bar of a window. If the call is successful, this API returns the number of bytes included in the return buffer.

C Prototype

```
int GetWindowText(HWND hWnd,
    LPTSTR lpString,
    int nMaxCount);
```

VB Declaration

```
Private Declare Function GetWindowText Lib "user32" _
    Alias "GetWindowTextA" _
    (ByVal hwnd As Long, _
    ByVal lpString As String, _
    ByVal cch As Long) As Long
```

Parameters

Parameter	Description
HWnd	Handle to the window whose text you wish to retrieve.
lpString	Pre-initialized string buffer used to return the window text.
cch	The maximum number of bytes to retrieve.
Returns	If successful, the length of the text is returned. If the returned value is zero, then either an invalid handle was used, the text is empty, or the window has no title bar.

Example

This code returns the title of the current window.

```
Public Function WindowTitle(hwnd As Long) As String
    Dim rc As Long
    Dim lpString As String
    Dim cch As Long

    'Allocate a buffer
    cch = 255
    lpString = String$(cch, Chr$(0))
```

```
    'Acll the API
    rc = GetWindowText(hwnd, lpString, cch)

    If rc > 0 Then
        WindowTitle = Left$(lpString, rc)
    Else
        WindowTitle = ""
    End If
End Function
```

SetWindowText

Description

The SetWindowText API sets the caption text in the title bar of the specified window.

C Prototype

```
BOOL SetWindowText(HWND hWnd,
    LPCTSTR lpString);
```

VBDeclaration

```
Private Declare Function SetWindowText Lib "user32" _
    Alias "SetWindowTextA" _
    (ByVal hwnd As Long, _
    ByVal lpString As String) As Long
```

Parameters

Parameter	Description
hWnd	Handle of the window whose caption you wish to set.
lpString	Null-terminated string containing the text to set the caption to.
Returns	If successful, a non-zero is returned. An error is indicated with a zero returned value. Use Get-LastError to retrieve extended information about the error.

Example

```
Dim rc As Long
Dim strTitle as String
strTitle = "New Title" & Chr$(0)
rc = SetWindowText( hwnd, strTitle )
```

SetForegroundWindow

Description

The SetForegroundWindow API is used to bring a window to the foreground.

C Prototype

```
BOOL SetForegroundWindow(HWND hWnd);
```

VB Declaration

```
Declare Function SetForegroundWindow Lib "user32" _
    Alias "SetForegroundWindow" _
    (ByVal hwnd As Long) As Long
```

Parameters

Parameter	Description
hwnd	Handle to the form you wish to bring to the foreground.
Returns	A non-zero indicates the window was brought to the foreground. A zero indicates the window was not brought to the foreground.

Example

```
Public Sub BringToForeground(Caption As String)
    Dim hwnd As Long

    'First, find the window
    hwnd = FindWindow("", Caption)

    'Then set it to the foreground...
```

```
        SetForegroundWindow hwnd
    End Sub
```

WindowFromPoint

Description

The WindowFromPoint API returns the window that contains the specified point.

C Prototype

```
HWND WindowFromPoint(POINT Point);
```

VB Declaration

```
Private Declare Function WindowFromPoint Lib "user32" _
    Alias "WindowFromPoint" _
    (ByVal xPoint As Long, _
    ByVal yPoint As Long) As Long
```

Parameters

Parameter	Description
xPoint	The horizontal point.
yPoint	The vertical point.
Returns	A handle to the window containing the point. Null is returned if no window exists at that point.

Example

```
Dim rc As Long
rc = WindowsFromPoint(xPoint, yPoint)
```

The examples in this chapter are found in the clsWindows class, which can be downloaded from the Sybex Web site at www.sybex.com.

CHAPTER
NINE

9

Shell APIs

- Launching Applications

- Working with the Recycle Bin

- Setting the Desktop Wallpaper

This chapter is a bit more fun, as it deals with more of the user interface aspects of the Windows API.

In this chapter you will learn how to launch applications both synchronously and asynchronously, work with Explorer and the Recycle Bin, as well as learn how to manipulate the desktop.

Launching Applications

There are several methods you can use to spawn another application. You can use Visual Basic's `Shell()` command or you can use an API, such as `CreateProcess` or `ShellExecute`.

The `Shell` command is handy for quick and dirty spawning operations. However, it spawns applications asynchronously and you can't start applications by calling their associated document. For example, you cannot start Word by shelling to `ReadMe.doc`.

You can use the `ShellExecute` API to launch a document or application. This launches the application asynchronously as well, but allows you to start applications based on a document's association.

The `CreateProcess` API is the most powerful of the three methods and is also the trickiest to use. If the API call is successful, it returns a handle to the newly created process. You can pass this handle to the `WaitForSingleObject` API to make Visual Basic wait until the spawned process has terminated.

This chapter takes a look at these APIs to give you a better understanding of what they actually do. Then all the APIs will be put together into a single `Spawn` function that you can use in your own applications.

ShellExecute

Description

The `ShellExecute` API is used to explore, open, or print a file or document.

C Prototype

```
HINSTANCE ShellExecute(HWND hwnd,
    LPCTSTR lpOperation,
    LPCTSTR lpFile,
    LPCTSTR lpParameters,
    LPCTSTR lpDirectory,
    INT nShowCmd);
```

VB Declaration

```
Private Declare Function ShellExecute Lib "shell32.dll" _
    Alias "ShellExecuteA" _
    (ByVal hWnd As Long, _
    ByVal lpOperation As String, _
    ByVal lpFile As String, _
    ByVal lpParameters As String, _
    ByVal lpDirectory As String, _
    ByVal nShowCmd As Long) As Long
```

Parameters

Parameter	Description
hWnd	Handle to the window that called this API.
lpOperation	A null-terminated string containing the command to carry out. This can be explore, properties, edit, open, or print.
lpFile	The file to open or print, or the folder to explore.
lpParameters	Null-terminated string containing the parameters to be passed to the command.
lpDirectory	Null-terminated string containing the default directory.
nShowCmd	Flag that determines how the application is displayed on the screen. You can use flags such as SW_SHOW, SW_HIDE, SW_MINIMIZE, SW_MAXIMIZE, SW_RESTORE, SW_SHOWNORMAL, and others.

Returns	If greater than 32, the call was successful. Less than 32 indicates an error.

Example

```
rc = ShellExecute(0, "Open", "calc.exe", _
        "", "c:\windows", SW_SHOWNORMAL)
```

CreateProcess

Description

The CreateProcess API creates a new process and thread, which it uses to run the specified executable file.

C Prototype

```
BOOL CreateProcess(LPCTSTR lpApplicationName,
    LPTSTR lpCommandLine,
    LPSECURITY_ATTRIBUTES lpProcessAttributes,
    LPSECURITY_ATTRIBUTES lpThreadAttributes,
    BOOL bInheritHandles,
    DWORD dwCreationFlags,
    LPVOID lpEnvironment,
    LPCTSTR lpCurrentDirectory,
    LPSTARTUPINFO lpStartupInfo,
    LPPROCESS_INFORMATION lpProcessInformation);
```

VB Declaration

```
Private Declare Function CreateProcess Lib "kernel32" _
    Alias "CreateProcessA" _
    (ByVal lpApplicationName As String, _
    ByVal lpCommandLine As String, _
    lpProcessAttributes As Any, _
    lpThreadAttributes As Any, _
    ByVal bInheritHandles As Long, _
    ByVal dwCreationFlags As Long, _
    lpEnvironment As Any, _
    ByVal lpCurrentDirectory As String, _
    lpStartupInfo As STARTUPINFO, _
    lpProcessInformation As PROCESS_INFORMATION) As Long
```

Parameters

Parameter	Description
lpApplicationName	Name of the executable or module. If lp-CommandLine is null, then CreateProcess executes the program specified in this parameter.
lpCommandLine	If lpApplicationName is null, then this parameter contains the name of the program to launch. If both lpApplicationName and lpCommandLine are not null, then the program name is specified in lpApplication-Name and its parameters are specified in lpCommandLine.
lpProcessAttributes	A SECURITY_ATTRIBUTES structure that determines if this process can be inherited. This can normally be set to 0.
lpThreadAttributes	A SECURITY_ATTRIBUTES structure that determines if this process can be inherited. This can normally be set to 0.
bInheritHandles	Boolean value indicating if the newly created process inherits handles from the calling process.
dwCreationFlags	Flags that specify additional configuration parameters for the process.
lpEnvironment	String containing a null-delimited list of environment parameters. If this parameter is set to null, the current environment is used in the new process.
lpCurrentDirectory	String pointing to the default directory for the new process.
lpStartupInfo	A STARTUPINFO structure that configures the appearance of the new process.

lpProcessInformation	A PROCESS_INFORMATION structure that returns information about the newly created process.
Returns	A non-zero value indicates it was successful. If zero is returned, then this call failed. Another call to GetLastError can be made to retrieve extended error information.

Notes

This function requires that the SECURITY_ATTRIBUTE, PROCESS_INFORMATION, and STARTUPINFO structures be used. These structures and their parameters are listed here.

```
Private Type SECURITY_ATTRIBUTES
    nLength As Long
    lpSecurityDescriptor As Long
    bInheritHandle As Long
End Type
```

Parameter	Description
nLength	Size of this structure.
lpSecurityDescriptor	A descriptor that controls the sharing of this process.
BInheritHandle	If set to True, the new process will inherit this handle. If set to False, the new process will not inherit this handle.

```
Private Type PROCESS_INFORMATION
    hProcess As Long
    hThread As Long
    dwProcessId As Long
    dwThreadId As Long
End Type
```

Parameter	Description
hProcess	Handle to the created process.
hThread	Handle to the primary thread for the new process.

| dwProcessId | Global process identifier for identifying the process. |
| dwThreadId | Global thread identifier for identifying the thread. |

```
Private Type STARTUPINFO
    cb As Long
    lpReserved As String
    lpDesktop As String
    lpTitle As String
    dwX As Long
    dwY As Long
    dwXSize As Long
    dwYSize As Long
    dwXCountChars As Long
    dwYCountChars As Long
    dwFillAttribute As Long
    dwFlags As Long
    wShowWindow As Integer
    cbReserved2 As Integer
    lpReserved2 As Long
    hStdInput As Long
    hStdOutput As Long
    hStdError As Long
End Type
```

Parameter	Description
cb	Size of this structure.
lpReserved	Set to null.
lpDesktop	Null-terminated name of desktop and window, or just desktop, for this process.
lpTitle	If console process, this is the title.
dwX	Ignored unless dwFlags is set to STARTF_USEPOSITION. If it is, then this is the x position for the upper-left corner of the window.

dwY	Ignored unless dwFlags is set to STARTF_USEPOSITION. If it is, then this is the y position for the upper-left corner of the window.
dwXSize	Ignored unless dwFlags is set to STARTF_USESIZE. If it is, then this is the width of the new window.
dwYSize	Ignored unless dwFlags is set to STARTF_USESIZE. If it is, then this is the height of the window.
dwXCountChars	Ignored unless dwFlags is set to STARTF_USECOUNTCHARS. If it is, then this is the screen buffer width, in pixels, for a console process.
dwYCountChars	Ignored unless dwFlags is set to STARTF_USECOUNTCHARS. If it is, then this is the screen buffer height, in pixels, for a console process.
dwFillAttribute	Ignored unless dwFlags is set to STARTF_USEFILLATTRIBUTE. If it is, then this is the initial colors (background and foreground) for the new window. It can be any one of the following values: FOREGROUND_BLUE, FOREGROUND_GREEN, FOREGROUND_RED, FOREGROUND_INTENSITY, BACKGROUND_BLUE, BACKGROUND_GREEN, BACKGROUND_RED, and BACKGROUND_INTENSITY.
dwFlags	This bit field can be any combination of the following: STARTF_FORCEONFEEDBACK, STARTF_FORCEOFFFEEDBACK, STARTF_RUNFULLSCREEN, STARTF_USECOUNTCHARS, STARTF_USEFILLATTRIBUTE, STARTF_USEPOSITION, STARTF_USESHOWWINDOW, STARTF_USESIZE, and STARTF_USESTDHANDLES, and is used to determine which part of the STARTUPINFO is used.

wShowWindow	Ignored unless dwFlags is set to STARTF _USESHOWWINDOW. Can be any constant SW_ value. There are too many to list here and it is recommended that you use the API Viewer to locate the SW_ flags to use.
cbReserved2	Must be zero.
lpReserved2	Must be null.
hStdInput	Ignored unless dwFlags is set to STARTF _USESTDHANDLES. If it is set, this is the handle to be used as the standard input.
hStdOutput	Ignored unless dwFlags is set to STARTF _USESTDHANDLES. If it is set, this is the handle to be used as the standard output.
hStdError	Ignored unless dwFlags is set to STARTF _USESTDHANDLES. If it is set, this is the handle to be used as the standard error.

Example

Refer to the CloseHandle API for an example of how to call this function.

WaitForSingleObject

Description

The WaitForSingleObject API simply waits for a process to return or a timeout to occur. This API is responsible for making a call to CreateProcess, a synchronous operation. If the API call is successful, it will return WAIT_ABANDONED if the process was not returned, WAIT_OBJECT_0 if the state of the process has been signaled, or WAIT_TIMEOUT to indicate the timeout period has elapsed.

C Prototype

```
DWORD WaitForSingleObject(HANDLE hHandle,
    DWORD dwMilliseconds);
```

VB Declaration

```
Private Declare Function WaitForSingleObject _
    Lib "kernel32" _
    (ByVal hHandle As Long, _
    ByVal dwMilliseconds As Long) As Long
```

Parameters

Parameter	Description
hHandle	Process handle to wait for.
dwMilliseconds	The waiting period in milliseconds. If this is set to INFINITE, the API will wait indefinitely for the process to return.
Returns	If successful, will return the value that caused the function to return. It can be one of the following: WAIT_ABANDONED, WAIT _OBJECT_0, or WAIT_TIMEOUT. Returns WAIT_FAILED if an error.

Example

Refer to the CloseHandle API for an example of how to call this function.

CloseHandle

Description

The CloseHandle API closes an object handle that was previously opened.

C Prototype

```
BOOL CloseHandle(HANDLE hObject);
```

VB Declaration

```
Private Declare Function CloseHandle Lib "kernel32" _
    (ByVal hObject As Long) As Long
```

Parameters

Parameter	Description
hObject	The handle to be closed.
Returns	Returns a non-zero if successful, zero if failed.

Example

The following example shows how to combine the previous APIs into a function that can spawn applications by executable name and by association. In addition, you can set this function to run synchronously or asynchronously.

```
Public Function Spawn(ByVal Filename As String, _
        Wait As Boolean) As Long

    Dim proc As PROCESS_INFORMATION
    Dim start As STARTUPINFO
    Dim rc As Long

    If Wait Then
        'Initialize the STARTUPINFO structure
        start.cb = Len(start)

        'Start the shelled application
        rc = CreateProcess(vbNullString, Filename, _
                ByVal 0, ByVal 0, 1, _
                NORMAL_PRIORITY_CLASS, ByVal 0, _
                vbNullString, start, proc)

        'Wait for the shelled application to finish
        rc = WaitForSingleObject(proc.hProcess, INFINITE)

        'Close its handle
        rc = CloseHandle(proc.hProcess)
    Else
        'Spawn the application asynchronously
        rc = ShellExecute(0, "Open", Filename, _
                "", "C:\", SW_SHOWNORMAL)
    End If
```

```
        'Return the result code
        Spawn = rc
    End Function
```

This example first checks to see if the user wants to run the application synchronously or asynchronously. It does this by checking the Wait parameter. If Wait is set to True, the application is started synchronously. Otherwise, an instance of the application is started asynchronously using the ShellExecute API.

When synchronous operation is requested, call the CreateProcess API first. In this example the concern is not with the STARTUPINFO structure, so just set its .cb member to the size of the structure.

If the call to CreateProcess is successful, it returns the handle to the new process in the hProcess member of the PROCESS_INFORMATION structure. Pass this handle to the WaitForSingleObject API using the INFINITE parameter to make it wait indefinitely for the application to terminate. Once the process terminates, WaitForSingleObject returns the appropriate result code and you release the process handle with a single call to CloseHandle.

This function is a great replacement for Visual Basic's Shell() command. It provides more flexibility for launching your own applications and documents. This function is especially useful when you need to create batch or text files that the application requires in a later step.

Working with the Recycle Bin

In this section you will see how easy it is to work with the Recycle Bin. Since Visual Basic doesn't natively allow you to send files to the Recycle Bin, you must revert to the Windows API to achieve this functionality.

You will build a Recycle Bin class that allows you to recycle files, display the contents of the Recycle Bin, as well as empty it.

Sending a File to the Recycle Bin

The following example shows how you can use the SHFileOperation API, which was discussed in Chapter 7, to send a file to the Recycle Bin.

```
Public Function Recycle(Filename As String, _
        Silent As Boolean) As Boolean
```

```
        Dim rc As Long
        Dim FileOperation As SHFILEOPSTRUCT

        On Error GoTo handler

        'Send the file to the recycle bin
        With FileOperation
            .wFunc = FO_DELETE
            .pFrom = Filename & Chr$(0)
            .fFlags = FOF_ALLOWUNDO + FOF_NOCONFIRMATION
            If Not Silent Then
                'Show the progress dialog
                .fFlags = .fFlags + FOF_SIMPLEPROGRESS
            End If
        End With

        'Do it
        rc = SHFileOperation(FileOperation)

        'Return the result
        Recycle = (rc = 0)

        'Bypass the error handler
        Exit Function

handler:
        'Return an error code
        Recycle = False
End Function
```

Exploring the Recycle Bin

This example shows how you can use the shell ShellExecute API to explore the Recycle Bin.

```
Public Sub Show()
    Dim rc As Long
Dim guid As String

    'Set the GUID for the bin
    guid = "::{645FF040-5081-101B-" & _
        "9F08-00AA002F954E}"

    'Explore it
```

```
    rc = ShellExecute(0&, _
            "Open", "explorer.exe", _
            "/root," & guid, _
            0&, SW_SHOWNORMAL)
End Sub
```

As you may have noticed, this example is a little unique in how it operates. In essence, it is a normal call to ShellExecute, but instead of passing a directory name as the startup folder, the Globally Unique Identifier (GUID) is passed, which represents the namespace for the Recycle Bin. You can pass other namespace GUIDs to browse other objects that can be represented by a namespace, such as the Windows desktop.

Another point to note here is the use of the /root switch before the GUID. This is actually a command line parameter for Explorer, which forces Explorer to restrict its view to the specified folder and all child folders. By using this parameter we are actually forcing Explorer to only show the Recycle Bin, while prohibiting navigation elsewhere.

Emptying the Recycle Bin

It is possible to empty a Recycle Bin using the SHEmptyRecycleBin API.

SHEmptyRecycleBin

Description

Calling the SHEmptyRecycleBin API allows you to empty the Windows Recycle Bin.

C Prototype

```
SHSTDAPI SHEmptyRecycleBin(HWND hwnd,
    LPCTSTR pszRootPath,
    DWORD dwFlags);
```

VB Declaration

```
Private Declare Function SHEmptyRecycleBin Lib "shell32" _
    Alias "SHEmptyRecycleBinA" _
    (ByVal hWnd As Long, _
    ByVal pszRootPath As String, _
    ByVal dwFlags As Long) As Long
```

Parameters

Parameter	Description
hWnd	Handle to the windows that called this API.
pszRootPath	A string containing the root drive, such as C:, that contains the Recycle Bin you wish to empty.
dwFlags	A mask of options that further configures the operation. Refer to the Notes below for further information on the flags.
Returns	Returns S_OK if successful. If not, returns an OLE-defined value.

Notes

This API is not declared in the API Viewer included with Visual Basic. The dwFlags mask can be a combination of the following constants:

Flags	Results
SHERB_NOCONFIRMATION	Suppresses the confirmation dialog before emptying the Recycle Bin.
SHERB_NOPROGRESSUI	Prevents the progress dialog from appearing during the procedure.
SHERB_NOSOUND	Prevents a sound from being played when the operation completes.

Example

This example shows how you can empty the Recycle Bin. As you can see in the code, this API call is very easy to use.

```
Public Function EmptyBin(Silent As Boolean, _
      Optional hWnd As Long, _
      Optional Drive As String) As Long

    Dim rc As Long
    Dim dwFlags As Long
```

```
'Make sure we have a handle
If IsNumeric(hWnd) = False Then hWnd = 0

'Set the options
dwFlags = SHERB_NOCONFIRMATION + _
            SHERB_NOSOUND
If Silent Then
    dwFlags = dwFlags + SHERB_NOPROGRESSUI
End If

'Empty the recycle bin
rc = SHEmptyRecycleBin(hWnd, ByVal Drive, dwFlags)
End Function
```

Setting the Desktop Wallpaper

This API is included in this chapter because the shell is like almost everything that is visible on the screen. For example, the desktop, start menu, Recycle Bin, and Explorer are all shell elements. In keeping with the object library approach to this book, this functionality has been added to the shell object.

Almost anything that can be accessed in the Control Panel can be accessed with the SystemParametersInfo API. Using this API you can set and retrieve the desktop wallpaper, icon spacing, screen saver options, and much more.

SystemParametersInfo

Description

The SystemParametersInfo API allows you to do much more than change the desktop wallpaper. You can use it to query or set almost every system-wide parameter found in the Control Panel. The API returns True if the call is successful.

C Prototype

```
BOOL SystemParametersInfo(UINT uiAction,
    UINT uiParam,
    PVOID pvParam,
    UINT fWinIni);
```

VB Declaration

```
Private Declare Function SystemParametersInfo _
    Lib "user32" _
    Alias "SystemParametersInfoA" _
    (ByVal uAction As Long, _
    ByVal uParam As Long, _
    ByRef lpvParam As Any, _
    ByVal fuWinIni As Long) As Long
```

Parameters

Parameter	Description
uAction	The parameter to retrieve or set. This will be one of the SPI_ constants listed in the API Viewer or API Explorer. These are self-explanatory.
uParam	Set to 0 when retrieving a value. Otherwise, set it to a value that depends on what uAction was used.
lpvParam	Returns the setting when uParam is set to 0. This returns null when setting a value.
fuWinIni	Flag to determine how the Win.Ini file is updated.
Returns	Returns a non-zero if successful, zero if failed. Place a call to GetLastError to obtain further error information.

Notes

The fuWinIni flag can be set to a combination of the following constants:

Flags	Results
SPIF_UPDATEINIFILE	Saves the setting to the user's profile.
SPIF_SENDCHANGE	Broadcasts a system settings change message to all other applications.
SPIF_SENDWININICHANGE	Same as SPIF_SENDCHANGE.

Example

```
Public Function SetWallpaper(Filename As String) As Boolean
    Dim rc As Long

    'Call the API
    rc = SystemParametersInfo(SPI_SETDESKWALLPAPER, _
            0&, _
            ByVal Filename, _
            SPIF_UPDATEINIFILE Or _
            SPIF_SENDWININICHANGE)

    'Return result
    SetWallpaper = (rc = 0)
End Function
```

There are many more things you can do using the shell APIs. Unfortunately, most of these APIs are undocumented by Microsoft, so you will need to scour the Internet for more information. If you download the API Explorer add-in from the Sybex Web site (www.sybex.com), you can add the undocumented declarations to your own database.

CHAPTER

TEN

Working with the Keyboard and Mouse

- Working with the Keyboard

- Working with the Mouse

There are several Windows APIs that let you work with your computer's keyboard or mouse. Understanding these APIs will allow you to program the keyboard or mouse in your application, if necessary.

Working with the Keyboard

You can use the subclassing techniques described in Chapter 3 to intercept keystrokes in your application and process them accordingly. You may want to do this if you wish to prevent certain keys from being pressed in your application. In other situations you may want to record all keystrokes for subsequent processing. In addition to trapping keystrokes, you can use the API to simulate keystrokes from your application. Some popular remote control applications use both of these techniques to send keystrokes to a remote computer, then the remote computer responds appropriately.

Before you read through the APIs, it is important for you to understand how a keyboard sends data to Windows.

The whole process is started when the user presses a key on the keyboard. When a key is pressed, a signal is sent to the computer and the keyboard driver translates it into a scan code. The scan code is a digital representation of the various signals sent from the keyboard.

Once a scan code is received it gets translated into a virtual key code. This key code is then sent to the keyboard buffer, where it waits to be processed. Keystrokes are processed on a first-in, first-out basis. This prevents any keystrokes from being lost or reorganized.

Finally, the virtual key code is sent to the window with the focus, where it gets translated into a character code so the application can process it. Figure 10.1 shows this process.

Now that you understand how the keyboard works, let's look at some keyboard APIs you can use to work with virtual keys, scan codes, and the keyboard buffer.

GetKeyState

Description

The GetKeyState API is used to determine the state of a virtual key. Use this API to determine if a key is pressed, released, or toggled.

How a keyboard processes keystrokes

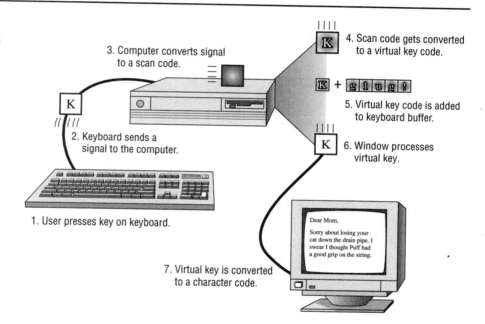

3. Computer converts signal to a scan code.

4. Scan code gets converted to a virtual key code.

5. Virtual key code is added to keyboard buffer.

2. Keyboard sends a signal to the computer.

6. Window processes virtual key.

1. User presses key on keyboard.

Dear Mom,

Sorry about losing your cat down the drain pipe. I swear I thought Puff had a good grip on the string.

7. Virtual key is converted to a character code.

C Prototype

```
SHORT GetKeyState(int nVirtKey);
```

VB Declaration

```
Private Declare Function GetKeyState Lib "user32" _
    (ByVal nVirtKey As Long) As Integer
```

Parameters

Parameter	Description
nVirtKey	The constant representing the virtual key you want to obtain information about.

Returns   Status of the key. If the high-order bit is 1, then the key is down, otherwise it is up. If the low-order bit is 1, the key is toggled. If the key is off and untoggled, then low-order will be 0.

Example

This example returns the state of the left control key:

```
Dim rc As Integer
rc = GetKeyState(VK_LCONTROL)
```

keybd_event

Description

The keybd_event API is used to send simulated keystrokes to the keyboard buffer.

C Prototype

```
VOID keybd_event(BYTE bVk,
    BYTE bScan,
    DWORD dwFlags,
    DWORD dwExtraInfo);
```

VB Declaration

```
Private Declare Sub keybd_event Lib "user32" _
    (ByVal bVk As Byte, _
    ByVal bScan As Byte, _
    ByVal dwFlags As Long, _
    ByVal dwExtraInfo As Long)
```

Parameters

Parameter	Description
bVk	The virtual key that will be sent to the keyboard buffer.
bScan	The hardware scan code for the key. This should not be used. Set it to 0.

dwFlags	A mask used to specify further information about the event. Refer to the Notes below.
dwExtraInfo	Additional information about the key.
Returns	None.

Notes

The dwFlags parameter can be composed of a combination of the following:

Flag	Results
KEYEVENTF_EXTENDEDKEY	Specifies that the key is an extended key.
KEYEVENTF_KEYUP	Specifies that the key is being released.

If the KEYEVENTF_KEYUP flag is not specified, it indicates the key is being pressed rather than released.

Example

This example sends a virtual key value of 32 to the window for processing:

```
keybd_event 32, 0, KEYEVENTF_KEYUP, 0
```

MapVirtualKey

Description

The MapVirtualKey API is used to translate a virtual key code to a scan code, and vice versa. This API returns a 0 if the call fails. Otherwise, it returns a virtual key, scan code, or character value, depending on the type of mapping action performed.

C Prototype

```
UINT MapVirtualKey(UINT uCode,
    UINT uMapType);
```

VB Declaration

```
Private Declare Function MapVirtualKey Lib "user32" _
    Alias "MapVirtualKeyA" _
    (ByVal wCode As Long, _
    ByVal wMapType As Long) As Long
```

Parameters

Parameter	Description
wCode	The virtual key or scan code to be converted.
wMapType	The type of mapping action to perform. Refer to the Notes below.
Returns	A scan code, virtual key, or character code. Depends on the value of wCode and wMapType.

Notes

You must pass one of the following values to the wMapType parameter to tell the API which conversion to perform:

0   Setting wMapType to 0 indicates you have passed a virtual key code to the wCode parameter and wish to return its scan code.

1   Setting wMapType to 1 indicates you have passed a scan code to the wCode parameter and wish to return a virtual key code that doesn't distinguish between left- and right-hand keys, such as the Control, Alt, and Shift keys.

2   Setting wMapType to 2 indicates you have passed a virtual key code to the wCode parameter and wish to return its character value. Note that the returned character value is unshifted.

3   Setting wMapType to 3 indicates you have passed a scan code to the wCode parameter and wish to return a virtual key code that distinguishes between left- and right-hand keys, such as the Control, Alt, and Shift keys.

Example

```
Dim rc As Long
rc = MapVirtualKey(VK_LCONTROL, 0)
```

MapVirtualKeyEx

Description

The MapVirtualKeyEx API is used to translate a virtual key code to a scan code, and vice versa. This API returns a 0 if the call fails. Otherwise, it returns a virtual key, scan code, or character value, depending on the action performed.

C Prototype

```
UINT MapVirtualKeyEx(UINT uCode,
    UINT uMapType,
    HKL dwhkl);
```

VB Declaration

```
Private Declare Function MapVirtualKeyEx Lib "user32" _
    Alias "MapVirtualKeyExA" _
    (ByVal uCode As Long, _
    ByVal uMapType As Long, _
    ByVal dwhkl As Long) As Long
```

Parameters

Parameter	Description
uCode	The code to be translated.
uMapType	The type of mapping to perform. Refer to the Notes for the MapVirtualKey API for more information.
dwhkl	Handle to a keyboard layout.
Returns	A scan code, virtual key, or character code. Depends on the value of uCode and uMapType. If there is no translation, it returns a zero.

OemKeyScan

Description

The OemKeyScan API returns the keyboard scan code for a specific ASCII character. The API returns the scan code in the low-order word of the return value and the shift state in the high-order word.

C Prototype

```
DWORD OemKeyScan(WORD wOemChar);
```

VB Declaration

```
Private Declare Function OemKeyScan Lib "user32" _
    (ByVal wOemChar As Long) As Long
```

Parameters

Parameter	Description
wOemChar	The ASCII value of the character whose scan code you wish to obtain.
Returns	Low-order contains the scan code, high-order contains the shift state and can be one of the following: 1=Shift key pressed, 2=Ctrl key pressed, and 4=Alt key pressed.

Example

This example returns the scan code for the space character:

```
Dim rc As Long
rc = OemKeyScan( 32 )
```

VkKeyScan

Description

The VkKeyScan API is used to translate a character code to its corresponding virtual key code and shift state. The API returns the virtual key code in the low-order word of the return value and the shift state in the high-order word.

C Prototype

```
SHORT VkKeyScan(TCHAR ch);
```

VB Declaration

```
Private Declare Function VkKeyScan Lib "user32" _
    Alias "VkKeyScanA" _
    (ByVal cChar As Byte) As Integer
```

Parameters

Parameter	Description
cChar	The character to translate.
Returns	If successful, the low-order contains the virtual key code, high-order contains the shift state and can be one of the following: 1=Shift key pressed, 2=Ctrl key pressed, and 4=Alt key pressed. Returns −1 if there is nothing to translate.

Example

```
Dim rc As Integer
rc = VkKeyScan( 32 )
```

VkKeyScanEx

Description

The VkKeyScanEx API is used to translate a character code to its corresponding scan code and shift state. The API returns the virtual key code in the low-order word of the return value and the shift state in the high-order word.

C Prototype

```
SHORT VkKeyScanEx(TCHAR ch,
    HKL dwhkl);
```

VB Declaration

```
Private Declare Function VkKeyScanEx Lib "user32" _
    Alias "VkKeyScanExA" _
    (ByVal ch As Byte, _
    ByVal dwhkl As Long) As Integer
```

Parameters

Parameter	Description
ch	The character to translate.
dwhkl	Handle to the keyboard layout to use in the translation.
Returns	If successful, the low-order contains the virtual key code, high-order contains the shift state and can be one of the following: 1=Shift key pressed, 2=Ctrl key pressed, and 4=Alt key pressed. Returns –1 if there is nothing to translate.

The following example shows how you can use the APIs described above to simulate sending keystrokes to the keyboard buffer. This method is handy when you want to send keys to other applications, especially when you don't know the handle to the application's destination window.

```
Private Sub SendText(Message As String)
    Dim vKey As Long
    Dim shift As Boolean
    Dim sc As Long
    Dim i As Integer

    For i = 1 To Len(Message)
        'Get the scan code for the character
        sc = OemKeyScan(Asc(Mid$(Message, i, 1)))

        'Do we need to use the shift key?
        shift = (HiWord(sc) And 2)

        'Get the virtual key, of the scan code
        vKey = MapVirtualKey(sc, 1)

        'Press the shift key if necessary...
        If shift Then keybd_event VK_SHIFT, _
                0, 0, 0

        'Press the key down
```

```
        keybd_event vKey, 0, 0, 0

        'Release the key
        keybd_event vKey, 0, KEYEVENTF_KEYUP, 0

        'Release the shift key if necessary
        If shift Then keybd_event VK_SHIFT, _
             0, KEYEVENTF_KEYUP, 0
    Next
End Sub
```

There are quite a few steps required to accomplish such a simple task! Since characters are sent to the keyboard buffer one at a time, it is necessary to process the text in the same manner. As a result, the keystroke APIs are placed in a loop that processes each character separately.

First, the OemKeyScan API is called with the ASCII value of the character to be sent. This API returns the virtual key code and shift state of the key being pressed. Since you need to separate these values, get the shift state by passing the scan code (sc) to the HiWord function. If the character requires the Shift key to be pressed, bit 2 will be set. As a result, AND the high-word portion with 2. If the result is true, then you know the Shift key must be pressed.

Once you have obtained the shift state, extract the virtual key from the scan code using the MapVirtualKey API. This will return the virtual key required by the keyboard buffer.

Now that you have all of the pieces to send a keystroke, determine if the Shift key must be pressed first. If the value of shift is true, then send the virtual key VK_SHIFT to the keyboard buffer.

Next, send the virtual key code to the keyboard buffer using keybd_event. This simulates the key press of the character within the string. Then release the key by calling keybd_event again, but this time with the KEYEVENTF_KEYUP option.

If the Shift key was pressed initially, then also call keybd_event along with KEYEVENTF_KEYUP and VK_SHIFT to release the Shift key. The result is a keystroke with the Shift key held down.

There are other shift states you may wish to check for, such as when the Ctrl and Alt keys are being held. You can easily add this functionality by ANDing the appropriate values with the high-word of the scan code. But for now, this example will show you how to send the basic keystrokes you may require in your own applications!

Working with the Mouse

Working with the mouse is much easier than working with the keyboard, perhaps because there are fewer combinations of code that can be processed by a mouse.

Fortunately, Visual Basic provides most of the mouse functionality that you need. It supports all the drag-and-drop operations, as well as changing the mouse pointer. It is much easier to use Visual Basic's intrinsic commands for these operations than to use APIs.

With all of its functionality there are still a few things that Visual Basic cannot do by itself, such as position the mouse pointer or simulate mouse movements. However, you can use the Windows API to build the additional functionality you require. The most useful APIs are described here.

GetCursorPos

Description

The GetCursorPos API returns the screen coordinates of the mouse pointer in pixels.

C Prototype

```
BOOL GetCursorPos(LPPOINT lpPoint);
```

VB Delcaration

```
Private Declare Function GetCursorPos Lib "user32" _
    (lpPoint As POINTAPI) As Long
```

Parameters

Parameter	Description
lpPoint	A POINTAPI structure that returns the x and y coordinates of the mouse.
Returns	If successful, returns a non-zero value. If fails, returns zero. For additional error information, call the GetLastError function.

Notes

Here is the POINTAPI structure that receives the information from this function call.

```
Private Type POINTAPI
        x As Long
        y As Long
End Type
```

Example

```
Public Sub GetScreenCoordinates(x As Long, y As Long)
    Dim rc As Long
    Dim lpPoint As POINTAPI

    'Get the cursor position
    rc = GetCursorPos(lpPoint)

    'Return the coordinates
    With lpPoint
        x = .x
        y = .y
    End With
End Sub
```

mouse_event

Description

The mouse_event API triggers a simulated mouse event.

C Prototype

```
VOID mouse_event(DWORD dwFlags,
    DWORD dx,
    DWORD dy,
    DWORD dwData,
    DWORD dwExtraInfo);
```

VB Delcaration

```
Private Declare Sub mouse_event Lib "user32" _
    (ByVal dwFlags As Long, _
```

```
ByVal dx As Long, _
ByVal dy As Long, _
ByVal cButtons As Long, _
ByVal dwExtraInfo As Long)
```

Parameters

Parameter	Description
dwFlags	A mask that specifies the type of mouse action to perform. Refer to the Notes below.
Dx	The position of the mouse pointer along the x-axis.
Dy	The position of the mouse pointer along the y-axis.
cButtons	A mask composed of the buttons that are being pressed.
dwExtraInfo	This contains an additional 32-bit value associated with the mouse event.
Returns	None

Notes

The dwFlags parameter can be a combination of the flags listed below:

Flag	Result
MOUSEEVENTF_ABSOLUTE	Use this flag to indicate that the dx and dy parameters contain absolute screen coordinates. If this flag is omitted, the dx and dy parameters contain coordinates relative to the current mouse location.
MOUSEEVENTF_MOVE	This flag indicates the mouse moved.
MOUSEEVENTF_LEFTDOWN	Simulates pressing the left mouse button.
MOUSEEVENTF_LEFTUP	Simulates releasing the left mouse button.
MOUSEEVENTF_RIGHTDOWN	Simulates pressing the right mouse button.
MOUSEEVENTF_RIGHTUP	Simulates releasing the right mouse button.

MOUSEEVENTF_MIDDLEDOWN	Simulates pressing the middle mouse button, if one exists.
MOUSEEVENTF_MIDDLEUP	Simulates releasing the middle mouse button, if one exists.
MOUSEEVENTF_WHEEL	When used in the Windows NT operating system, this flag specifies that the mouse wheel was moved. The amount of movement is passed through the dwData parameter.

Example

The following example is used to move the mouse pointer to the specified coordinates on the screen:

```
Public Sub Move(ByVal x As Long, ByVal y As Long)
    'Simulate a mouse move event
    mouse_event MOUSEEVENTF_ABSOLUTE + MOUSEEVENTF_MOVE, _
            (x * 65535) / (Screen.Width / 15), _
            (y * 65535) / (Screen.Height / 15), _
            0, _
            0
End Sub
```

ShowCursor

Description

The ShowCursor API is used to display or hide the mouse pointer. This API is commonly used in screen savers where the mouse is hidden while the screen saver is running, and then shown again when the screen saver is deactivated.

C Prototype

```
int ShowCursor( BOOL bShow // cursor visibility flag);
```

VB Declaration

```
Private Declare Function ShowCursor Lib "user32" _
    (ByVal bShow As Long) As Long
```

Parameters

Parameter	Description
bShow	A Boolean value used to toggle the state of the mouse pointer.
Returns	Display counter is returned.

Example

```
Public Sub Show()
    ShowCursor True
End Sub

Public Sub Hide()
    ShowCursor False
End Sub
```

CHAPTER

ELEVEN

Programming the Registry

- Overview of the Registry

- Registry APIs

- Using the Registry APIs

The registry is the database that Windows uses to store most of your computer settings. For the most part, the registry has replaced the initialization files left over from Windows 3.*x*. Everything from hardware configuration to applications, file associations, and Internet settings are stored in the registry.

Visual Basic has two functions that are used to access the registry. These are GetSetting and SaveSetting. So if Visual Basic has these, why would anyone want to learn the difficult registry APIs? The answer is simple: Visual Basic only writes to one small section of the registry. If you want to query values from other applications or system settings, you need something more powerful than the stock Visual Basic functions.

The GetSetting and SaveSetting functions read and write from the HKEY_CURRENT_USER\Software\VB and VBA Program Settings keys of the registry. Notice that when you use the CURRENT_USER registry key, all of the settings you work with are specific to the user who is currently logged in and not the default user ID. Therefore, each time a new user logs into that computer the settings will probably be different. This means you cannot create or access global settings when the computer is configured for multiple users. In Windows 9*x* this may not be much of a problem, as most machines are configured for single users. But if you use Windows NT, every computer maintains individual user settings. Therefore, you must maintain separate settings for each user.

Because GetSetting is a single-user style registry function, you would not be able to retrieve values such as the registered owner, which for Windows 95/98 is stored in the RegisteredOwner key under the HKEY_LOCAL_MACHINE\Software\ Microsoft\Windows\CurrentVersion key of the registry. Windows NT/2000 stores the same information under the HKEY_LOCAL_MACHINE\Software\ Microsoft\ Windows NT\CurrentVersion key. Since GetSetting cannot access this area of the registry, you must use the Windows registry APIs.

Overview of the Registry

The registry is the central component to almost everything within the 32-bit Windows environment. Applications store information in the registry. Hardware configuration is stored and retrieved. Even the operating system's configuration is stored in the registry. The registry is a convenient repository of information as long as you know how to use it. You may have snooped around in it, which is perfectly safe if you don't modify anything. Modifying the registry can be like neurosurgery for your computer. If you work with it properly the benefits are great and the possibilities are abundant. However, if you don't know what you are doing you could give your computer amnesia.

WARNING   Exercise caution when working with the registry. It is safe to read information, but if you must add or modify data within the registry, make sure you don't inadvertently modify data used to configure something else.

The registry is laid out much like the file system on your hard drive. It consists of keys and values, which are analogous to folders and files, respectively. If you are familiar with Windows NT security, you know that each folder has some level of security attached to it. Some folders permit all access while others restrict access. In the same manner, under Windows NT, each key in the registry has its own security descriptor that permits or restricts access to the key.

When you work with the registry you will be enumerating, reading, and writing keys and values. You don't need to worry about some of the more complex registry functions; chances are you will never need or use them. However, if you are interested, check out the Microsoft Developer Network Online at `http://msdn .microsoft.com`. It contains all of the registry information you could ever want.

The registry is organized by separate keys that logically group other keys and values together. There are six main keys in the registry for Windows 95/98 and five for Windows NT/2000. Windows NT/2000 maintains the first five keys shown below and Windows 95/98 uses all of them.

- HKEY_CLASSES_ROOT
- HKEY_CURRENT_USER
- HKEY_LOCAL_MACHINE
- HKEY_USERS
- HKEY_CURRENT_CONFIG
- HKEY_DYN_DATA

The Registry Editor, shown in Figure 11.1, gives you a picture of how the registry is organized. As you will soon see, each of these keys serves a specific purpose.

The registry editor

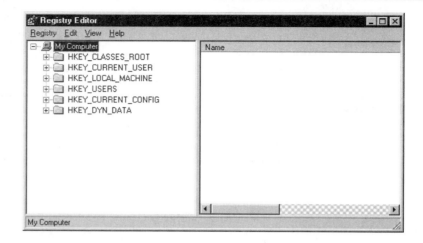

HKEY_CLASSES_ROOT

The HKEY_CLASSES_ROOT key is a copy of the information found under the HKEY _LOCAL_MACHINE\Software\Classes key of the registry. This key stores all information about ActiveX (COM) components, as well as file associations. The HKEY _CLASSES_ROOT key is provided for backward compatibility with Windows 3.x. If you need to access information about COM objects, look in the \Software\ Classes key under HKEY_LOCAL_MACHINE.

HKEY_CURRENT_USER

The HKEY_CURRENT_USER key contains profile information for the user who is currently logged onto the system. This profile can contain information such as the user's desktop arrangement, color configuration, network connections, and more. This key is more specific than the HKEY_USERS key, which contains all loaded user profiles.

HKEY_LOCAL_MACHINE

The HKEY_LOCAL_MACHINE key stores your computer's hardware, software, and operating system configurations. You can find a wealth of information about your system under this key. In fact, when you complete the example at the end of this chapter you will see how to obtain a list of all the printers installed on your system. You will find that you will spend most of your time working with keys and values under this key.

HKEY_USERS

The HKEY_USERS key contains all of the active user profiles on the computer.

This key contains two sub-keys. The first is called DEFAULT and contains information about the default user profile. When new users log onto the computer for the first time, their profile is cloned from information stored under this sub-key.

The second sub-key varies depending on which version of Windows you are running. Under Windows NT/2000 this sub-key is named after the Secure ID (SID) of the current user. Windows NT/2000 maintains every person's SID in its own sub-key, so more than one SID may be listed. Under Windows 95/98 this second sub-key is named Software and maintains the current user's software profile. However, if user profiles are being used, then this sub-key maintains very little information because the user.dat file populates the keys with the appropriate user ID.

HKEY_CURRENT_CONFIG

The HKEY_CURRENT_CONFIG key points to the \System\CurrentControlSet\ Hardware Profiles\Current key under HKEY_LOCAL_MACHINE. This key contains the current hardware configuration information for the computer. Unfortunately, the information is not easy to work with, so you would be better served to configure your hardware through the Control Panel. You probably won't spend too much time with this key.

HKEY_DYN_DATA

The HKEY_DYN_DATA key stores Windows 9x performance data ranging from how much memory is in use to how fast your file system is moving data. You can locate this information under the PerfStats key. If after reading this chapter you decide to get creative, you could place the code inside the Timer event of a Timer control that reads these values and displays them like a performance monitor. This key is not available on Windows NT.

Registry APIs

If you have spent time working with the Registry Editor you know that when you want to reach a specific key or value, you simply drill down the folders until you get there. Unfortunately, the registry APIs are not organized that easily. Before you can pass the name of the key you wish to access, you must specify a handle to the appropriate key. Then you specify the sub-key of the key. This is how all of the registry APIs are designed.

Go through this chapter and familiarize yourself with the APIs so you get a better understanding of what is going on. After you have read through and understand the APIs, the Visual Basic code necessary to use these APIs and create a reusable registry class will be presented.

RegOpenKeyEx

Description

The RegOpenKeyEx API opens the requested key in the registry.

C Prototype

```
LONG RegOpenKeyEx(HKEY hKey,
    LPCTSTR lpSubKey,
    DWORD ulOptions,
    REGSAM samDesired,
    PHKEY phkResult);
```

VB Declaration

```
Private Declare Function RegOpenKeyEx Lib "advapi32.dll" _
    Alias "RegOpenKeyExA" _
    (ByVal hKey As Long, _
    ByVal lpSubKey As String, _
    ByVal ulOptions As Long, _
    ByVal samDesired As Long, _
    phkResult As Long) As Long
```

Parameters

Parameter	Description
hKey	Handle of the root-level key, such as HKEY_CURRENT_MACHINE.
lpSubKey	The sub-key portion of the key you wish to open.

ulOptions	Reserved. Pass 0 as the argument when calling this API.
samDesired	Security access desired for the specified key. This can have one of the following values: KEY_CREATE_LINK, KEY_CREATE_SUB_KEY, KEY_ENUMERATE_SUB_KEYS, KEY_EXECUTE, KEY_NOTIFY, KEY_QUERY_VALUE, KEY_SET_VALUE, KEY_ALL_ACCESS, KEY_READ, and KEY_WRITE.
phkResult	Handle to the opened key if the API call is successful.
Returns	Returns ERROR_SUCCESS if the registry is opened successfully. Otherwise, it returns an error code.

Notes

On Windows 9x you can also specify the HKEY_DYN_DATA key.

RegConnectRegistry

Description

The RegConnectRegistry API opens the registry on a remote computer.

C Prototype

```
LONG RegConnectRegistry(LPTSTR lpMachineName,
    HKEY hKey,
    PHKEY phkResult);
```

VB Declaration

```
Private Declare Function RegConnectRegistry _
    Lib "advapi32.dll" _
    Alias "RegConnectRegistryA" _
    (ByVal lpMachineName As String, _
    ByVal hKey As Long, _
    phkResult As Long) As Long
```

Parameters

Parameter	Description
lpMachineName	The name of the remote computer to connect to.
hKey	Handle to the key you want to access on the remote computer.
phkResult	Handle to the remote registry key if the API call is successful.
Returns	Returns ERROR_SUCCESS if the registry is opened successfully. Otherwise, it returns an error code.

RegCloseKey

Description

The RegCloseKey API closes and releases the handle of an open registry key.

C Prototype

```
int RegCloseKey(HANDLE hKey);
```

VB Declaration

```
Private Declare Function RegCloseKey _
    Lib "advapi32.dll" _
    (ByVal hKey As Long) As Long
```

Parameters

Parameter	Description
hKey	Handle to the open key you wish to close.
Returns	Returns ERROR_SUCCESS if the registry is closed successfully. Otherwise, it returns an error code.

RegQueryValueEx

Description

The RegQueryValueEx API retrieves a value from the registry.

C Prototype

```
LONG RegQueryValueEx(HKEY hKey,
    LPTSTR lpValueName,
    LPDWORD lpReserved,
    LPDWORD lpType,
    LPBYTE lpData,
    LPDWORD lpcbData);
```

VB Declaration

```
Private Declare Function RegQueryValueEx Lib "advapi32.dll" _
    Alias "RegQueryValueExA" _
    (ByVal hKey As Long, _
    ByVal lpValueName As String, _
    ByVal lpReserved As Long, _
    lpType As Long, _
    lpData As Any, _
    lpcbData As Long) As Long
```

Parameters

Parameter	Description
hKey	Handle to the open registry key.
lpValueName	The value to query in the selected key.
lpReserved	Reserved. Pass 0 as an argument when calling this API.
lpType	Data type of the registry value.
lpData	Data that value gets set to if the API call is successful.
lpcbData	Size of lpData.
Returns	Returns ERROR_SUCCESS if the value is read successfully. Otherwise, it returns an error code.

Notes

Because this API is used to read multiple data types, it is a great candidate to be typecast with multiple declarations. To query string data, add the following declaration to your project:

```
Private Declare Function RegQueryValueExString Lib "advapi32.dll" _
    Alias "RegQueryValueExA" _
    (ByVal hKey As Long, _
    ByVal lpValueName As String, _
    ByVal lpReserved As Long, _
    lpType As Long, _
    lpData As String, _
    lpcbData As Long) As Long
```

To read DWORD data, use the following declaration:

```
Private Declare Function RegQueryValueExDword Lib "advapi32.dll" _
    Alias "RegQueryValueExA" _
    (ByVal hKey As Long, _
    ByVal lpValueName As String, _
    ByVal lpReserved As Long, _
    lpType As Long, _
    lpData As Long, _
    lpcbData As Long) As Long
```

RegSetValueEx

Description

The RegSetValueEx API is used to write a value in the registry.

C Prototype

```
LONG RegSetValueEx(HKEY hKey,
    LPCTSTR lpValueName,
    DWORD Reserved,
    DWORD dwType,
    CONST BYTE *lpData,
    DWORD cbData);
```

VB Declaration

```
Private Declare Function RegSetValueEx Lib "advapi32.dll" _
    Alias "RegSetValueExA" _
    (ByVal hKey As Long, _
    ByVal lpValueName As String, _
    ByVal Reserved As Long, _
    ByVal dwType As Long, _
    lpData As Long, _
    ByVal cbData As Long) As Long
```

Parameters

Parameter	Description
hKey	Handle to the open registry key.
lpValueName	The value to set in the selected key.
Reserved	Reserved. Pass 0 as an argument when calling this API.
dwType	Data type of the registry value.
lpData	Data the value gets set to if the API call is successful. If you use this API to pass a string, precede the argument with ByVal when calling the API.
cbData	Length of cbData including the null-terminating character.
Returns	If the value is written successfully, the API returns ERROR_SUCCESS. Otherwise, it returns an error code.

Notes

As the registry grows in size, system performance will degrade. As a result, it is best not to store large amounts of data in a single key within the registry. In some situations you may wish to store a pointer or reference, such as a filename, to data stored on a hard disk or network path.

RegDeleteValue

Description

The RegDeleteValue API removes a value from the specified registry key.

C Prototype

```
LONG RegDeleteValue(HKEY hKey,
    LPCTSTR lpValueName);
```

VB Declaration

```
Private Declare Function RegDeleteValue Lib "advapi32.dll" _
    Alias "RegDeleteValueA" _
    (ByVal hKey As Long, _
    ByVal lpValueName As String) As Long
```

Parameters

Parameter	Description
hKey	Handle to the key that contains the value you wish to delete.
lpValueName	The name of the value you wish to delete from the selected key.
Returns	Returns ERROR_SUCCESS if the value is successfully deleted. Otherwise, it returns an error code.

RegEnumKeyEx

Description

The RegEnumKeyEx API enumerates the sub-keys of the selected registry key.

C Prototype

```
LONG RegEnumKeyEx(HKEY hKey,
    DWORD dwIndex,
    LPTSTR lpName,
```

```
LPDWORD lpcbName,
LPDWORD lpReserved,
LPTSTR lpClass,
LPDWORD lpcbClass,
PFILETIME lpftLastWriteTime);
```

VB Declaration

```
Private Declare Function RegEnumKeyEx Lib "advapi32.dll" _
    Alias "RegEnumKeyExA" _
    (ByVal hKey As Long, _
    ByVal dwIndex As Long, _
    ByVal lpName As String, _
    lpcbName As Long, _
    ByVal lpReserved As Long, _
    ByVal lpClass As String, _
    lpcbClass As Long, _
    lpftLastWriteTime As FILETIME) As Long
```

Parameters

Parameter	Description
hKey	Handle to the open key to be enumerated.
dwIndex	The index position of the key to be returned.
lpName	If the API call is successful, lpName will contain the name of the enumerated key.
lpcbName	Size of the lpName buffer.
lpReserved	Reserved. Pass 0 in place of this argument when calling the API.
lpClass	This argument can be set to vbNullString if it is not required by your application.
lpcbClass	This argument can be set to 0 if you pass vbNullString to lpClass.
lpftLastWriteTime	Returns a FILETIME structure containing the last time this key was modified.
Returns	Returns ERROR_SUCCESS on success. Otherwise, it returns an error code.

RegEnumValue

Description

The RegEnumValue API lists all the key values within an open registry key. Each value is retrieved with a separate call to RegEnumValue, passing a new index for each call.

C Prototype

```
LONG RegEnumValue(HKEY hKey,
    DWORD dwIndex,
    LPTSTR lpValueName,
    LPDWORD lpcbValueName,
    LPDWORD lpReserved,
    LPDWORD lpType,
    LPBYTE lpData,
    LPDWORD lpcbData);
```

VB Declaration

```
Private Declare Function RegEnumValue Lib "advapi32.dll" _
    Alias "RegEnumValueA" _
    (ByVal hKey As Long, _
    ByVal dwIndex As Long, _
    ByVal lpValueName As String, _
    lpcbValueName As Long, _
    ByVal lpReserved As Long, _
    lpType As Long, _
    lpData As Byte, _
    lpcbData As Long) As Long
```

Parameters

Parameter	Description
hKey	Handle to the open key to be enumerated.
dwIndex	Index to the value within the key.
lpValueName	Name of the value to be queried.
lpcbValueName	Length of the lpValueName, including the null-terminating character.

lpReserved	Reserved.
lpType	Type of the value, such as REG_DWORD or REG_SZ.
lpData	Buffer containing the results of the query.
lpcbData	Size of the lpData buffer.
Returns	Returns ERROR_SUCCESS if a value is read. In addition, the name of the value is returned in the buffer specified in lpData. Otherwise, it returns an error code.

RegCreateKeyEx

Description

The RegCreateKeyEx API creates a new key in the registry. If the key already exists, then this API opens it.

C Prototype

```
LONG RegCreateKeyEx(HKEY hKey,
    LPCTSTR lpSubKey,
    DWORD Reserved,
    LPTSTR lpClass,
    DWORD dwOptions,
    REGSAM samDesired,
    LPSECURITY_ATTRIBUTES lpSecurityAttributes,
    PHKEY phkResult,
    LPDWORD lpdwDisposition);
```

VB Declaration

```
Private Declare Function RegCreateKeyEx Lib "advapi32.dll" _
    Alias "RegCreateKeyExA" _
    (ByVal hKey As Long, _
    ByVal lpSubKey As String, _
    ByVal Reserved As Long, _
    ByVal lpClass As String, _
    ByVal dwOptions As Long, _
    ByVal samDesired As Long, _
```

```
        lpSecurityAttributes As SECURITY_ATTRIBUTES, _
        phkResult As Long, _
        lpdwDisposition As Long) As Long
```

Parameters

Parameter	Description
hKey	Handle to the root key.
lpSubKey	Name of the new sub-key.
Reserved	Reserved. Pass 0 as an argument.
lpClass	Returns the name of the class for the newly created key.
dwOptions	Options required to create the key.
samDesired	A combination of security access masks that specify the access rights for the newly created key.
lpSecurityAttributes	A SECURITY_ATTRIBUTES structure. For further details, refer to the Notes below.
phkResult	Handle to the newly created key.
lpdwDisposition	A Long integer indicating whether the key was newly created, or if it already exists and was opened.
Returns	Returns ERROR_SUCCESS if the key is created or opened. Otherwise, it returns an error code.

Notes

The samDesired argument is used to define what level of security should be placed on the new registry key. This argument can be a combination of constants, such as KEY_READ, KEY_WRITE, KEY_EXECUTE, and KEY_ALL_ACCESS.

The SECURITY_ATTRIBUTES structure, shown below, contains the security descriptor for an object.

```
Private Type SECURITY_ATTRIBUTES
    nLength As Long
    lpSecurityDescriptor As Long
    bInheritHandle As Long
End Type
```

Set the nLength member to the size of the structure using the Len() function. The lpSecurityDescriptor member is unused on Windows 9x computers. When bInheritedHandle is set to True, new processes will inherit the handle.

RegDeleteKey

Description

The RegDeleteKey API deletes a key from the registry.

C Prototype

```
LONG RegDeleteKey(HKEY hKey,
    LPCTSTR lpSubKey);
```

VB Declaration

```
Private Declare Function RegDeleteKey Lib "advapi32.dll" _
    Alias "RegDeleteKeyA" _
    (ByVal hKey As Long, _
    ByVal lpSubKey As String) As Long
```

Parameters

Parameter	Description
hKey	Handle to the root level key.
lpSubKey	Long pointer to a string containing the sub-key to be deleted.
Returns	If the key is deleted, the API returns ERROR_SUCCESS. Otherwise, it returns an error code.

Using the Registry APIs

The registry APIs are especially good candidates to be wrapped in a class. The registry class has been included with this chapter, which you can download from the Sybex Web site at www.sybex.com. This class is by no means a complete component, but you can use it for most of your registry work and can easily add functionality as you see fit. The code shown below will work for Windows 95/98. Some slight adjustment is needed to certain keys for the application to function properly under Windows NT/2000.

As you know, the basic things you do within the registry are reading and writing values, as well as creating, listing, and removing keys. The registry class included with this chapter will allow you to perform all of these tasks easily and reliably. Not only will wrapping them help you keep your code smaller by allowing you to reuse the registry code, it will help you avoid the many pitfalls of parameter mismatches and incorrect memory allocations.

NOTE   The sample code for this chapter can be downloaded from the Sybex Web site at http://www.sybex.com. Included is a reusable registry class you can include in your own projects!

Creating a Registry Key

Listing 11.1 shows the function that allows you to create a registry key.

LISTING 11.1   **Creating a Registry Key**

```
Public Function CreateKey(PredefinedKey As HKEYs, _
    KeyName As String) As Boolean

    Dim hNewKey As Long
    Dim rc As Long

    On Error GoTo handler

    'Make sure there is no backslash preceding the branch
    If Left$(KeyName, 1) = "\" Then
        KeyName = Right$(KeyName, Len(KeyName) - 1)
    End If
```

```
'Create the branch
rc = RegCreateKeyEx(PredefinedKey, _
        KeyName, _
        0&, _
        vbNullString, _
        REG_OPTION_NON_VOLATILE, _
        KEY_ALL_ACCESS, _
        0&, _
        hNewKey, _
        rc)

If rc = ERROR_SUCCESS Then
    'Close the registry
    rc = RegCloseKey(hNewKey)

    'Return the result code
    CreateKey = True
Else
    CreateKey = False
End If

'Bypass the error handler
Exit Function

handler:
    CreateKey = False
End Function
```

The code is straightforward. The calling function passes the handle to the key and the name of the sub-key you wish to create. After setting the error trap, check to make sure there are no backslashes preceding the sub-key. Calls to any registry API will fail if the sub-key is preceded with a backslash. If a backslash is found, it is stripped off so a valid sub-key can be passed. After the API call is made the registry key is closed and an error code is returned.

Assuming you have a valid handle and sub-key, call the RegCreateKeyEx API. The first two arguments are the handle to the key and the sub-key. If the API call is successful, the result code (rc) will be set to ERROR_SUCCESS. If the call is successful, then you must close the handle and return True to indicate that the command was successful.

Deleting a Registry Key

Deleting a key from the registry is a simple process. Just pass the handle to the key and the name of the sub-key to be removed. The code is shown in Listing 11.2.

LISTING 11.2   **Deleting a Registry Key**

```
Public Function DeleteKey(PredefinedKey As HKEYs, _
        KeyName As String) As Boolean

    Dim rc As Long

    On Error GoTo handler

    'Make sure there is no backslash preceding the branch
    If Left$(KeyName, 1) = "\" Then
        KeyName = Right$(KeyName, Len(KeyName) - 1)
    End If

    'Call the API
    rc = RegDeleteKey(PredefinedKey, KeyName)
    If rc = ERROR_SUCCESS Then
        'Return result code
        DeleteKey = True
    Else
        DeleteKey = False
    End If

    'Bypass the error handler
    Exit Function

handler:
    DeleteKey = False
End Function
```

Again, make sure there are no preceding backslashes before you make the API call. Then the call is made to the API. If the call is successful, the result code will be ERROR_SUCCESS.

Enumerating Registry Keys

Now that you know how to create and delete registry keys, you need to know how to enumerate them. To accomplish this you must make repeated calls to the RegEnumKeyEx API. The function shown in Listing 11.3 is a bit more complicated, but it is still manageable.

LISTING 11.3   **Enumerating Registry Keys**

```
Public Function ListSubKey(PredefinedKey As HKEYs, _
        KeyName As String, _
        Index As Long) As String

    Dim rc As Long
    Dim hKey As Long
    Dim dwIndex As Long
    Dim lpName As String
    Dim lpcbName As Long
    Dim lpClass As String
    Dim lpcbClass As Long
    Dim lpReserved As Long
    Dim lpftLastWriteTime As FILETIME
    Dim i As Integer

    On Error GoTo handler

    'Make sure there is no backslash preceding the branch
    If Left$(KeyName, 1) = "\" Then
        KeyName = Right$(KeyName, Len(KeyName) - 1)
    End If

    'Attempt to open the registry
    rc = RegOpenKeyEx(PredefinedKey, KeyName, _
            0, KEY_ALL_ACCESS, hKey)

    If rc = ERROR_SUCCESS Then
        'Allocate buffers for lpName & lpClass
        lpcbName = 255
        lpName = String$(lpcbName, Chr(0))
        lpcbClass = 255
        lpClass = String$(lpcbClass, Chr(0))

        'Get the subkey
```

```
        rc = RegEnumKeyEx(hKey, Index, lpName, _
                lpcbName, lpReserved, vbNullString, _
                0, lpftLastWriteTime)

        If rc = ERROR_SUCCESS Then
            'Return the result
            ListSubKey = Left$(lpName, lpcbName)
        Else
            'Return nothing
            ListSubKey = ""
        End If

        'Close the registry
        RegCloseKey hKey
    End If

    'Bypass the error handler
    Exit Function

handler:
    ListSubKey = ""
End Function
```

The argument list for this function is a little different than before. You will notice the Index argument at the end of the list. Before calling this function, increment Index by one. This will tell RegEnumKeyEx to look for the next sub-key in the key. When no more sub-keys can be returned, the API returns an error result. You then pass back an empty string to indicate there is nothing left.

Before you can enumerate a sub-key, the parent key needs to be opened with the RegOpenKeyEx API. If the key is opened successfully, a handle to the opened key is returned through hKey and the result code is ERROR_SUCCESS.

After the key is successfully opened and you have a handle to it, allocate a buffer to hold the name of the sub-key (remember, you must manage your own memory). It is unlikely you will ever return a sub-key over 255 characters in length. Since the API also needs to know how large the buffer is, set lpcbName to 255. Then allocate 255 bytes of memory using the String$() function. If you anticipate retrieving more data than 255 bytes in length, you can always create larger buffers. The requisite is that the buffer be large enough to return all of the data. It is good programming practice to keep your registry data small, since everything added to the registry slightly degrades system performance.

Now that you have an adequate buffer for the return data, call the RegEnum-KeyEx API, passing the standard arguments in addition to a few others. Of particular note is the vbNullString value. If you recall from Chapter 2, if you don't want to pass data to a string argument, pass it vbNullString. This was done for the lpClass argument. Since a null string has no length, pass zero to the lpcb-Class argument. Finally, pass lpftLastWriteTime, which is a UDT based on the FILETIME structure. Notice that nothing is done with this argument. You can read the values returned in this structure if you want to find out when the returned sub-key was last modified.

If the API call is successful, lpName will contain the name of the sub-key and lpcbName will contain the length of the text in the buffer. Call the Left$() function to trim off the remaining null characters.

Retrieving Values from the Registry

Retrieving values from the registry is similar to listing sub-keys. Once you open the registry key and get a valid handle, allocate the appropriate buffers and make the API call. The function in Listing 11.4 shows you how this is done.

LISTING 11.4   **Retrieving a Value from the Registry**

```
Public Function GetValue(PredefinedKey As HKEYs, _
        ByVal KeyName As String, _
        ByVal ValueName As String) As Variant

    Dim rc As Long
    Dim hKey As Long
    Dim lpData As String
    Dim lpDataDWORD As Long
    Dim lpcbData As Long
    Dim lpType As Long


    On Error GoTo handler

    'Make sure there is no backslash preceding the branch
    If Left$(KeyName, 1) = "\" Then
        KeyName = Right$(KeyName, Len(KeyName) - 1)
    End If

    'Attempt to open the registry
    rc = RegOpenKeyEx(PredefinedKey, KeyName, _
```

```
           0, KEY_ALL_ACCESS, hKey)

If rc = ERROR_SUCCESS Then
    'Create a buffer so we can retrieve the data type
    'of the key. We'll need this to determine which
    'API we should call.
    lpcbData = 255
    lpData = String(lpcbData, Chr(0))

    'Get the value type first.
    'It will be returned via lpType argument
    rc = RegQueryValueEx(hKey, _
        ValueName, _
        0, lpType, _
        ByVal lpData, _
        lpcbData)

    If rc = ERROR_SUCCESS Then
        'Then read the value using the
        'appropriate data type...
        Select Case lpType
            Case REG_SZ
                rc = RegQueryValueExString(hKey, _
                    ValueName, _
                    0, lpType, _
                    ByVal lpData, _
                    lpcbData)

                'Return the value
                If rc = 0 Then
                    GetValue = Left$(lpData, _
                            lpcbData - 1)
                Else
                    GetValue = ""
                End If
            Case REG_DWORD
                rc = RegQueryValueEx(hKey, _
                    ValueName, _
                    0, lpType, _
                    lpDataDWORD, _
                    lpcbData)

                'Return the value
```

```
                If rc = 0 Then
                        GetValue = CLng(lpDataDWORD)
                Else
                        GetValue = 0
                End If
            End Select
        End If

        'Close the registry
        RegCloseKey hKey
    End If

    'Bypass the error handler
    Exit Function

handler:
    'Return a null value
    GetValue = Null
End Function
```

Notice that the return type of this function is a Variant. I don't ordinarily like to use Variant data types, but this function can return both strings and Long integers. Since most of the code is similar to the previous example, only the design specifics of this function will be explained.

The functionality of this routine is similar to the Visual Basic functions you ordinarily use. Why call a separate routine to retrieve a string from the registry one time and a Long integer another? You would first have to determine what type of data you are retrieving. As you know, passing the wrong data type to an API can lead to disaster. So rather than leave the guesswork to you, the function makes an initial call to the API to retrieve the data type and the size of the buffer required. Based on what is returned, you can call the appropriate API so your program won't crash. Notice that REG_SZ is the constant that represents the string data type for all registry APIs. REG_DWORD represents C's DWORD data type, which can be translated to Visual Basic's Long data type.

Now that you have an idea how the registry APIs work you can modify the registry class to suit your own needs. You can write your own wrapper functions to store and retrieve licensing information. Or if you are a bit more adventurous you could write your own performance monitor. Take a look at the code in the class and see how it works. It will point you in the right direction to make your own registry functions.

CHAPTER
TWELVE

12

Graphics

- Graphics Theory

- Device Contexts

- Drawing Objects

- Drawing Functions

- Moving On

Graphics play a vital role in Windows. In fact, graphics make the interface what it is: a Graphical User Interface, or GUI.

Graphics Theory

Think of all the graphics components a typical user interacts with in a given day at the computer console. There are the basic forms, the mouse pointer, desktop, icons, command buttons, combo and list boxes, and much, much more.

The reason GUIs are so popular is that they present an interface people can relate to. The text-based operating systems require the user to remember commands, which can be cryptic and difficult to use, especially for new computer users. In contrast, it is easier for people to remember images than numbers and text. In fact, your brain actually uses mental images (icons) to represent many thoughts and memories. This is why icons are so prevalent in GUIs. Icons make it easier for the user to remember what various programs and components do.

Graphics contribute significantly to the user's overall experience on the computer. How many applications have you seen that disregard basic symmetry? For example, when was the last time you saw an application that used ambient light coming from the upper-left rather than the upper-right corner, which is used throughout the Windows environment?

Colors greatly enhance the GUI but must be used judiciously. The colors must blend nicely within the application, as well as the Windows environment. This is why you can apply themes in the Display properties of the Control Panel. Imagine if you really liked lavender and you made all of your forms that color. Although it may look a bit odd at first, if the user likes that color there won't be a problem. But imagine forcing this color scheme on a user who likes yellows, greens, and browns. Perhaps they have a forest of them on their desktop. Lavender on brown would cause a serious color clash.

Basic oversights like these create a visual nightmare for the user. Not to mention, when the GUI looks sloppy, the user will most likely think the application is sloppy and unreliable. It is very important to use graphics effectively and consistently, not only throughout your application, but throughout the Windows environment as well.

Fortunately, Windows manages many of these graphics issues for you. But inevitably you will have to write code that requires you to work with graphics of some sort. Visual Basic provides many graphics routines for you to use, but many are limited in their functionality or require significant coding to achieve the results you desire.

If it were not for the Windows API most graphics routines would be extremely difficult to implement, especially in a hardware-independent environment such as Windows. Imagine what it would be like if you had to write hardware-dependent graphics routines. You might have to write hundreds of versions of the same routine. If you had several graphics routines the code would really add up! Fortunately, the Windows API simplifies the daunting task of generating graphics, even on multiple hardware and software platforms.

As you progress through this chapter you will learn to use the various Windows graphics objects to build the rotating topographical map of the Earth, as shown in Figure 12.1. This project uses many of the Windows graphics routines.

FIGURE 12.1:

Map of the earth

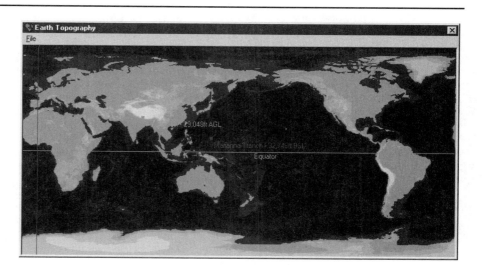

Device Contexts

With all the different hardware devices, how can Windows use one set of APIs that works across multiple platforms? How can one graphics routine work the same on Windows 95/98, Windows NT, Windows 2000, and Windows CE? The answer lies in *Device Contexts*.

A Device Context (DC) is like an artist's canvas. It is the actual object you draw on in Windows. You can create DCs for the display as well as printers. A DC insulates you from the hardware-specific display drivers used to drive your monitor and printer. Once you know how to draw on a DC you can send graphics to the monitor as well as the printer.

A DC is a powerful graphics object. It doesn't just hold graphics, it also performs all scale conversions for you. You don't have to worry about adjusting an 800 by 600 pixel display image to a 1200 dpi printer. This feature alone makes a DC worth its weight in gold.

A DC is actually a chunk of memory whose bits are manipulated through graphics objects rather than bitwise operators. Since most DCs reside in memory rather than on your display, it is faster to draw on a DC in memory. Graphics routines are intensive and slow. As a result, most applications render graphics on a memory DC and then copy the entire image onto the screen to a window DC. Depending on the graphics routine, this technique can be several hundred times faster than drawing directly to the window DC.

Now that you have a basic idea of how a DC works, let's look at some of the DC APIs. Then we'll look at drawing objects.

CreateCompatibleDC

Description

The CreateCompatibleDC API is used to create a new DC in memory that is based on the attributes of another DC.

C Prototype

```
HDC CreateCompatibleDC(HDC hdc);
```

VB Declaration

```
Private Declare Function CreateCompatibleDC Lib "gdi32" _
    (ByVal hDC As Long) As Long
```

Parameters

Parameter	Description
hDC	Handle to the DC to be copied.
Returns	On success, this API returns the handle to the new DC. If the call fails, it returns Null.

Example

```
hNewDC = CreateCompatibleDC(hDC)
```

CreateDC

Description

The CreateDC API is used to create a new memory DC.

C Prototype

```
HDC CreateDC(LPCTSTR lpszDriver,
    LPCTSTR lpszDevice,
    LPCTSTR lpszOutput,
    CONST DEVMODE *lpInitData);
```

VB Declaration

```
Private Declare Function CreateDC Lib "gdi32" _
    Alias "CreateDCA" _
    (ByVal lpDriverName As String, _
    ByVal lpDeviceName As String, _
    ByVal lpOutput As String, _
    lpInitData As DEVMODE) As Long
```

Parameters

Parameter	Description
lpDriverName	A null-terminated string specifying either DISPLAY or WINSPOOL. This parameter exists for backward compatibility with previous versions of Windows. On Windows 9x systems, this parameter is set to vbNullChar.

lpDeviceName	Unused in Win32. Set this to vbNullChar.
LpOutput	Unused. Set to vbNullChar.
LpInitData	If lpDriverName is DISPLAY, then this should be vbNullChar. Otherwise, a DEVMODE structure used to specify the initialization parameters of the DC.
Returns	Returns the handle to the new DC. If the call fails, the API returns NULL.

Notes

Here is the DEVMODE structure and the accompanying table for each variable:

```
Public Type DEVMODE
        dmDeviceName As String * CCHDEVICENAME
        dmSpecVersion As Integer
        dmDriverVersion As Integer
        dmSize As Integer
        dmDriverExtra As Integer
        dmFields As Long
        dmOrientation As Integer
        dmPaperSize As Integer
        dmPaperLength As Integer
        dmPaperWidth As Integer
        dmScale As Integer
        dmCopies As Integer
        dmDefaultSource As Integer
        dmPrintQuality As Integer
        dmColor As Integer
        dmDuplex As Integer
        dmYResolution As Integer
        dmTTOption As Integer
        dmCollate As Integer
        dmFormName As String * CCHFORMNAME
        dmUnusedPadding As Integer
        dmBitsPerPel As Long
        dmPelsWidth As Long
        dmPelsHeight As Long
        dmDisplayFlags As Long
        dmDisplayFrequency As Long
    End Type
```

Parameter	Description
dmDeviceName	Name of the device, like PCL/HP LaserJet.
dmSpecVersion	Version number.
dmDriverVersion	Printer driver version number.
dmSize	Size of this structure.
dmDriverExtra	Set to 0.
dmFields	Used to tell if a member variable has been initialized.
dmOrientation	Can be either DMORIENT_PORTRAIT or DMORIENT_LANDSCAPE.
dmPaperSize	Size of the paper. One type is DMPAPER_10x11. Another is DMPAPER_A4. Use the API Viewer for more constants for this variable. Can use any constant that begins with DMPAPER_.
dmPaperLength	Overrides the length of dmPaperSize.
dmPaperWidth	Overrides the width of dmPaperSize.
dmScale	Factor to scale the output.
dmCopies	Number of copies.
dmDefaultSource	Paper source. The more frequently used sources include DMBIN_UPPER, DMBIN_FIRST, DMBIN_ONLYONE, and DMBIN_LOWER. Use the API Viewer to find more values under the DMBIN_ constant.
dmPrintQuality	Printer resolution. Can be DMRES_HIGH, DMRES_MEDIUM, DMRES_LOW, or DMRES_DRAFT.
dmColor	Color or Monochrome. Can be DMCOLOR_COLOR or DMCOLOR_MONOCHROME.
dmDuplex	Duplex or double-sided printing. Can be DMDUP_SIMPLEX, DMDUP_VERTICAL, or DMDUP_HORIZONTAL.

dmYResolution	Dots per inch of the y resolution.
dmTTOption	TrueType fonts. Can be DMTT_BITMAP, DMTT_DOWNLOAD, or DMTT_SUBDEV.
dmCollate	Collate or not. Can be DMCOLLATE_FALSE or DMCOLLATE_TRUE.
dmFormName	Name of form. Can be Letter or Legal.
dmUnusedPadding	Set to 0.
dmBitsPerPel	Color resolution.
dmPelsWidth	Width of device surface in pixels.
dmPelsHeight	Height of device surface in pixels.
dmDisplayFlags	Display mode. Can be DM_GRAYSCALE or DM_INTERLACED.
dmDisplayFrequency	Frequency in Hertz.

Example

```
Dim hDC As Long

HDC = CreateDC( "DISPLAY", 0, 0, 0)
```

GetDC

Description

The GetDC API is used to retrieve the DC belonging to a window.

C Prototype

```
HDC GetDC(HWND hWnd);
```

VB Declaration

```
Private Declare Function GetDC Lib "user32" _
    (ByVal hwnd As Long) As Long
```

Parameters

Parameter	Description
hwnd	Handle to the window whose DC you wish to obtain.
Returns	If the call is successful, the API returns the handle to the DC of the window.

Example

```
Dim hDC As Long

hDC = GetDC(frmMain.hWnd)
```

GetWindowDC

Description

The GetWindowDC API is used to get the DC for an entire window or form. This includes the caption bar and borders.

C Prototype

```
HDC GetWindowDC(HWND hWnd);
```

VB Declaration

```
Private Declare Function GetWindowDC Lib "user32" _
    (ByVal hwnd As Long) As Long
```

Parameters

Parameter	Description
hwnd	Handle to the form whose DC you wish to obtain.
Returns	If the call is successful, the API returns the handle to the DC of the entire form. Otherwise it returns NULL, or 0.

Example

```
Dim hDC As Long

hDC = GetWindowDC(frmMain.hWnd)
```

ReleaseDC

Description

The `ReleaseDC` API is called to remove a DC from memory. Call this API when you are done working with a DC that you created using the `CreateDC` or `CreateCompatibleDC` APIs.

C Prototype

```
int ReleaseDC(HWND hWnd, HDC hDC);
```

VB Declaration

```
Private Declare Function ReleaseDC Lib "user32" _
    (ByVal hwnd As Long, _
    ByVal hdc As Long) As Long
```

Parameters

Parameter	Description
hwnd	Handle to the window containing the DC to be released.
hdc	Handle to the DC being released.
Returns	This API returns a Boolean value specifying whether the call was successful or not.

Example

```
DIM rc As Long

Rc = ReleaseDC( hwnd, hDC )
```

Drawing Objects

Just like an artist cannot paint a picture without some paint and a brush, you cannot create graphics without drawing objects. In Windows you use drawing objects such as pens, brushes, fonts, and bitmaps to draw graphics on a DC.

A pen works much the same as a real pen. It is used to draw lines and text. When you draw a polygon, the outline is drawn with a pen object.

Brush objects are used to paint colors on a DC. Windows uses brushes to fill polygons and backgrounds.

If you wanted to create a solid square you would create a pen and set its color. Next you would create a brush and set it to the same color as the pen. Then you would call the `Rectangle` API described later in this chapter. The result would be a solid, red square. If you set the color of the pen to black and call the `Rectangle` API, the result would be a red square outlined in black.

As you already know, fonts are used to describe every attribute of text. A font describes the text style, size, color, underline, bold, italics, and many other attributes of the text.

A bitmap object is a complete graphic. Actually it is much like a stencil when used on a DC. It has dimensions and color attributes that get applied to a DC when a bitmap object is used to paint a graphic.

When you want to use a drawing object on a DC you must select it into the DC. This is much like grabbing or switching paintbrushes while painting. You select an object to use by calling the `SelectObject` API. Once a drawing object is selected into a DC, it will be used as appropriate. For example, it is not practical to use a wide brush to paint window trim. You would want to use a narrow brush. In much the same manner the `SetPixel` API will not use a brush to draw a pinpoint.

Like you learned in kindergarten, it is important to put things back when you are done with them. This rule applies to drawing objects as well. Once you are done using a drawing object you must put the original drawing object back on the DC. Do this by selecting the old drawing object back into the DC. You will see this technique used in the next section.

After you have selected the original drawing object back into the DC, you must delete the new drawing object using the `DeleteObject` API.

CreateBitmap

Description

The CreateBitmap API is used to create a generic bitmap object, which will be applied to a DC.

C Prototype

```
HBITMAP CreateBitmap(int nWidth,
    int nHeight,
    UINT cPlanes,
    UINT cBitsPerPel,
    CONST VOID *lpvBits);
```

VB Declaration

```
Private Declare Function CreateBitmap Lib "gdi32" _
    Alias "CreateBitmap" _
    (ByVal nWidth As Long, _
    ByVal nHeight As Long, _
    ByVal nPlanes As Long, _
    ByVal nBitCount As Long, _
    lpBits As Any) As Long
```

Parameters

Parameter	Description
Nwidth	The width of the new bitmap in pixels.
Nheight	The height of the new bitmap in pixels.
Nplanes	The number of color planes used in the bitmap.
NbitCount	The bit depth of the bitmap. A bit count of 1 specifies a monochrome bitmap, 8 indicates a 256-color bitmap, and 24 indicates true color.
LpBits	Pointer to the pixel data for the bitmap.
Returns	On success, this API returns a handle to the new bitmap object. Otherwise it returns 0.

Example

```
Dim hDC As Long
HDC = CreateBitmap( width, height, 1, 1, ByVal o&)
```

CreateCompatibleBitmap

Description

The CreateCompatibleBitmap API creates a bitmap object based on another bitmap object that exists in another DC.

C Prototype

```
HBITMAP CreateCompatibleBitmap(HDC hdc,
    int nWidth,
    int nHeight);
```

VB Declaration

```
Private Declare Function CreateCompatibleBitmap Lib "gdi32" _
    (ByVal hdc As Long, _
    ByVal nWidth As Long, _
    ByVal nHeight As Long) As Long
```

Parameters

Parameter	Description
hDC	The DC containing the bitmap object that will be cloned.
nWidth	The width of the new bitmap in pixels.
nHeight	The depth of the new bitmap in pixels.
Returns	If the call is successful, the API returns a handle to the new bitmap, otherwise it returns 0.

Example

```
Dim rc As Long
rc = CreateCompatibleBitmap(hDC, nWidth, nHeight)
```

CreatePalette

Description

The CreatePalette API is used to create a palette object that can be used to define the colors used within a DC.

C Prototype

```
HPALETTE CreatePalette(CONST LOGPALETTE *lplgpl);
```

VB Declaration

```
Private Declare Function CreatePalette Lib "gdi32" _
    (lpLogPalette As LOGPALETTE) As Long
```

Parameters

Parameter	Description
lpLogPalette	A LOGPALETTE structure that specifies the color information for the palette.
Returns	On success, this API returns a handle to the new palette. If the call fails, the API returns 0.

Notes

The LOGPALETTE structure is required before calling the function. Here is that structure:

```
Private Type LOGPALETTE
    palVersion As Integer
    palNumEntries As Integer
    palPalEntry(1) As PALETTEENTRY
End Type
```

Parameter	Description
palVersion	Version number of the system.
palNumEntries	Number of logical palettes.
palPalEntry(1)	Array of colors.

Here is the structure for the PALETTEENTRY:

```
Private Type PALETTEENTRY
    peRed As Byte
    peGreen As Byte
    peBlue As Byte
    peFlags As Byte
End Type
```

Parameter	Description
peRed	Value for red intensity.
peGreen	Value for green intensity.
peBlue	Value for blue intensity.
peFlags	How the palette entry is to be used. Can be PC_EXPLICIT, PC_NOCOLLAPSE, or PC_RESERVED.

Example

```
Dim rc As Long
Dim logpal As LOGPALETTE

Rc = CreatePalette( logpal )
```

CreatePen

Description

The CreatePen API is used to create a pen object that defines the width, style, and color of a new pen object. When this object is selected into a DC, lines and many functions that draw polygons use the attributes when drawing the line.

C Prototype

```
HPEN CreatePen(int fnPenStyle,
    int nWidth,
    COLORREF crColor);
```

VB Declaration

```
Private Declare Function CreatePen Lib "gdi32" _
    (ByVal nPenStyle As Long, _
```

```
ByVal nWidth As Long, _
ByVal crColor As Long) As Long
```

Parameters

Parameter	Description
nPenStyle	The style of the pen, such as solid or dotted. Refer to the Notes below.
nWidth	The width, in pixels, of the line that will be drawn.
crColor	The RGB color of the line that will be drawn.
Returns	If the call is successful, the API returns the handle to the new pen object.

Notes

The nPenStyle argument can be one of the following constants:

- PS_SOLID
- PS_DASH
- PS_DASHDOT
- PS_DASHDOTDOT
- PS_DOT
- PS_NULL
- PS_INSIDEFRAME

Example

```
hNewPen = CreatePen(PS_SOLID, 1, Color)
```

CreateSolidBrush

Description

The CreateSolidBrush API is used to create a brush object, which is used with APIs that create polygons that can be filled.

C Prototype

```
HBRUSH CreateSolidBrush(COLORREF crColor);
```

VB Declaration

```
Private Declare Function CreateSolidBrush Lib "gdi32" _
    (ByVal crColor As Long) As Long
```

Parameters

Parameter	Description
crColor	The RGB value of the color you wish to use.
Returns	On success, this API returns the handle to the new brush. Otherwise it returns 0.

Example

The following example creates a solid red brush:

```
hNewBrush = CreateSolidBrush(RGB(255,0,0))
```

DeleteObject

Description

You must call the DeleteObject API to delete a drawing object after you have created and used it. This destroys the object and releases it from memory.

C Prototype

```
BOOL DeleteObject(HGDIOBJ hObject);
```

VB Declaration

```
Private Declare Function DeleteObject Lib "gdi32" _
    (ByVal hObject As Long) As Long
```

Parameters

Parameter	Description
hObject	The handle of the object to be deleted.
Returns	Returns True on success, False on failure.

Example

```
rc = DeleteObject( hObject )
```

SelectObject

Description

The SelectObject API is used to apply a drawing object to a DC. A drawing object must be selected into the DC before it can be used.

C Prototype

```
HGDIOBJ SelectObject(HDC hdc,
    HGDIOBJ hgdiobj);
```

VB Declaration

```
Private Declare Function SelectObject Lib "gdi32" _
    (ByVal hdc As Long, _
    ByVal hObject As Long) As Long
```

Parameters

Parameter	Description
hDC	Handle to the DC.
hObject	Handle to the drawing object.
Returns	If the API call is successful, the API returns the handle to the original drawing object. This must be selected back into the DC once the drawing operation is complete.

Example

This example shows how to create a pen, select it into a DC, draw, and then restore the original pen. Finally, the newly created pen is destroyed once the drawing function is complete. Most drawing functions will follow this structure. Note that this example uses the Ellipse function, which is discussed later in this chapter.

```
Dim hOldPen As Long
Dim hNewPen As Long
```

```
'Get a pen
hNewPen = CreatePen(0, 1, Color)
hOldPen = SelectObject(mDC, hNewPen)

'Draw a circle
Ellipse mDC, Left, Top, Left + Radius, Top + Radius

'Reset the pen
SelectObject mDC, hOldPen

'Destroy the pen
DeleteObject hNewPen
```

Drawing Functions

There are many drawing APIs you can choose from. In fact, there are so many that it would be difficult to cover them all in this book. However, most of the APIs are self-explanatory and don't require a lengthy explanation. In addition, each API is used pretty much in the same manner.

Arc

Description

The ARC API draws an arc on a DC.

C Prototype

```
BOOL Arc(
    HDC hdc,          // handle to device context
    int nLeftRect,    // x-coord of rectangle's upper-left corner
    int nTopRect,     // y-coord of rectangle's upper-left corner
    int nRightRect,   // x-coord of rectangle's lower-right corner
    int nBottomRect,  // y-coord of rectangle's lower-right corner
    int nXStartArc,   // x-coord of first radial ending point
    int nYStartArc,   // y-coord of first radial ending point
    int nXEndArc,     // x-coord of second radial ending point
    int nYEndArc      // y-coord of second radial ending point
);
```

VB Declaration

```
Private Declare Function Arc Lib "gdi32" _
    (ByVal hdc As Long, _
    ByVal X1 As Long, _
    ByVal Y1 As Long, _
    ByVal X2 As Long, _
    ByVal Y2 As Long, _
    ByVal X3 As Long, _
    ByVal Y3 As Long, _
    ByVal X4 As Long, _
    ByVal Y4 As Long) As Long
```

Parameters

Parameter	Description
X1	The horizontal position of the upper-left corner of the arc.
Y1	The vertical position of the upper-left corner of the arc.
X2	The horizontal position of the lower-right corner of the arc.
Y2	The vertical position of the lower-right corner of the arc.
X3	The horizontal position of the ending point of the first radial.
Y3	The vertical position of the ending point of the first radial.
X4	The horizontal position of the end point of the arc.
Y4	The vertical position of the end point of the arc.
Returns	Returns True on success, False on failure.

BitBlt

Description

The BitBlt API stands for *Bit-Block Transfer*. This API is used to move large amounts of bitmapped data from one DC to another.

C Prototype

```
BOOL BitBlt(HDC hdcDest,
    int nXDest,
    int nYDest,
    int nWidth,
    int nHeight,
    HDC hdcSrc,
    int nXSrc,
    int nYSrc,
    DWORD dwRop);
```

VB Declaration

```
Private Declare Function BitBlt Lib "gdi32" _
    (ByVal hDestDC As Long, _
    ByVal x As Long, _
    ByVal y As Long, _
    ByVal nWidth As Long, _
    ByVal nHeight As Long, _
    ByVal hSrcDC As Long, _
    ByVal xSrc As Long, _
    ByVal ySrc As Long, _
    ByVal dwRop As Long) As Long
```

Parameters

Parameter	Description
hDestDC	Handle to the DC the graphics will be transferred to.
x	The horizontal position of the upper-left corner of the destination in the DC.
y	The vertical position of the upper-left corner of the destination in the DC.

nWidth	The width of the portion of the graphic you want to transfer.
nHeight	The height of the portion of the graphic you want to transfer.
hSrcDC	The handle to the DC that contains the image to be transferred.
xSrc	The horizontal position of the upper-left corner where the image will be transferred from.
ySrc	The vertical position of the upper-left corner where the image will be transferred from.
dwROP	The Raster Operation (ROP) code that will be applied to the transfer. Refer to the Notes below.
Returns	Returns True on success, False on failure.

Notes

Rather than selecting the dimensions of the data to be copied from the source DC, the dimensions are specified using the destination DC. For example, you would normally specify the top-left corner, as well as the width and height of the source bitmap, and copy that rectangle to the destination. Instead, specify the upper-left corner on the source DC and set the width and height to be displayed on the destination.

NOTE   The clipping is performed on the destination DC, not the source DC.

Table 12.1 is a listing of some of the ROP codes. For a more detailed list of ROP codes, use the API Viewer.

TABLE 12.1: Raster Operation Codes

ROP Code	Description
NOTSRCCOPY	The bit patterns of the image are inverted as they are transferred to the destination DC.
SRCAND	The bits of the source and destination DCs will be ANDed together to provide a composite graphic.

Continued on next page

TABLE 12.1 CONTINUED: Raster Operation Codes

ROP Code	Description
SRCCOPY	The bits are copied directly from the source DC to the destination DC.
SRCERASE	This ROP logically ORs the pixels and then inverts them on the destination DC.
SRCINVERT	Inverts the pixels.
SRCPAINT	Logically ORs the pixels on the source and destination DCs.

Example

This example performs a direct copy of an image from one DC to another.

```
rc = BitBlt(dcCopy, 0, 0, mWidth, mHeight, _
            dcOriginal, mLeft, mTop, SRCCOPY)
```

DrawText

Description

The DrawText API is used to output text to a DC.

C Prototype

```
int DrawText(HDC hDC,
    LPCTSTR lpString,
    int nCount,
    LPRECT lpRect,
    UINT uFormat);
```

VB Declaration

```
Private Declare Function DrawText Lib "user32" _
    Alias "DrawTextA" _
    (ByVal hdc As Long, _
    ByVal lpStr As String, _
    ByVal nCount As Long, _
    lpRect As RECT, _
    ByVal wFormat As Long) As Long
```

Parameters

Parameter	Description
hDC	Handle to the destination DC.
lpStr	A null-terminated string containing the text to be drawn on the DC.
nCount	The length of the text, minus the null-terminating character.
lpRect	A RECT structure that defines the bounding rectangle the text will be drawn in.
wFormat	A flag that describes the layout of the text within the rectangle.
Returns	Returns True on success, False on failure.

Example

```
Public Sub DrawText(Text As String, _
       Left As Long, _
       Top As Long, _
       Optional Color As Long, _
       Optional Transparent As Boolean)

   Dim lpRect As RECT
   Dim wFormat As Long
   Dim tWidth As Long
   Dim tHeight As Long

   'Adjust the text color if necessary
   If IsNumeric(Color) Then SetTextColor mDC, Color

   'Get the text dimensions
   tWidth = 400
   tHeight = 20

   'Create a bounding rectangle
   With lpRect
       .Left = Left
       .Top = Top
```

```
        .Right = Left + tWidth
        .Bottom = Top + tHeight
    End With

    'Align the text
    wFormat = DT_LEFT

    'Draw the text
    DrawTextAPI mDC, ByVal Text, Len(Text), lpRect, wFormat
End Sub
```

Ellipse

Description

The Ellipse API draws an ellipse on a DC.

C Prototype

```
BOOL Ellipse(HDC hdc,
    int nLeftRect,
    int nTopRect,
    int nRightRect,
    int nBottomRect);
```

VB Declaration

```
Private Declare Function Ellipse Lib "gdi32" _
    (ByVal hdc As Long, _
    ByVal X1 As Long, _
    ByVal Y1 As Long, _
    ByVal X2 As Long, _
    ByVal Y2 As Long) As Long
```

Parameters

Parameter	Description
hDC	Handle to the DC.
X1	The horizontal position of the upper-left corner of the rectangle that bounds the circle.

Y1	The vertical position of the upper-left corner of the rectangle that bounds the circle.
X2	The horizontal position of the lower-right corner of the rectangle that bounds the circle.
Y2	The vertical position of the lower-right corner of the rectangle that bounds the circle.
Returns	Returns True on success, False on failure.

Example

```
Public Sub DrawEllipse(Left As Long, _
        Top As Long, _
        Width As Long, _
        Height As Long, _
        Color As Long, _
        Optional Fill As Boolean)

    Dim hOldBrush As Long
    Dim hNewBrush As Long
    Dim hOldPen As Long
    Dim hNewPen As Long

    'Get a pen
    hNewPen = CreatePen(0, 1, Color)
    hOldPen = SelectObject(mDC, hNewPen)

    If Fill Then
        'Get a brush
        hNewBrush = CreateSolidBrush(Color)

        'Set the color
        hOldBrush = SelectObject(mDC, hNewBrush)
    End If

    'Draw an ellipse
    Ellipse mDC, Left, Top, Left + Width, Top + Height

    If Fill Then
        'Reset the brush
        SelectObject mDC, hOldBrush
```

```
        'Delete the brush
        DeleteObject hNewBrush
    End If

    'Reset the pen
    SelectObject mDC, hOldPen

    'Destroy the pen
    DeleteObject hNewPen
End Sub
```

FillRect

Description

The FillRect API is used to fill a rectangular area on the DC.

C Prototype

```
int FillRect(HDC hDC,
    CONST RECT *lprc,
    HBRUSH hbr);
```

VB Declaration

```
Private Declare Function FillRect Lib "user32" _
    (ByVal hdc As Long, _
    lpRect As RECT, _
    ByVal hBrush As Long) As Long
```

Parameters

Parameter	Description
hdc	Handle to the destination DC.
lpRect	A RECT structure that defines the area to be filled.
hBrush	Handle to a previously created brush object.
Returns	Returns True on success, False on failure.

FloodFill

Description

The FloodFill API is used to fill a polygon with color. If the point to be filled is not in a bounding polygon the entire DC will be filled. Otherwise the polygon is filled. If you have used Microsoft Paint, then you are familiar with this function.

C Prototype

```
BOOL FloodFill(HDC hdc,
    int nXStart,
    int nYStart,
    COLORREF crFill);
```

VB Declaration

```
Private Declare Function FloodFill Lib "gdi32" _
    (ByVal hdc As Long, _
    ByVal x As Long, _
    ByVal y As Long, _
    ByVal crColor As Long) As Long
```

Parameters

Parameter	Description
hdc	Handle to the destination DC.
x	The horizontal position of a point in the area that will be filled.
y	The vertical position of a point in the area that will be filled.
crColor	The RGB value of the color you wish to fill.
Returns	Returns True on success, False on failure.

Example

```
Public Sub Fill(x As Long, y As Long, Color As Long)
    'Perform a flood fill around the specified point
    FloodFill mDC, x, y, Color
End Sub
```

LineTo

Description

The LineTo API draws a line from the current pixel position to the coordinates passed to the API.

C Prototype

```
BOOL LineTo(HDC hdc,
    int nXEnd,
    int nYEnd);
```

VB Declaration

```
Private Declare Function LineTo Lib "gdi32" _
    (ByVal hdc As Long, _
    ByVal x As Long, _
    ByVal y As Long) As Long
```

Parameters

Parameter	Description
hDC	Handle to the DC.
x	The horizontal position of the end point of the line.
y	The vertical position of the end point of the line.
Returns	Returns True on success, False on failure.

Notes

This example uses a POINTAPI structure. To help you understand this example, here is more information on that structure.

```
Private Type POINTAPI
    x As Long
    y As Long
End Type
```

Parameter	Description
x	The horizontal position of the end point of the line.
y	The vertical position of the end point of the line.

Example

```
Public Sub DrawLine(StartX As Long, _
        StartY As Long, _
        EndX As Long, _
        EndY As Long, _
        Color As Long)

    Dim hOldPen As Long
    Dim hNewPen As Long
Dim lpPoint As POINTAPI

    'Get a bruch
    hNewPen = CreatePen(0, 1, Color)

    'Set the color
    hOldPen = SelectObject(mDC, hNewPen)

    'Set the starting point
    MoveToEx mDC, StartX, StartY, lpPoint

    'Draw the line
    LineTo mDC, EndX, EndY

    'Reset the brush
    SelectObject mDC, hOldPen
End Sub
```

In this example, notice the call to the MoveToEx API. This call positions the pixel to the starting point. Then LineTo draws a line from that point to the destination point specified in the arguments to the LineTo API.

MoveToEx

Description

The MoveToEx API is used to move the current pixel location within a DC.

C Prototype

```
BOOL MoveToEx(HDC hdc,
    int X,
    int Y,
    LPPOINT lpPoint);
```

VB Declaration

```
Private Declare Function MoveToEx Lib "gdi32" _
    (ByVal hdc As Long, _
    ByVal x As Long, _
    ByVal y As Long, _
    lpPoint As POINTAPI) As Long
```

Parameters

Parameter	Description
hdc	Handle to the DC.
x	The horizontal position of the new starting point.
y	The vertical position of the new starting point.
lpPoint	A POINTAPI structure that returns the coordinates of the previous position of the pixel. If you don't require this information, pass an un-initialized POINTAPI structure. Refer to the previous example to see how the POINTAPI is defined.
Returns	Returns True on success, False on failure.

Rectangle

Description

The Rectangle API is used to draw a rectangle on a DC.

C Prototype

```
BOOL Rectangle(HDC hdc,
    int nLeftRect,
    int nTopRect,
```

```
    int nRightRect,
    int nBottomRect);
```

VB Declaration

```
Private Declare Function Rectangle Lib "gdi32" _
    (ByVal hdc As Long, _
    ByVal X1 As Long, _
    ByVal Y1 As Long, _
    ByVal X2 As Long, _
    ByVal Y2 As Long) As Long
```

Parameters

Parameter	Description
hdc	Handle to the DC to be drawn on.
X1	The leftmost coordinate of the rectangle.
Y1	The topmost coordinate of the rectangle.
X2	The rightmost coordinate of the rectangle.
Y2	The lowest coordinate of the rectangle.
Returns	Returns True on success, False on failure.

Example

```
Public Sub DrawRectangle(Left As Long, _
        Top As Long, _
        Width As Long, _
        Height As Long, _
        Color As Long, _
        Optional Fill As Boolean)

    Dim hOldBrush As Long
    Dim hNewBrush As Long
    Dim hOldPen As Long
    Dim hNewPen As Long

    'Get a pen
    hNewPen = CreatePen(0, 1, Color)
    hOldPen = SelectObject(mDC, hNewPen)
```

```
If Fill Then
    'Get a brush
    hNewBrush = CreateSolidBrush(Color)

    'Set the color
    hOldBrush = SelectObject(mDC, hNewBrush)
End If

'Draw the rectangle
Rectangle mDC, Left, Top, Left + Width, Top + Height

If Fill Then
    'Reset the brush
    SelectObject mDC, hOldBrush

    'Delete the brush
    DeleteObject hNewBrush
End If

'Reset the pen
SelectObject mDC, hOldPen

'Destroy the pen
DeleteObject hNewPen
End Sub
```

SetBkColor

Description

The SetBkColor API is used to set the background color of a DC.

C Prototype

```
COLORREF SetBkColor(HDC hdc,
    COLORREF crColor);
```

VB Declaration

```
Private Declare Function SetBkColor Lib "gdi32" _
    (ByVal hdc As Long, _
    ByVal crColor As Long) As Long
```

Parameters

Parameter	Description
hdc	Handle to the DC to be colored.
crColor	The RGB color you wish to use. You can use Visual Basic's RGB() function in this parameter.
Returns	On success, the API returns the RGB value of the previous background color.

Example

The following line of code sets the background color of the destination DC dcDest to red:

```
rc = SetBkColor(dcDest, RGB(255, 0, 0))
```

SetBkMode

Description

The SetBkMode API is used to set the background of a DC to transparent or opaque.

C Prototype

```
int SetBkMode(HDC hdc,
    int iBkMode);
```

VB Declaration

```
Private Declare Function SetBkMode Lib "gdi32" _
    (ByVal hdc As Long, _
    ByVal nBkMode As Long) As Long
```

Parameters

Parameter	Description
hDC	Handle to the DC.
nBkMode	A constant representing either an OPAQUE or TRANSPARENT background.

Returns	On success, the previous background mode is returned. Otherwise, the API returns 0.

SetPixel

Description

The SetPixel API is used to draw a single pixel on a DC.

C Prototype

```
COLORREF SetPixel(HDC hdc,
    int X,
    int Y,
    COLORREF crColor);
```

VB Declaration

```
Private Declare Function SetPixel Lib "gdi32" _
    (ByVal hdc As Long, _
    ByVal x As Long, _
    ByVal y As Long, _
    ByVal crColor As Long) As Long
```

Parameters

Parameter	Description
hdc	Handle to the DC to draw on.
x	The horizontal position of the pixel.
y	The vertical position of the pixel.
crColor	The RGB value that determines the color of the pixel.
Returns	The RGB value the pixel gets set to. This value may be different than what you set in crColor. For example, you may specify a color that is not represented in the color palette on a 256-color system. If the API call fails, the return will be –1.

Example

```
Public Sub DrawPoint(x As Long, y As Long, Color)
    'Set the pixel
    SetPixel mDC, x, y, Color
End Sub
```

SetTextColor

Description

The SetTextColor API is used to set the color of the text that will be drawn on a DC using the DrawText API.

C Prototype

```
COLORREF SetTextColor(HDC hdc,
    COLORREF crColor);
```

VB Declaration

```
Private Declare Function SetTextColor Lib "gdi32" _
    (ByVal hdc As Long, _
    ByVal crColor As Long) As Long
```

Parameters

Parameter	Description
hdc	Handle to the DC.
crColor	The RGB value representing the color of the text.
Returns	On success, the API returns the RGB value of the previous color.

Example

The following code is used in the DrawText method of the graphics class in the example for this chapter. The Color argument is optional, so to check if the user specified a color, use Visual Basic's IsNumeric() function.

```
If IsNumeric(Color) Then SetTextColor mDC, Color
```

StretchBlt

Description

The StretchBlt API is like BitBlt, except that it can be used to rapidly shrink or stretch the bitmap while copying it to the destination DC.

C Prototype

```
BOOL StretchBlt(HDC hdcDest,
    int nXOriginDest,
    int nYOriginDest,
    int nWidthDest,
    int nHeightDest,
    HDC hdcSrc,
    int nXOriginSrc,
    int nYOriginSrc,
    int nWidthSrc,
    int nHeightSrc,
    DWORD dwRop);
```

VB Declaration

```
Private Declare Function StretchBlt Lib "gdi32" _
    (ByVal hdc As Long, _
    ByVal x As Long, _
    ByVal y As Long, _
    ByVal nWidth As Long, _
    ByVal nHeight As Long, _
    ByVal hSrcDC As Long, _
    ByVal xSrc As Long, _
    ByVal ySrc As Long, _
    ByVal nSrcWidth As Long, _
    ByVal nSrcHeight As Long, _
    ByVal dwRop As Long) As Long
```

Parameters

Parameter	Description
hdc	Handle of the destination DC.
x	The horizontal position of the upper-left corner in the destination DC.

y	The vertical position of the upper-left corner in the destination DC.
nWidth	The width of the destination image.
nHeight	The height of the destination image.
hSrcDC	Handle to the source DC.
xSrc	The horizontal coordinate of the upper-left corner of the clipping area in the destination DC.
ySrc	The vertical coordinate of the upper-left corner of the clipping area in the destination DC.
nSrcWidth	The width, in pixels, of the source area to be transferred.
nSrcHeight	The height, in pixels, of the source area to be transferred.
dwRop	Raster operation code. Refer to the Notes under the BitBlt API for more information on raster operation codes.
Returns	Returns True on success, False on failure.

Moving On

As you can see, most graphics operations are very easy to use. Windows does a great job of insulating you from the underlying complexities of each graphics routine. Most drawing operations can be accomplished by following these steps:

1. Create a drawing object such as a pen or brush.

2. Select the new object into the destination DC. Remember to save the original drawing object!

3. Perform the drawing operation.

4. Restore the original drawing object into the DC.

5. Destroy the drawing object you created in Step 1.

Now that you have seen many APIs in the code listings in this chapter, take a look at the sample project, which draws a topographical map of the Earth. Most of the graphics routines are encapsulated in a graphics class that you can enhance and reuse in your own applications. There are many more methods that could be added, but I'll leave these up to you to develop. The only limits are your imagination!

CHAPTER
THIRTEEN

13

Multimedia

- Playing a Wave File

- The Multimedia Command Interface

- Working with Digital Audio

- Playing Digital Video

- Programming the Mixer

Every programmer should have the capability to play waveform audio, or wave files, in their applications. Sound bites not only add to the overall experience in your applications, but they can also be useful usability aids. The key to playing wave files is the sndPlaySound API, as described below.

Playing a Wave File

sndPlaySound

Description

The sndPlaySound API allows you to easily play a wave file synchronously or asynchronously.

C Prototype

```
BOOL sndPlaySound(LPCSTR lpszSound,
    UINT fuSound);
```

VB Declaration

```
Private Declare Function sndPlaySound Lib "winmm.dll" _
    Alias "sndPlaySoundA" _
    (ByVal lpszSoundName As String, _
    ByVal uFlags As Long) As Long
```

Parameters

Parameter	Description
lpszSoundName	A null-terminated string containing the filename of the wave file.
uFlags	Flags for specifying how the command should be executed.
Returns	Returns True on success, False on failure.

Notes

The following constants are used in the uFlags parameter:

Constant	Result
SND_ASYNC (&H1)	Plays a wave file asynchronously.
SND_LOOP (&H8)	Plays a wave file repetitively.
SND_MEMORY (&H4)	Plays a wave file stored in memory.
SND_NODEFAULT (&H2)	Disregards playing the default wave file, such as Ding, if the file specified in lpszSoundName cannot be found.
SND_NOSTOP (&H10)	Aborts a request to play a wave file if another wave file is currently playing.
SND_SYNC (&H0)	Plays the wave file synchronously.

Example

Listing 13.1 is a function taken from the clsWavePlayer class and demonstrates how to use sndPlaySound to play a wave file once, or repetitively.

LISTING 13.1   Playing a Wave File Using sndPlaySound

```
Public Function Play(Optional Repeat As Boolean)
    Dim rc As Long
    Dim uFlags As Long

    If Repeat Then
        'Play the file asynchronously
        'and loop it
        uFlags = SND_ASYNC + SND_LOOP
    Else
        'Play the file once
        uFlags = SND_ASYNC
    End If

    'Play the file
    rc = sndPlaySound(mFilename, uFlags)
End Function
```

The sndPlaySound API is not the only method you can use to play audio on your computer. Using the Multimedia Command Interface (MCI) you can play wave files, MIDI files, compact disks, and more!

The Multimedia Command Interface

Windows makes it easy to play multimedia files using the MCI. There are several MCI device types you can access. These include, but are not limited to, cdaudio, avivideo, dvdvideo, and many more.

There are many MCI APIs, but few offer any benefit over the mciSendString command. For example, the mciSendCommand API achieves the same functionality, but uses MCI messages rather than strings.

There are many derivatives of MCI commands and each MCI-compatible device can have its own unique commands, as well as the standard commands, and possibly some derivatives. When working with an MCI device be sure to obtain the MCI command specification for that device.

The first thing to look at is the mciSendString API. Then on to some specific examples of how to use it to play various multimedia formats. By the end of this chapter you will know how to work with several media types, including digital audio and digital video!

mciSendString

Description

The mciSendString API is used to send MCI command strings to an MCI device.

C Prototype

```
MCIERROR mciSendString(LPCTSTR lpszCommand,
    LPTSTR lpszReturnString,
    UINT cchReturn,
    HANDLE hwndCallback);
```

VB Declaration

```
Private Declare Function mciSendString Lib "winmm.dll" _
    Alias "mciSendStringA" _
    (ByVal lpstrCommand As String, _
    ByVal lpstrReturnString As String, _
    ByVal uReturnLength As Long, _
    ByVal hwndCallback As Long) As Long
```

Parameters

Parameter	Description
lpstrCommand	An ASCII string containing the MCI command to execute.
lpstrReturnString	A pre-allocated buffer used to return the result of the MCI command.
uReturnLength	The length of the data returned in the buffer specified in lpstrReturnString.
hwndCallback	If the Notify option is specified in the command, this parameter must specify the address of a callback function that will be triggered.
Returns	Returns 0 on success or an error number on failure. You can retrieve the results by reading the value returned in the buffer specified in the lpstrReturnString parameter. The error can be one of the following: MCIERR_BAD_CONSTANT, MCIERR_BAD_INTEGER, MCIERR_DUPLICATE_FLAGS, MCIERR_MISSING_COMMAND_STRING, MCIERR_MISSING_DEVICE_NAME, MCIERR_MISSING_STRING_ARGUMENT, MCIERR_NEW_REQUIRES_ALIAS, MCIERR_NO_CLOSING_QUOTE, MCIERR_NOTIFY_ON_AUTO_OPEN, MCIERR_PARAM_OVERFLOW, MCIERR_PARSER_INTERNAL, or MCIERR_UNRECOGNIZED_KEYWORD.

Example

The following example plays a CD audio device that has been previously opened with the MCI open command:

```
Public Function Play() As Boolean
     Dim rc As Long
     Dim ret As String
     Dim cmd As String

     cmd = "play cdaudio"

     'Send the command
     rc = mciSendString(cmd, ret, 0, 0)

     'Return the result
     Play = (rc = 0)
End Function
```

Working with Digital Audio

As you noticed in the first section of this chapter you can use the sndPlaySound API to easily play wave files. If you require more sophistication you can use MCI commands to play and record your own digital audio and video files.

Playing Wave Audio Using MCI

Another method to play wave files, as well as other sound types, is to use MCI commands. Even though it requires a few more steps, the process is still quite easy.

This is the procedure for playing a wave file:

1.   Open the wave file using the MCI open waveaudio commands.

2.   Play the file by issuing the play filename commands.

3.   Close the file using close waveaudio.

Listing 13.2 is from the clsWavePlayer class. It shows how to use MCI commands to play a wave file.

LISTING 13.2   Playing a Wave File Using MCI

```
Public Function PlayMCI() As Boolean
    Dim rc As Long
    Dim ret As String
    Dim cmd As String

    'Open the file
    cmd = "open waveaudio"
    ret = String$(256, Chr$(0))
    rc = mciSendString(cmd, ret, 256, 0)

    'Play it
    cmd = "play " & mFilename
    ret = String$(256, Chr$(0))
    rc = mciSendString(cmd, ret, 256, 0)

    'Close it
    cmd = "close waveaudio"
    ret = String$(256, Chr$(0))
    rc = mciSendString(cmd, ret, 256, 0)

    'Return the result
    PlayMCI = (rc = 0)
End Function
```

Recording Wave Audio

It's fun to play audio on your computer. Sound stimulates your sense of hearing, and if you have the bass or volume turned up the sense of touch is also involved. But sometimes you may need to provide audio recording functionality in your application.

Fortunately, recording wave audio isn't difficult. Again, using simple MCI commands you can record your own wave files. Listing 13.3 shows how to do this.

LISTING 13.3   Recording a Wave File Using MCI

```
Public Function Record() As Boolean
    Dim rc As Long
    Dim ret As String
    Dim cmd As String

    'Set the bit rate
    cmd = "set wave bitspersample 16"
    ret = String$(256, Chr$(0))
    rc = mciSendString(cmd, ret, 256, 0)

    'Start recording
    cmd = "set wave samplespersec 44100"
    ret = String$(256, Chr$(0))
    rc = mciSendString(cmd, ret, 256, 0)

    'Start recording
    cmd = "record wave insert"
    ret = String$(256, Chr$(0))
    rc = mciSendString(cmd, ret, 256, 0)

    'Return the result
    Record = (rc = 0)
End Function
```

As you can see there are a few more commands in this example, but they are not too difficult.

Once you are done recording your wave file, issue a stop command, and then save it using the save command. The methods for stopping and saving the file are listed below:

```
Public Function StopRecording() As Boolean
    Dim rc As Long
    Dim ret As String
    Dim cmd As String

    'Stop the recorder
    cmd = "stop wave"
    ret = String$(256, Chr$(0))
    rc = mciSendString(cmd, ret, 256, 0)
```

```
        'Return the result
        StopRecording = (rc = 0)
End Function

Public Function Save(Filename As String) As Boolean
        Dim rc As Long
        Dim ret As String
        Dim cmd As String

        'Save the file
        cmd = "save wave " & _
                Chr$(34) & Filename & Chr$(34)

        ret = String$(256, Chr$(0))
        rc = mciSendString(cmd, ret, 256, 0)

        'Return the result
        Save = (rc = 0)
End Function
```

Notice that in the Save method the filename is surrounded by quotation marks. Make sure you do this because long filenames often contain spaces. By omitting the quotes the MCI may misinterpret the filename as an invalid MCI command.

Playing CD Audio

Once again you can use the MCI to work with multiple formats. Compact Disk is another one of the supported devices. You can write to your own CD player using MCI commands.

Before you play a CD you must open it using code similar to the following:

```
Private Sub Class_Initialize()
    .
    .
    .
    'Open the CD drive
    cmd = "open " & mDrive & _
            " type cdaudio alias cdaudio"
    rc = mciSendString(cmd, ret, 0, 0)
    .
    .
    .
End Sub
```

When the CD device is open you can issue commands to make the CD play, stop, fast-forward, rewind, and more. You can even query status information from the CD while it is playing. Start playing the CD with the following lines of code:

```
cmd = "play cdaudio"

'Send the command
rc = mciSendString(cmd, ret, 0, 0)
```

When you are done, you need to stop and close the device:

```
Private Sub Class_Terminate()
    Dim rc As Long
    Dim ret As String
    Dim cmd As String

    'Make sure the CD is stopped
    cmd = "stop cdaudio"
    rc = mciSendString(cmd, ret, 0, 0)

    'Close the CD drive
    cmd = "close cdaudio"
    rc = mciSendString(cmd, ret, 0, 0)
End Sub
```

As you can see, MCI makes it extremely easy to work with multimedia files and devices. And remember that many devices also support their own MCI commands, so be sure to find out if the manufacturer provides a Software Development Kit (SDK) that supports MCI commands. Such an SDK will make your development efforts easy and much more enjoyable.

Playing Digital Video

The more popular audio formats have been covered in the previous section, but I would be remiss to leave out a section dealing with digital video. While the ability to play Audio Video Interleave (AVI) files has been around for a few years, the explosion of DVD players opens up a whole new digital video arena. Not only can you play movies and animations, you can also develop your own applications, such as games and impressive multimedia kiosks, all utilizing DVD.

Playing digital video is just as easy as digital audio, but the MCI command set provides additional commands that help contribute to your overall visual experience.

Unlike audio you can resize video. This means you can play your movies full screen or in a window in a multimedia kiosk or game. Your implementation method depends on your application, but I guarantee that watching your application come to life with digital video is a rewarding experience. The example in this chapter shows how you can play the sample AVI file shown in Figure 13.1.

FIGURE 13.1:

Spinning globe

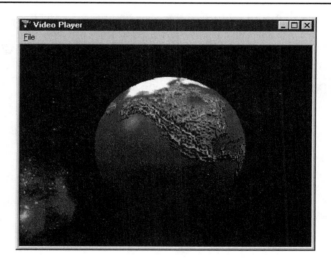

In the clsVCR class, the mciSendString API is wrapped in a function called mci. This was done to keep the code neater.

Opening a digital video file, such as an AVI file, is pretty much the same as opening a sound file. You simply issue the open MCI command and specify the name of the video file using the AVIVideo type, as shown in Listing 13.4.

LISTING 13.4   Opening an AVI File

```
Public Sub OpenScene()
    Dim rc As String
    Dim cmd As String
```

```
'Open the video
cmd = "open " & mFilename & _
        " alias " & mAlias & _
        " type AVIVideo"

rc = mci(cmd)
        .
        .
        .
End Sub
```

A cool feature of the MCI command set is the ability to resize a video file on the fly. Do this by issuing the MCI put command. An example is shown below. Listing 13.5 shows the code that positions the video display on its target.

LISTING 13.5   **Positioning a Video Window**

```
Public Sub Resize()
    Dim rc As String
    Dim cmd As String

    'Project it on the screen
    cmd = "window " & mAlias & _
            " handle " & _
            Trim$(Str$(mhWnd))

    rc = mci(cmd)

    'Set the size
    cmd = "put " & mAlias & _
            " destination at " & _
            Trim$(Str$(mLeft)) & " " & _
            Trim$(Str$(mTop)) & " " & _
            Trim$(Str$(mWidth)) & " " & _
            Trim$(Str$(mHeight))

    'Send the command
    rc = mci(cmd)
End Sub
```

In this example, the first thing is to make sure the video image is projected on the target window by issuing the MCI `window` command, followed by the alias of the device and the keyword `handle`, followed by the handle of the destination window. This command ensures that the video is rendered on the proper window.

After the `window` command is issued, tell MCI to put the device alias, in this case `video`, at a destination specified by the coordinates that follow. This example tells the MCI to position the video at the upper left-hand corner, making the video 320 pixels wide and 240 pixels high.

When you want to play the video file, issue the MCI `play` command. If you want the file to repeat, specify the keyword `repeat` at the end of the MCI command. A sample command is shown below:

```
play video repeat
```

If you want the video to play synchronously, add the keyword `wait` to the MCI command string.

Finally, when you are done playing the video file make sure you stop and close it. This is accomplished with the following code:

```
Public Sub CloseScene()
    Dim rc As String
    Dim cmd As String

    'Set command to stop the video
    cmd = "stop " & mAlias
    rc = mci(cmd)

    'Set command to close the video
    cmd = "close " & mAlias
    rc = mci(cmd)
End Sub
```

Now that you have seen how to play an AVI video in a Visual Basic application you can play any video format supported by MCI. MPEG video files are supported if you have an MPEG video player installed. What's better is that there are many video clips available on the Internet. And if you are really a video buff you can purchase video capture hardware fairly inexpensively. The more you work with digital video, the more fun multimedia becomes!

Programming the Mixer

An often-overlooked multimedia device is the mixer control. Many books seem to overlook this basic device when covering multimedia programming. I felt compelled to touch upon it because audio contributes so much to the entire multimedia experience.

The presence of audio is not what is important, but the dynamics of the audio. Volume control allows your program to present antagonistic speed metal when you are shooting up your mutant enemies, and provides a gentle buzz of a motor while flying a single-engine plane. Imagine how boring your applications would be if everything was played at the same volume!

To spruce up the CD Player sample application I decided it needed a volume control. The volume control object was created by wrapping various mixer APIs into an easy-to-use object that operates more like a volume control than a set of complex APIs. Let's look at the mixer APIs and construct the volume control class and you will see what I mean.

mixerClose

Description

The mixerClose API closes a mixer object opened with the mixerOpen API.

C Prototype

```
MMRESULT mixerClose(HMIXER hmx);
```

VB Declaration

```
Private Declare Function mixerClose Lib "winmm.dll" _
    (ByVal hmx As Long) As Long
```

Parameters

Parameter	Description
hmx	Handle to the mixer object to close.
Returns	Returns MMSYSERR_NOERROR on success, MMSYSERR_INVALHANDLE on error.

Example

```
Private Sub Class_Terminate()
    'Close the mixer
    mixerClose hMixer
End Sub
```

mixerGetControlDetails

Description

The mixerGetControlDetails API returns information specific to a particular mixer device.

C Prototype

```
MMRESULT mixerGetControlDetails(HMIXEROBJ hmxobj,
    LPMIXERCONTROLDETAILS pmxcd,
    DWORD fdwDetails);
```

VB Declaration

```
Private Declare Function mixerGetControlDetails Lib "winmm.dll" _
    Alias "mixerGetControlDetailsA" _
    (ByVal hmxobj As Long, _
    pmxcd As MIXERCONTROLDETAILS, _
    ByVal fdwDetails As Long) As Long
```

Parameters

Parameter	Description
hmxobj	Handle to the mixer object.
pmxcd	Pointer to a MIXERCONTROLDETAILS structure that will return information about the mixer control.
fdwDetails	A combination of flags that specify what information to retrieve.
Returns	On success, this API returns MMSYSERR_NOERROR. Otherwise, it returns one of the following error codes: MIXERR_INVALCONTROL, MMSYSERR_BADDEVICEID, MMSYSERR_INVALFLAG, MMSYSERR_INVALHANDLE, MMSYSERR_INVALPARAM, or MMSYSERR_NODRIVER.

Notes

The MIXERCONTROLDETAILS structure is described below:

```
Private Type MIXERCONTROLDETAILS
    cbStruct As Long
    dwControlID As Long
    cChannels As Long
item As Long
    cbDetails As Long
    paDetails As Long
End Type
```

Each member is described below:

Member	Description
cbStruct	Handle to the mixer object.
dwControlID	Pointer to a MIXERCONTROLDETAILS structure that will return information about the mixer control.
cChannels	A combination of flags that specify what information to retrieve.
item	Set to 0.
cbDetails	Size of the structure pointed to in the paDetails parameter.
paDetails	Address pointing to the first structure in an array of structures, such as MIXERCONTROLDETAILS_UNSIGNED.

Example

```
Dim rc As Long
rc = mixerGetControlDetails( hmxobj, _
    Pmxcd, fdwDetails )
```

mixerGetDevCaps

Description

The mixerGetDevCaps API is used to retrieve the capabilities of a mixer object.

C Prototype

```
MMRESULT mixerGetDevCaps(UINT uMxId,
    LPMIXERCAPS pmxcaps,
    UINT cbmxcaps);
```

VB Declaration

```
Private Declare Function mixerGetDevCaps Lib "winmm.dll" _
    Alias "mixerGetDevCapsA" _
    (ByVal uMxId As Long, _
    ByVal pmxcaps As MIXERCAPS, _
    ByVal cbmxcaps As Long) As Long
```

Parameters

Parameter	Description
uMxId	Handle to a mixer device.
pmxcaps	Pointer to a MIXERCAPS structure.
cbmxcaps	Length of the MIXERCAPS structure passed in the pmxcaps parameter.
Returns	On success, this API returns MMSYSERR_NOERROR. Otherwise, it returns one of these error codes: MMSYSERR_BADDEVICEID, MMSYSERR_INVALHANDLE, or MMSYSERR_INVALPARAM.

Notes

The MIXERCAPS structure is described below:

```
Private Type MIXERCAPS
    wMid As Integer
    wPid As Integer
    vDriverVersion As Long
    szPname As String * MAXPNAMELEN
    fdwSupport As Long
    cDestinations As Long
End Type
```

Each member is described below:

Member	Description
wMid	Returns the manufacturer ID.
wPid	Returns the product ID.
vDriverVersion	Returns the version of the driver for this device.
szName	Returns the product name of the device.
fdwSupport	Unused.
cDestinations	Returns the number of destinations (outputs) for this device.

Example

```
Dim mixCaps As MIXERCAPS
Dim rc As Long

rc = mixerGetDevCaps(0, mixCaps, _
    LenB(mixCaps))
```

mixerGetID

Description

The mixerGetID API is used to retrieve the identifier for a mixer object with a specific handle.

C Prototype

```
MMRESULT mixerGetID(HMIXEROBJ hmxobj,
    UINT * puMxId,
    DWORD fdwId);
```

VB Declaration

```
Private Declare Function mixerGetID Lib "winmm.dll" _
    (ByVal hmxobj As Long, _
    pumxID As Long, _
    ByVal fdwId As Long) As Long
```

Parameters

Parameter	Description
hmxobj	Handle of the mixer object.
pmuxID	A variable that will return the identifier of the mixer object.
fdwId	Flags that configure the mixer object. Can be one or more of the following: MIXER_OBJECTF_AUX, MIXER_OBJECTF_HMIDIIN, MIXER_OBJECTF_HMIDIOUT, MIXER_OBJECTF_HMIXER, MIXER_OBJECTF_HWAVEIN, MIXER_OBJECTF_HWAVEOUT, MIXER_OBJECTF_MIDIIN, MIXER_OBJECTF_MIDIOUT, MIXER_OBJECTF_MIXER, MIXER_OBJECTF_WAVEIN, or MIXER_OBJECTF_WAVEOUT.
Returns	On success, this API returns MMSYSERR_NOERROR. Otherwise, it returns one of these error codes: MMSYSERR_BADDEVICEID, MMSYSERR_INVALFLAG, MMSYSERR_INVALHANDLE, MMSYSERR_INVALPARAM, or MMSYSERR_NODRIVER.

Example

```
Dim mixCaps As MIXERCAPS
Dim rc As Long

rc = mixerGetID( hmxobj, pumxID, _
    MIXER_OBJECTF_HMIDIIN )
```

mixerGetLineControls

Description

The mixerGetLineControls API is used to retrieve the audio objects associated with a mixer object.

C Prototype

```
MMRESULT mixerGetLineControls(HMIXEROBJ hmxobj,
    LPMIXERLINECONTROLS pmxlc,
    DWORD fdwControls);
```

VB Declaration

```
Private Declare Function mixerGetLineControls Lib "winmm.dll" _
    Alias "mixerGetLineControlsA" _
    (ByVal hmxobj As Long, _
    pmxlc As MIXERLINECONTROLS, _
    ByVal fdwControls As Long) As Long
```

Parameters

Parameter	Description
hmxobj	The handle of a mixer object.
pmxlc	A pointer to a MIXERLINECONTROLS structure.
fdwControls	Flags identifying the information to be retrieved about an audio object.
Returns	On success, this API returns MMSYSERR_NOERROR. Otherwise, it returns one of these error codes: MIXERR_INVALCONTROL, MIXERR_INVALLINE, MMSYSERR_BADDEVICEID, MMSYSERR_INVALFLAG, MMSYSERR_INVALHANDLE, MMSYSERR_INVALPARAM, or MMSYSERR_NODRIVER.

Notes

The MIXERLINECONTROLS structure is described below:

```
Private Type MIXERLINECONTROLS
    cbStruct As Long
    dwLineID As Long
    dwControl As Long
    cControls As Long
    cbmxctrl As Long
    pamxctrl As Long
End Type
```

Each member is described below:

Member	Description
cbStruct	The size of the structure.
dwLineID	The ID of the line being queried.

dwControl	The type of control being queried.
cControls	Count of controls pmxctrl points to.
cbmxctrl	The size of the MIXERCONTROL structure.
pamxctrl	Pointer to an array of MIXERCONTROL structures.

Example

```
    .
    .
    .
'Get the control
If mixerGetLineControls(mhMixer, _
        mxlc, _
        MIXER_GETLINECONTROLSF_ONEBYTYPE) = _
        MMSYSERR_NOERROR Then
    .
    .
    .
```

mixerGetLineInfo

Description

The mixerGetLineInfo API is used to retrieve information about a specific line device of a mixer, such as wave, CD, or MIDI output.

C Prototype

```
MMRESULT mixerGetLineInfo(HMIXEROBJ hmxobj,
    LPMIXERLINE pmxl,
    DWORD fdwInfo);
```

VB Declaration

```
Private Declare Function mixerGetLineInfo Lib "winmm.dll" _
    Alias "mixerGetLineInfoA" _
    (ByVal hmxobj As Long, _
    pmxl As MIXERLINE, _
    ByVal fdwInfo As Long) As Long
```

Parameters

Parameter	Description
hmxobj	Handle to the mixer object.
pmxl	Pointer to a MIXERLINE structure used to return information about the line device.
Returns	On success, this API returns MMSYSERR_NOERROR. Otherwise, it returns one of these error codes: MIXERR_INVALLINE, MMSYSERR_BADDEVICEID, MMSYSERR_INVALFLAG, MMSYSERR_INVALHANDLE, MMSYSERR_INVALPARAM, or MMSYSERR_NODRIVER.

Notes

The MIXERLINE structure is described below:

```
Private Type MIXERLINE
    cbStruct As Long
    dwDestination As Long
    dwSource As Long
    dwLineID As Long
    fdwLine As Long
    dwUser As Long
    dwComponentType As Long
    cChannels As Long
    cConnections As Long
    cControls As Long
    szShortName As String * MIXER_SHORT_NAME_CHARS
    szName As String * MIXER_LONG_NAME_CHARS
    dwType As Long
    dwDeviceID As Long
    wMid  As Integer
    wPid As Integer
    vDriverVersion As Long
    szPname As String * MAXPNAMELEN
End Type
```

Each member is described below:

Member	Description
cbStruct	Size of the MIXERLINE structure.
dwDestination	Zero-based destination index.
dwSource	Zero-based source index (if source).
dwLineID	A unique line ID for the mixer device.
fdwLine	Will let you know if the audio line is active, disconnected, or if it is a source with a single destination.
dwUser	Driver-specific information.
dwComponentType	The type of device the line connects to.
cChannels	The number of channels a line supports. This will be 1 for single channel (monaural) devices and 2 for stereo devices.
cConnections	Set to 0 for output devices.
cControls	Number of controls at this line.
szShortName	A null-terminated buffer containing the short name for the audio device.
szName	A null-terminated buffer containing the name of the audio device.
dwType	The type of device associated with the audio line.
dwDeviceID	Returns the ID of the device.
wMid	Returns the manufacturer's ID for the device.
wPid	Returns the product ID for the device.
wDriverVersion	Returns the version of the audio driver.
szPname	Returns the product name of the device.

Example

```
Dim mxlc As MIXERLINECONTROLS
Dim mxl As MIXERLINE
```

```
With mx1
    .cbStruct = Len(mx1)
    .dwComponentType = MIXERLINE_COMPONENTTYPE_DST_SPEAKERS
End With
    .
    .
    .
'Obtain a line corresponding to the component type
rc = mixerGetLineInfo(mhMixer, _
        mx1, _
        MIXER_GETLINEINFOF_COMPONENTTYPE)
    .
    .
    .
```

mixerGetNumDevs

Description

The mixerGetNumDevs API retrieves the number of mixer devices installed in the system.

C Prototype

```
UINT mixerGetNumDevs(VOID);
```

VB Declaration

```
Private Declare Function mixerGetNumDevs _
    Lib "winmm.dll" () As Long
```

Parameters

Parameter	Description
None	
Returns	The number of mixer devices installed.

Example

```
rc = mixerGetNumDevs()
```

mixerOpen

Description

The mixerOpen API is used to open a mixer device.

C Prototype

```
MMRESULT mixerOpen(LPHMIXER phmx,
    UINT uMxId,
    DWORD dwCallback,
    DWORD dwInstance,
    DWORD fdwOpen);
```

VB Declaration

```
Private Declare Function mixerOpen Lib "winmm.dll" _
    (phmx As Long, _
    ByVal uMxId As Long, _
    ByVal dwCallback As Long, _
    ByVal dwInstance As Long, _
    ByVal fdwOpen As Long) As Long
```

Parameters

Parameter	Description
phmx	A variable that will return the handle of the mixer device.
uMxId	An identifier for the mixer device to be opened.
dwCallback	The address of the callback function.
dwInstance	Instance data that will be passed back to the callback function specified in the dwCallback parameter.
fdwOpen	Flags that define how the mixer device is opened.
Returns	On success, this API returns MMSYSERR_NOERROR. Otherwise, it returns one of these error codes: MMSYSERR_ALLOCATED, MMSYSERR_BADDEVICEID, MMSYSERR_INVALFLAG, MMSYSERR_INVALHANDLE, MMSYSERR_INVALPARAM, MMSYSERR_NODRIVER, or MMSYSERR_NOMEM.

Example

```
        .
        .
        .
'Open the mixer with DeviceID 0.
If mixerOpen(mhMixer, 0, 0, 0, 0) = _
        MMSYSERR_NOERROR Then
        .
        .
        .
```

mixerSetControlDetails

Description

The mixerSetControlDetails API sets information about a specific mixer object.

C Prototype

```
MMRESULT mixerSetControlDetails(HMIXEROBJ hmxobj,
    LPMIXERCONTROLDETAILS pmxcd,
    DWORD fdwDetails);
```

VB Declaration

```
Private Declare Function mixerSetControlDetails Lib "winmm.dll" _
    (ByVal hmxobj As Long, _
    pmxcd As MIXERCONTROLDETAILS, _
    ByVal fdwDetails As Long) As Long
```

Parameters

Parameter	Description
hmxobj	Handle to the mixer object.
pmxcd	A pointer to a MIXERCONTROLDETAILS structure that contains the details to be set.
fdwDetails	Flags that specify what information will be set.

Returns   On success, this API returns MMSYSERR_NOERROR.
Otherwise, it returns one of these error codes:
MIXERR_INVALCONTROL, MMSYSERR_BADDEVICEID,
MMSYSERR_INVALFLAG, MMSYSERR_INVALHANDLE,
MMSYSERR_INVALPARAM, or MMSYSERR_NODRIVER.

Notes

See the Notes section under the mixerGetControlDetails API for more information on the MIXERCONTROLDETAILS structure.

Example

```
.
.
.
'Allocate a buffer for the control value buffer
hmem = GlobalAlloc(&H40, Len(vol))

    With mxcd
        .item = 0
        .dwControlID = ControlID
        .cbStruct = Len(mxcd)
        .cbDetails = Len(vol)
        .paDetails = GlobalLock(hmem)
        .cChannels = 1
    End With

    'Set the volume
    vol.dwValue = Volume

    'Copy the data from the volume structure to
    'the mixer structure
    CopyPtrFromStruct mxcd.paDetails, vol, Len(vol)

    'Set the control volume
    rc = mixerSetControlDetails(mhMixer, mxcd, 0)

'Release the buffer
GlobalFree hmem
.
.
.
```

CHAPTER
FOURTEEN

14

Windows Networking

- The Basics

- Enumerating Network Resources

- Connecting to Network Resources

As more and more computers are being connected by networks, it is important that you be prepared to write applications that can help the user discover and utilize the services available on the network.

The Basics

In its inception, Windows NT was the little brother to Microsoft's LAN Manager. LAN Manager was Microsoft's answer to Novell's NetWare and IBM's LAN Server products.

Pieces of LAN Manager are evident in almost every Windows platform, including Windows for Workgroups, Windows 9x, and Windows NT.

The WNet APIs, often referred to as the *LANMan*, or LAN Manager APIs, are still available and useful. These APIs allow you to perform many basic networking tasks such as browsing networks, as well as connecting to and disconnecting from networked resources. There are several APIs that perform these tasks, but first let's look at the two most basic networking functions.

Two of the most common questions in network programming are how to determine the user and workstation names. These requests can easily be fulfilled using two APIs: GetComputerName and GetUserName. You may want to retrieve and include these values in your application, either for simple aesthetics or to provide detailed logging information for your database application. If you design your application correctly you can even use these values to allow user's access to applications, rather than implementing a logon screen where the user is required to remember yet another password.

GetComputerName

Description

The GetComputerName API returns the name of the workstation the API is called on. This is useful if you want to track where a user is located or want to send network messages.

C Prototype

```
BOOL GetComputerName(LPTSTR lpBuffer,
    LPDWORD nSize);
```

VB Declaration

```
Private Declare Function GetComputerName Lib "kernel32" _
    Alias "GetComputerNameA" _
    (ByVal lpBuffer As String, _
    nSize As Long) As Long
```

Parameters

Parameter	Description
lpBuffer	A pre-initialized buffer used to return the name of the computer.
nSize	The size of the buffer specified in the lpBuffer parameter.
Returns	Returns True if the computer's name was retrieved successfully. Otherwise it returns False.

Example

Listing 14.1 shows a sample property that retrieves and returns the computer name to the calling program.

LISTING 14.1   Workstation Name

```
Public Property Get ComputerName() As String
    Dim nSize As Long
    Dim lpBuffer As String

    'Create a buffer large ennough to hold
    'the computer name
    nSize = 255
    lpBuffer = Space$(nSize)

    'Get the computer name
    If GetComputerName(lpBuffer, nSize) Then
        'Return the computer name
        ComputerName = Left$(lpBuffer, nSize)
    Else
        ComputerName = ""
    End If
End Property
```

GetUserName

Description

The GetUserName API retrieves the logon name of the user currently logged on.

C Prototype

```
BOOL GetUserName(LPTSTR lpBuffer,
    LPDWORD nSize);
```

VB Declaration

```
Private Declare Function GetUserName Lib "advapi32.dll" _
    Alias "GetUserNameA" _
    (ByVal lpBuffer As String, _
    nSize As Long) As Long
```

Parameters

Parameter	Description
lpBuffer	A pre-initialized buffer used to return the user's logon name.
nSize	The size of the buffer specified in the lpBuffer parameter.
Returns	Returns True if the user's name was retrieved successfully. Otherwise it returns False.

Notes

Although the documentation says that the nSize parameter returns the number of bytes that make up the user name, it actually returns the number of characters, plus the null-terminating character. As a result, you need to trim the last character off.

Example

Listing 14.2 retrieves and returns the user name for the person currently logged on.

LISTING 14.2   Network User Name

```
Public Property Get UserName() As String
    Dim lpBuffer As String
    Dim nSize As Long

    'initialize the buffer
    nSize = 255
    lpBuffer = Space$(nSize)

    'Get the name of the current user
    If GetUserName(lpBuffer, nSize) Then
        'Return the user name
        'Remember that the API returns
        'an extra character!
        UserName = Left$(lpBuffer, nSize - 1)
    Else
        UserName = ""
    End If
End Property
```

Enumerating Network Resources

Sometimes your applications will need to know the status of a networked resource. For example, a document management application may need to ensure that a connection to the document archive share is available before attempting to start, thus preventing other network-related errors as the user utilizes the application.

To obtain connection information you can enumerate (list) the network connections using the WNet enumeration APIs.

To enumerate networked resources you must first obtain a handle to an enumeration object by calling the WNetOpenEnum API. If this call is successful you can make repeated calls to WNetEnumResource until all resources have been enumerated. Finally, call the WNetCloseEnum API to free the enumeration handle when you are done. The enumeration APIs are described below.

WNetOpenEnum

Description

The WNetOpenEnum API is used to start an enumeration of network resources for the local computer.

C Prototype

```
DWORD WNetOpenEnum(DWORD dwScope,
    DWORD dwType,
    DWORD dwUsage,
    LPNETRESOURCE lpNetResource,
    LPHANDLE lphEnum);
```

VB Declaration

```
Private Declare Function WNetOpenEnum Lib "mpr.dll" _
    Alias "WNetOpenEnumA" _
    (ByVal dwScope As Long, _
    ByVal dwType As Long, _
    ByVal dwUsage As Long, _
    lpNetResource As NETRESOURCE, _
    lphEnum As Long) As Long
```

Parameters

Parameter	Description
dwScope	This specifies the scope of the objects to be enumerated. Refer to the Notes below.
dwType	This parameter specifies which types of resources are to be enumerated. Refer to the Notes below.
dwUsage	This specifies the usage of the objects to be enumerated. Refer to the Notes below.
lpNetResource	Pointer to a NETRESOURCE structure. Refer to the Notes below for more details on this structure.
lphEnum	Returns a handle to the enumeration object, which is used to enumerate the network resources.
Returns	On success, the API returns NO_ERROR. Otherwise, it returns an error code.

Notes

The dwScope parameter can be any of the following:

RESOURCE_CONNECTED	Lists currently connected resources, ignoring the dwUsage parameter.
RESOURCE_CONTEXT	Provides a Network Neighborhood view.
RESOURCE_GLOBALNET	Lists all resources on the network.
RESOURCE_REMEMBERED	Lists all persistent connections, ignoring the dwUsage parameter.

The dwType parameter is used to indicate which resource type to enumerate. It can be set to one of the following:

RESOURCETYPE_DISK	Lists networked drive resources.
RESOURCETYPE_PRINT	Lists networked printer resources.
RESOURCETYPE_ANY	Lists all networked resource types.

The dwUsage parameter is used to distinguish between resources you can directly connect to, or container objects such as servers or the Network Neighborhood. You can specify which type to enumerate using the following constants:

RESOURCEUSAGE_CONNECTABLE	A connectable resource.
RESOURCEUSAGE_CONTAINER	A container resource.

The lpNetResource parameter is a pointer to a NETRESOURCE structure. Here is the definition of that structure:

```
Private Type NETRESOURCE
    dwScope As Long
    dwType As Long
    dwDisplayType As Long
    dwUsage As Long
    lpLocalName As String
    lpRemoteName As String
    lpComment As String
    lpProvider As String
End Type
```

Each member is described below:

Member	Description
dwScope	Returns the scope of the connection, such as RESOURCE_CONNECTED.
dwType	Returns the type of device you wish to connect to. This can be set to RESOURCETYPE_DISK or RESOURCE-TYPE_PRINT.
dwDisplayType	Specifies how the resource should be displayed. This can be RESOURCEDISPLAYTYPE_DOMAIN, RESOURCEDIS-PLAYTYPE_GENERIC, RESOURCEDISPLAYTYPE_SERVER, or RESOURCEDISPLAYTYPE_SHARE.
dwUsage	Returns the usage characteristics of the enumerated object.
lpLocalName	Returns the local name of the network device, such as P: or LPT2:.
lpRemoteName	The Universal Naming Convention (UNC) path to the resource you want to connect to. This parameter must be in the format \\server\resource.
lpComment	This member is unused with this API.
lpProvider	The provider used to make the connection. It is recommended that you leave this parameter set to NULL.

Example

```
Dim rc As Long
Dim n As NETRESOURCE
Dim hEnum As Long

'Open the enum object
rc = WNetOpenEnum(RESOURCE_CONNECTED, _
        RESOURCETYPE_DISK, _
        RESOURCEUSAGE_CONNECTABLE, _
        n, _
        hEnum)
.
.
.
```

WNetEnumResource

Description

The WNetEnumResource API lists one or more resources specified in the call to the WNetOpenEnum API. This API does not perform like normal Windows enumeration APIs, but instead is used to populate an array of NETRESOURCE structures.

C Prototype

```
DWORD WNetEnumResource(HANDLE hEnum,
    LPDWORD lpcCount,
    LPVOID lpBuffer,
    LPDWORD lpBufferSize);
```

VB Declaration

```
Private Declare Function WNetEnumResource Lib "mpr.dll" _
    Alias "WNetEnumResourceA" _
    (ByVal hEnum As Long, _
    lpcCount As Long, _
    lpBuffer As Any, _
    lpBufferSize As Long) As Long
```

Parameters

Parameter	Description
Henum	Handle to the enumeration object returned from the call to the WNetOpenEnum API.
LpcCount	The number of items to return.
LpBuffer	A pointer to an array of NETRESOURCE structures, which will be used to return information about the enumerated objects.
lpBufferSize	The size of the buffer specified in the lpBuffer parameter.
Returns	On success, the API returns NO_ERROR. Otherwise, it returns an error code.

Notes

The heart of this API is the NETRESOURCE structure, which is used to return resource information from the API. Refer to the WNetOpenEnum function described above for more details on this structure.

WNetCloseEnum

Description

The WNetCloseEnum API is used to close an open enumeration operation.

C Prototype

```
DWORD WNetCloseEnum(HANDLE hEnum);
```

VB Declaration

```
Private Declare Function WNetCloseEnum Lib "mpr.dll" _
    (ByVal hEnum As Long) As Long
```

Parameters

Parameter	Description
hEnum	The handle of the enumeration object created in the call to WNetOpenEnum.
Returns	On success, the API returns NO_ERROR. Otherwise, it returns an error code.

Example

```
WNetCloseEnum hEnum
```

Connecting to Network Resources

Once you know which resources are available to your application you can connect to additional resources or disconnect existing ones. There are myriad reasons to perform these two tasks, which are mainly dependent on the requirements of your application. How many setup applications have you created that required you to connect to a server to install files? This is not an easy task using the Package and Deployment Wizard! But if you use the following APIs you can write Help applets that can help install your applications automatically. There are many reasons why you may need to connect to a server.

Although many network applications are based on the three-tier architecture, many servers still perform basic file and printer sharing services, and these services are likely to remain for many years to come. Let's take a look at the APIs you can use to utilize resources on file and print servers.

WNetAddConnection

Description

The WNetAddConnection API is used to connect a local device to a remote device on another computer, such as a Windows NT server or Windows workstation. This is the most basic network connection API, the most widely used on Windows 9x, and is provided for backward compatibility on older Win 3.x workstations.

C Prototype

```
DWORD WNetAddConnection(LPTSTR lpRemoteName,
    LPTSTR lpPassword,
    LPTSTR lpLocalName);
```

VB Declaration

```
Private Declare Function WNetAddConnection Lib "mpr.dll" _
    Alias "WNetAddConnectionA" _
    (ByVal lpszNetPath As String, _
    ByVal lpszPassword As String, _
    ByVal lpszLocalName As String) As Long
```

Parameters

Parameter	Description
lpszNetPath	The Universal Naming Convention (UNC) path to the resource you want to connect to. This parameter must be in the format \\server\resource.

lpszPassword	A password used to connect to the resource, if required.
lpszLocalName	The name of the local drive or printer device that will map to the remote device. Local names should be in a format such as P: or LPT2:.
Returns	On success, the API returns NO_ERROR. Otherwise, it returns an error code.

Notes

This API is primarily used for backward compatibility with Windows 3.x workstations. If you are only developing for Win32 platforms, use WNetAddConnection2.

WNetAddConnection2

Description

The WNetAddConnection2 API is used to connect a local device to a remote device on another computer, such as a Windows NT server or Windows workstation. This API allows you to specify additional connection options to provide advanced connections on Windows NT machines. This API now supercedes WNetAddConnection.

C Prototype

```
DWORD WNetAddConnection2(LPNETRESOURCE lpNetResource,
    LPCTSTR lpPassword,
    LPCTSTR lpUsername,
    DWORD dwFlags);
```

VB Declaration

```
Private Declare Function WNetAddConnection2 Lib "mpr.dll" _
    Alias "WNetAddConnection2A" _
    (lpNetResource As NETRESOURCE, _
    ByVal lpPassword As String, _
    ByVal lpUserName As String, _
    ByVal dwFlags As Long) As Long
```

Parameters

Parameter	Description
lpNetResource	A pointer to a NETRESOURCE structure containing information about the resource you want to connect to.
lpPassword	A password used to connect to the resource, if required.
lpUserName	The name of the user account you wish to use to complete the connection.
DwFlags	A bit flag used to determine if the system should remember this connection when the system restarts. Set this value to 1 if you want to make the connection persistent. Otherwise set it to 0.
Returns	On success, the API returns NO_ERROR. Otherwise, it returns an error code.

Notes

The heart of this API is the NETRESOURCE structure, which is used to pass additional connection information to the API. This structure was described above under the WNetOpenEnum function.

Example

Listing 14.3 shows how to use a generic Connect function that makes the call to WNetAddConnection2.

LISTING 14.3   Connecting to a Remote Resource

```
Public Function Connect(Optional LocalResource As String, _
Optional RemoteResource As String, _
        Optional UserID As String, _
        Optional Password As String) As Long

    Dim rc As Long
    Dim n As NETRESOURCE

    If LocalResource = "" Or IsMissing(RemoteResource) Then
```

```
            .
            .
            .
        'Populate the structure
        With n
            .lpLocalName = LocalResource
            .lpRemoteName = RemoteResource
            If InStr(UCase$(LocalResource), "LPT") Then
                .dwType = RESOURCETYPE_PRINT
            Else
                .dwType = RESOURCETYPE_DISK
            End If
        End With

        'Connect to the remote resource
        rc = WNetAddConnection2(n, Password, UserID, 1)
    End If

    'Return result code
    Connect = rc
End Function
```

WNetCancelConnection

Description

The WNetCancelConnection API is used to disconnect a network resource. This API is provided for backward compatibility with Windows 3.x machines.

C Prototype

```
DWORD WNetCancelConnection(LPTSTR lpName,
    BOOL fForce);
```

VB Declaration

```
Private Declare Function WNetCancelConnection _
    Lib "mpr.dll" _
    Alias "WNetCancelConnectionA" _
    (ByVal lpszName As String, _
    ByVal bForce As Long) As Long
```

Parameters

Parameter	Description
lpszName	The local name of a connected resource, such as P: or LPT2:.
bForce	Set to True to force the device to be disconnected. If you don't want the device to disconnect, for example when you are browsing a networked drive, set this to False.
Returns	Returns True on success, False if the API call fails.

Notes

This API is primarily used for backward compatibility with Windows 3.x workstations. If you are only developing for Win32 platforms, use WNetcancel-Connection2.

WNetCancelConnection2

Description

The WNetCancelConnection2 API is the Win32 equivalent of the WNetCancel-Connection API. It is used to disconnect a local resource from a shared resource on a remote computer.

C Prototype

```
DWORD WNetCancelConnection2(LPTSTR lpName,
    DWORD dwFlags,
    BOOL fForce);
```

VB Declaration

```
Private Declare Function WNetCancelConnection2 _
    Lib "mpr.dll" _
    Alias "WNetCancelConnection2A" _
    (ByVal lpName As String, _
    ByVal dwFlags As Long, _
    ByVal fForce As Long) As Long
```

Parameters

Parameter	Description
lpName	The local name of a connected resource, such as P: or LPT2:.
DwFlags	Set this to 0 if you want this connection to remain persistent, but is not needed if for the current session. Otherwise, set it to CONNECT_UPDATE_PROFILE or 1.
FForce	Set to True to force the device to be disconnected. If you don't want the device to disconnect, for example when you are browsing a networked drive, set this to False.
Returns	If the device is successfully disconnected, this API returns NO_ERROR or 0. Otherwise, it returns an error code.

Example

Listing 14.4 shows a generic Disconnect function that in turn calls the WNet-CancelConnection2 function for removing a network resource from your machine.

LISTING 14.4   **Removing a Network Resource**

```
Public Function Disconnect( _
        Optional LocalResource As String) As Long

    Dim rc As Long

    'Disconnect the resource
    If LocalResource = "" Then

        .
        .
        .

    Else
        'Force a permanent disconnection
        rc = WNetCancelConnection2(LocalResource, _
            CONNECT_UPDATE_PROFILE, _
            True)
```

```
        End If

        'Return result code
        Disconnect = rc
    End Function
```

WNetConnectionDialog

Description

The WNetConnectionDialog API displays a dialog used to connect to a remote resource. For more information, refer to Chapter 6, *Dialog APIs*.

C Prototype

```
DWORD WNetConnectionDialog(HWND hwnd,
    DWORD dwType);
```

VB Declaration

```
Private Declare Function WNetConnectionDialog _
    Lib "mpr.dll" _
    (ByVal hwnd As Long, _
    ByVal dwType As Long) As Long
```

Parameters

Parameter	Description
hwnd	The handle of the parent form that called this API.
dwType	This value must be RESOURCETYPE_DISK or RESOURCETYPE_PRINT.
Returns	If the device is successfully disconnected, this API returns NO_ERROR or 0. Otherwise, it returns an error code.

Example

Listing 14.5 provides the code necessary to make a generic Connect call. This code causes the generic Map Network Drive dialog box to appear.

LISTING 14.5   **Use the Network Dialog Box to make a Connection**

```
Public Function Connect(Optional LocalResource As String, _
Optional RemoteResource As String, _
        Optional UserID As String, _
        Optional Password As String) As Long

    Dim rc As Long
    Dim n As NETRESOURCE

    If IsMissing(LocalResource) Or _
            IsMissing(RemoteResource) Then

        'Connect using the dialog
        If InStr(UCase$(LocalResource), "LPT") Then
            rc = WNetConnectionDialog(0, _
                    RESOURCETYPE_PRINT)
        Else
            rc = WNetConnectionDialog(0, _
                    RESOURCETYPE_DISK)
        End If
        .
        .
        .
    End If

    'Return result code
    Connect = rc
End Function
```

WNetDisconnectDialog

Description

The WNetDisconnectDialog API displays a dialog containing a list of devices that are currently connected to remote resources. For more information, refer to Chapter 6, *Dialog APIs*.

C Prototype

```
DWORD WNetDisconnectDialog(HWND hwnd,
    DWORD dwType);
```

VB Declaration

```
Private Declare Function WNetDisconnectDialog _
    Lib "mpr.dll" _
    (ByVal hwnd As Long, _
    ByVal dwType As Long) As Long
```

Parameters

Parameter	Description
hwnd	The handle of the parent form that called this API.
dwType	This value must be RESOURCETYPE_DISK or RESOURCETYPE_PRINT.
Returns	If the device is successfully disconnected, this API returns NO_ERROR or 0. Otherwise, it returns an error code.

Example

Listing 14.6 displays the standard Disconnect Network Drive dialog box. This allows you to then remove a network drive from your system.

LISTING 14.6   **Disconnecting with the Network Dialog Box**

```
Public Function Disconnect( _
        Optional LocalResource As String) As Long

    Dim rc As Long

    'Disconnect the resource
    If LocalResource = "" Then
        'Disconnect through the dialog
        rc = WNetDisconnectDialog(0, RESOURCETYPE_DISK)
        .
        .
        .
```

```
        End If

        'Return result code
        Disconnect = rc
    End Function
```

WNetGetConnection

Description

The WNetGetConnection API is used to return the Universal Naming Convention (UNC) path to a connected network resource.

C Prototype

```
DWORD WNetGetConnection(LPCTSTR lpLocalName,
    LPTSTR lpRemoteName,
    LPDWORD lpnLength);
```

VB Declaration

```
Private Declare Function WNetGetConnection Lib "mpr.dll" _
    Alias "WNetGetConnectionA" _
    (ByVal lpszLocalName As String, _
    ByVal lpszRemoteName As String, _
    cbRemoteName As Long) As Long
```

Parameters

Parameter	Description
lpszLocalName	The name of the local resource to query.
lpszRemoteName	A buffer used to return the UNC path to the network resource.
cbRemoteName	The length of the buffer specified in lpszRemoteName.
Returns	On success, this API returns NO_ERROR, and the length of the return data is specified in cbRemoteName. Otherwise, it returns an error code.

Example

Listing 14.7 demonstrates how to get the UNC for a given device.

LISTING 14.7 **Get Device UNC**

```
Public Function UNC(LocalName As String) As String
    Dim rc As Long
    Dim lpBuff As String
    Dim cbBuff As Long

    'Initailize the buffer
    cbBuff = 255
    lpBuff = String$(cbBuff, Chr$(0))

    'Call the API
    If WNetGetConnection(LocalName, _
            lpBuff, cbBuff) = 0 Then

        'Return the data in the buffer
        UNC = Left$(lpBuff, cbBuff)
    Else
        UNC = ""
    End If
End Function
```

CHAPTER
FIFTEEN

Internet Programming

- ■ Introduction to Windows Sockets

- ■ Winsock APIs

- ■ Accessing TCP/IP Services

Windows Sockets 2, commonly referred to as Winsock, is the foundation of Internet communications for all Windows platforms. Winsock was derived from the original Berkeley Sockets developed for the UNIX platform.

Introduction to Windows Sockets

Before you develop any Winsock applications you must be familiar with how Transmission Control Protocol/Internet Protocol (TCP/IP) works. You will also need to know the various protocols, as well as ports, used by TCP/IP services.

Servers and Ports

As you know, there are hundreds of thousands of servers on the Internet. Many of these servers also host multiple services. For example, some Internet Service Providers (ISPs) provide both e-mail and Web hosting on the same server. For a single computer to host multiple services, each service must use a separate port.

Table 15.1 lists some of the common services and ports used by servers with multiple services.

TABLE 15.1: Common IP Ports

Port	Service
25	Simple Mail Transfer Protocol (SMTP) - Outbound E-mail
17	Quote of the Day
37	Time Service
43	Whois
70	Gopher
80	Hypertext Transfer Protocol (HTTP) - Used for the World Wide Web
110	Post Office Protocol 3 (POP3) - Inbound E-mail
20 & 21	File Transfer Protocol (FTP)
6667	Internet Relay Chat (IRC)

For a more comprehensive list you might want to search the Web for lists of services and their ports. One URL that shows the RFC for the ports is `http://info .internet.isi.edu/in-notes/rfc/files/rfc1700.txt`. There are other sites as well. There are many good lists, but each seems to have its benefits and drawbacks. I'll leave you to decide which list is best for you.

Protocols

There are three types of Internet protocols used in Windows. These include the Transmission Control Protocol (TCP), the User Datagram Protocol (UDP), and the Internet Message Control Protocol (IMCP).

Transmission Control Protocol

TCP is a stateful protocol. It is used when you want to establish a persistent connection between a client and server.

As you can see in Figure 15.1, using TCP is much like using a telephone. In a telephone call you must first dial the telephone number. Likewise in Winsock you must first attempt to establish a connection with the remote host. This is called a session. When someone answers the phone, the connection is established and you can talk back and forth to your heart's content. In Winsock, once the host accepts your connection, you have a session. Now you can transmit and receive data all you want. When you are done with the telephone, both parties hang up. In Winsock, both computers disconnect when the session is complete.

FIGURE 15.1:

Using TCP

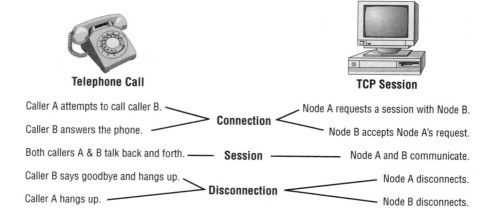

Telephone Call

Caller A attempts to call caller B.
Caller B answers the phone.

Connection

Node A requests a session with Node B.
Node B accepts Node A's request.

Both callers A & B talk back and forth. — **Session** — Node A and B communicate.

Caller B says goodbye and hangs up.
Caller A hangs up.

Disconnection

TCP Session

Node A disconnects.
Node B disconnects.

User Datagram Protocol

UDP is a connectionless protocol. It is used primarily for rapid transmissions and broadcasts where a persistent connection would be cumbersome, difficult, or inefficient to use.

In contrast to the telephone metaphor used previously, communicating with UDP is much like talking on a CB radio, as shown in Figure 15.2. You are not required to establish a session with the remote host. You simply send it a request, and it may or may not respond depending on the nature of the request. No permanent connection is made.

FIGURE 15.2:

Using UDP

CB Broadcast

CB Operator A broadcasts on channel 25.

CB Operator B replies on channel 25.

UDP Session

Computer A transmits on port 25.

Computer B replies on port 25.

Internet Control Message Protocol

ICMP is a messaging protocol rarely used in Windows. In fact, it is generally used to ping another computer. It isn't used much beyond that.

Winsock APIs

There are many Winsock APIs available to you. Fortunately, you only need a few to provide most of the functionality required in a client or server application.

Basic Winsock client functions include connecting to remote host computers, sending and receiving data, and disconnecting. Examples of client applications include Web browsers, FTP, and Internet Relay Chat (IRC) clients.

Server applications generally involve listening for connection requests, accepting them, reading requests and replying to them, and finally disconnecting.

The specifics of what each component does and how it does it lie in the logic and design of your application. The Winsock APIs listed in this chapter provide the connectivity framework that allows you to write your own Internet-enabled applications.

accept

Description

The accept API is used to accept an incoming connection request from a remote client.

C Prototype

```
SOCKET accept (SOCKET s,
    struct sockaddr FAR* addr,
    int FAR* addrlen);
```

VB Declaration

```
Declare Function SocketAccept Lib "wsock32.dll" _
    Alias "accept" _
    (ByVal s As Long, _
    addr As sockaddr, _
    addrlen As Long) As Long
```

Parameters

Parameter	Description
s	Descriptor for the socket that is waiting for connections.
addr	Pointer to an optional sockaddr structure that is used to return address information about the socket being accepted.
addrlen	The length of the sockaddr buffer.
Returns	On success, the API returns the descriptor for the socket that actually connected to the client. Otherwise it returns INVALID_SOCKET.

Notes

As you will see throughout this chapter, many Winsock applications use the sockaddr structure as a parameter to their APIs. The sockaddr structure is described below:

```
Private Type sockaddr
    sin_family As Integer
    sin_port As Integer
    sin_addr As Long
    sin_zero As String * 8
End Type
```

Each member is described below:

Member	Description
sin_family	The protocol family you will use. For your Winsock applications this will be set to AF_INET.
sin_port	Specifies the IP port you wish to use. This must be in network order so you must use the hton() API to convert it.
sin_addr	The IP address to use, again in network order.
sin_zero	An 8-byte, zero-filled string. Unused with the IP protocols.

The following example configures a sockaddr structure to use the AF_INET protocol on port 80:

```
With sck
    .sin_family = AF_INET
    .sin_port = htons(80)
    .sin_addr = 0
    .sin_zero = String$(8, Chr$(0))
End With
```

In most host applications a single socket is set up to listen for a connection request. When the request is received, a new socket is created and it actually accepts the socket making the request. This architecture allows your application to continue listening for, as well as accepting, multiple connections.

Example

```
Dim sck As sockaddr

'Return the port that the call was accepted on
Accept = SocketAccept(mSocket, sck, Len(sck))
```

bind

Description

The bind API is used to associate an unconnected socket with a local address.

C Prototype

```
int bind (SOCKET s,
    const struct sockaddr FAR* name,
    int namelen);
```

VB Declaration

```
Function bind Lib "wsock32.dll" _
    (ByVal s As Long, _
    addr As sockaddr, _
    ByVal namelen As Long) As Long
```

Parameters

Parameter	Description
s	A descriptor for a socket that has not been previously bound.
addr	A sockaddr structure. Refer to the Notes under the accept API.
namelen	The length of the sockaddr structure passed in the addr parameter.
Returns	Returns 0 on success, SOCKET_ERROR on failure.

Example

The following example obtains a descriptor for a socket using the socket API, and then it attempts to bind it:

```
Public Function Listen(Port As Long) As Boolean
    Dim sck As sockaddr
    Dim rc As Long

    'Get a new socket
    mSocket = Socket(AF_INET, SOCK_STREAM, 0)

    If mSocket > 0 Then
        'Prepare the socket
        With sck
            .sin_family = AF_INET
            .sin_port = htons(Port)
            .sin_addr = 0
            .sin_zero = String$(8, Chr$(0))
        End With

        'Bind it to the adapter
        rc = bind(mSocket, sck, Len(sck))
        .
        .
        .
End Function
```

closesocket

Description

The closesocket API is used to close a socket when you are done using it.

C Prototype

```
int closesocket (SOCKET s);
```

VB Declaration

```
Declare Function closesocket Lib "wsock32.dll" _
    (ByVal s As Long) As Long
```

Parameters

Parameter	Description
s	The descriptor of the socket to be closed.
Returns	This API will return 0 if the socket is successfully closed. Otherwise, it will return SOCKET_ERROR.

Notes

This API is extremely simple, but you must always remember to match each closesocket API with its corresponding socket API.

Example

```
Public Sub Disconnect()
    'Close the socket
    closesocket mSocket

    'Raise the Disconnect event
    RaiseEvent Disconnect

    mSocket = 0
End Sub
```

connect

Description

Use the connect API to request a connection with another computer.

C Prototype

```
int connect (SOCKET s,
    const struct sockaddr FAR* name,
    int namelen );
```

VB Declaration

```
Private Declare Function connect Lib "wsock32.dll" _
    (ByVal s As Long, _
    addr As sockaddr, _
    ByVal namelen As Long) As Long
```

Parameters

Parameter	Description
s	A descriptor for an unused socket.
addr	A sockaddr structure containing the IP address and port in network order.
namelen	The length of the sockaddr structure passed in the addr parameter.
Returns	Returns 0 on success, SOCKET_ERROR on failure.

Example

The following code shows how to create a socket, populate the sockaddr structure, and pass it to the connect API. Note that the SocketConnect function is actually an alias for the connect API because the member function's name is Connect.

```
        .
        .
        .
'Create the socket
mSocket = socket(AF_INET, SOCK_STREAM, 0)
If mSocket <> SOCKET_ERROR Then
    'Populate the socket
    With sck
        .sin_family = AF_INET
        .sin_addr = Resolve(Host)
        If Service <> "" Then
            .sin_port = getservbyname(ByVal Service, _
                    ByVal "TCP")
        Else
            .sin_port = htons(Port)
        End If
        .sin_zero = String$(8, 0)
    End With

    'Attempt to connect
    rc = SocketConnect(mSocket, sck, Len(sck))
        .
        .
        .
```

gethostbyname

Description

The gethostbyname API is used to perform a DNS-type lookup of a URL and return its IP address in network order.

C Prototype

```
struct hostent FAR * gethostbyname
    (const char FAR * name );
```

VB Declaration

```
Private Declare Function gethostbyname Lib "wsock32.dll" _
    (ByVal host_name As String) As Long
```

Parameters

Parameter	Description
host_name	A null-terminated string containing the name of the host to resolve.
Returns	On success, this API returns the pointer to a HOSTENT structure that contains the IP address of the host. Otherwise, it returns SOCKET_ERROR. Refer to the Notes below for more information on the HOSTENT structure.

Notes

The HOSTENT structure is used to return information about a particular host entry.

```
Private Type HOSTENT
    h_name As Long
    h_aliases As Long
    h_addrtype As Integer
    h_length As Integer
    h_addr_list As Long
End Type
```

Each member is described below:

Member	Description
h_name	Returns a pointer to the name of the host.
h_aliases	Returns a pointer to an array of null-terminated names that can be used to contact the host.
h_addrtype	The type of address being returned.
h_length	The length of each address returned, in bytes.
h_addr_list	Returns a list of network-order IP addresses for the host. Each address is separated by a null-terminating byte.

Example

The following code is taken from the Socket control in the WinsockAPI project. It is used to return the IP address of the host name passed in the Host parameter. This function can take both dotted IP addresses, as well as URL addresses. URLs are resolved using the gethostbyname API.

```
Private Function Resolve(Host As String) As Long
    Dim he As Long
    Dim heDestHost As HOSTENT
    Dim addrList As Long
    Dim rc As Long

        .
        .
        .

    'If we couldn't resolve by IP,
    'then try by host name
    If rc = SOCKET_ERROR Then
        he = gethostbyname(ByVal Host)
        If he <> 0 Then
            'Copy the memory of he to the
            'HOSTENT structure heDestHost
            CopyMemory heDestHost, _
                    ByVal he, _
                    Len(heDestHost)
```

```
                'Get the address of the address array
                CopyMemory addrList, _
                        ByVal heDestHost.h_addr_list, _
                        4

                'Copy the pointer of the first
                'address in the array to rc
                CopyMemory rc, _
                        ByVal addrList, _
                        heDestHost.h_length
            Else
                rc = INADDR_NONE
            End If
        End If

        'Return the address
        Resolve = rc
    End Function
```

This example deserves a bit of scrutiny. Calling gethostbyname is the easy part. The real work lies in extracting the address from the array returned by the API. This is done through a series of calls to the CopyMemory API.

The first call to the CopyMemory API copies the data from the structure pointed to by he, to the structure created called heDestHost. This allows you to reference each member of the structure.

The second call to CopyMemory gives you the address of the first host address returned in the .h_address_list array. This address is copied to the addrList variable.

Once you have this address you can extract the first address by calling Copy-Memory and copying the first four bytes of addrList to the rc variable. Fortunately, the address is returned in network order, so it is ready for use with other APIs.

gethostname

Description

The gethostname API returns the name of the local host computer.

C Prototype

```
int gethostname (char FAR * name,
    int namelen);
```

VB Declaration

```
Private Declare Function gethostname Lib "wsock32.dll" _
    (ByVal host_name As String, _
    ByVal namelen As Long) As Long
```

Parameters

Parameter	Description
host_name	A buffer used to return the name of the local host.
namelen	The length of the buffer specified in host_name.
Returns	If successful, this API returns the length of the host name, in bytes. In addition, the actual name is passed back via the buffer specified in the host_name parameter.

Example

```
Public Function LocalHost() As String
    Dim buf As String
    Dim rc As Long

    'Allocate a buffer
    buf = Space$(255)

    'Call the API
    rc = gethostname(buf, Len(buf))
    rc = InStr(buf, vbNullChar)

    'Return the host name
    If rc > 0 Then
        LocalHost = Left$(buf, rc - 1)
    Else
        LocalHost = ""
    End If
End Function
```

getservbyname

Description

The getservbyname API returns the IP port used to access a particular TCP/IP service. This API is particularly useful if you know the name of the service you wish to access, but not its port.

C Prototype

```
struct servent FAR * getservbyname
    (const char FAR * name,
    const char FAR * proto);
```

VB Declaration

```
Private Declare Function getservbyname Lib "wsock32.dll" _
    (ByVal serv_name As String, _
    ByVal proto As String) As Long
```

Parameters

Parameter	Description
serv_name	A null-terminated string containing the name of the services whose port you want to retrieve.
proto	A null-terminated string containing either TCP or UDP, depending on which protocol you are using.
Returns	If successful, this API returns the port of the service in network order. Otherwise, it returns SOCKET_ERROR.

Example

The following example uses the getservbyname API to get the port or the File Transfer Protocol (FTP), and return it in network order. This result is passed to the .sin_port member of a SOCKADDR structure.

```
Dim sck As SOCKADDR

With sck
    .sin_family = AF_INET
    .sin_addr = Resolve(Host)
```

```
        .sin_port = getservbyname(ByVal "FTP", ByVal "TCP")
        .sin_zero = String$(8, 0)
End With
```

htonl

Description

The htonl API is used to convert a 32-bit unsigned integer in host-byte order (big-endian) to a 32-bit unsigned value in network-byte order (little-endian), which is suitable for Winsock.

C Prototype

```
u_long htonl (u_long hostlong);
```

VB Declaration

```
Private Declare Function htonl Lib "wsock32.dll" _
    (ByVal hostlong As Long) As Long
```

Parameters

Parameter	Description
hostlong	A Long integer in host-byte order.
Returns	Returns a Long integer in network-byte order.

Notes

On most UNIX-based networks, numbers are passed in host-byte order, which is big-endian. That is, the most significant byte is the first byte and the least significant byte is the last byte. On Intel platforms, byte order is little-endian, meaning the least significant byte comes first and the most significant byte comes last.

It is important to understand these differences, since results will be returned in host-byte order, which is big-endian.

htons

Description

The htons API is used to convert an unsigned *short* integer in host-byte order (big-endian) to network-byte order (little-endian), which is suitable for Winsock.

C Prototype

```
u_short htons (u_short hostshort);
```

VB Declaration

```
Private Declare Function htons Lib "wsock32.dll" _
    (ByVal hostshort As Long) As Integer
```

Parameters

Parameter	Description
hostshort	A Long integer in host-byte order.
Returns	An integer in network-byte order.

Notes

Refer to the Notes under the htonl API.

Example

The following example uses htons to set the .sin_port member of the SOCKADDR structure to host-byte order:

```
With sck
    .
    .
    .
    .sin_port = htons(Port)
    .
    .
    .
End With
```

IcmpCloseHandle

Description

The `IcmpCloseHandle` API closes an ICMP handle that was opened using `IcmpCreateFile`.

C Prototype

```
BOOL WINAPI IcmpCloseHandle (HANDLE IcmpHandle);
```

VB Declaration

```
Private Declare Function IcmpCloseHandle Lib "ICMP.DLL" _
    (ByVal hIcmpHandle As Long) As Integer
```

Parameters

Parameter	Description
hIcmpHandle	Handle to the ICMP file to be closed.
Returns	Returns a Boolean value indicating if the API call was successful or not.

Example

```
'Start ICMP
hICMP = IcmpCreateFile()
  .
  .
  .
'Close ICMP
IcmpCloseHandle hICMP
```

IcmpCreateFile

Description

The `IcmpCreateFile` API creates a handle that can be used in other ICMP APIs.

C Prototype

```
HANDLE WINAPI IcmpCreateFile (VOID);
```

VB Declaration

```
Private Declare Function IcmpCreateFile Lib "ICMP.DLL" _
    () As Long
```

Parameters

Parameter	Description
None	
Returns	On success, a handle to the ICMP file is returned. Otherwise, INVALID_HANDLE_VALUE is returned.

Example

```
'Start ICMP
hICMP = IcmpCreateFile()
```

IcmpSendEcho

Description

The IcmpSendEcho API sends a standard echo request to a destination IP address. This is the API used when a computer pings another device.

C Prototype

```
DWORD WINAPI IcmpSendEcho (HANDLE IcmpHandle,
    IPAddr DestinationAddress,
    LPVOID RequestData,
    WORD RequestSize,
    PIP_OPTION_INFORMATION RequestOptions,
    LPVOID ReplyBuffer,
    DWORD ReplySize,
    DWORD Timeout);
```

VB Declaration

```
Private Declare Function IcmpSendEcho Lib "ICMP.DLL" _
    (ByVal IcmpHandle As Long, _
    ByVal DestinationAddress As Long, _
    RequestData As String, _
    ByVal RequestSize As Integer, _
```

```
RequestOptions As ICMPReqOpt, _
ReplyBuffer As Byte, _
ByVal ReplySize As Long, _
ByVal TimeOut As Long) As Long
```

Parameters

Parameter	Description
IcmpHandle	Handle to the ICMP file opened when using IcmpCreateFile.
DestinationAddress	The IP address of the computer you want to ping, in network-byte order.
RequestData	A buffer containing data to be sent in the request.
RequestSize	The length of the buffer specified in the RequestData parameter.
RequestOptions	Pointer to an ICMPReqOpt structure containing options specific to the API request.
ReplyBuffer	A pointer to a buffer that will be used to return the reply from the other computer.
ReplySize	The length of the buffer specified in ReplyBuffer.
Timeout	The length of time in milliseconds to wait for a reply.
Returns	If the call is successful, the API returns the number of replies received from the computer being pinged. The API returns 0 if it fails.

Notes

The ICMPReqOpt structure is used to configure the IcmpSendEcho API.

```
Private Type ICMPReqOpt
    TTL As Byte
    tos As Byte
    flags As Byte
    optsize As Byte
```

```
        options As String
End Type
```

Each member is described below:

Member	Description
TTL	The total time to live.
tos	The type of service requested. This should be set to ICMP_ECHO_REQUEST.
flags	Set to ICMP_FLAG_NO_FRAGMENT.
optsize	The length of this structure.
options	Additional options. Pass an empty string to this member.

Example

The following code shows how you can use ICMP to ping another computer. It creates a handle to ICMP using IcmpCreateFile(). Once the handle is created, an ICMPReqOpt structure is populated and a call to IcmpSendEcho() is made. If the remote computer responds, a non-zero value is returned and the ping is successful. When everything is complete, the ICMP handle is closed by calling Icmp-CloseHandle().

```
Public Function Ping(Address As String, _
        Timeout As Long) As Boolean

    Dim IRO As ICMPReqOpt
    Dim Response(1 To 4096) As Byte
    Dim lAddress As Long
    Dim rc As Long

    'Start ICMP
    hICMP = IcmpCreateFile()

    If hICMP <> INVALID_HANDLE_VALUE Then
        'Convert IP Address
        lAddress = Resolve(Address)

        'Build request packet
```

```
With IRO
    .TTL = 64
    .tos = ICMP_ECHO_REQUEST
    .options = ""
    .optsize = Len(IRO.options)
    .flags = ICMP_FLAG_NO_FRAGMENT
End With

'Call the Ping API
rc = IcmpSendEcho(hICMP, _
        lAddress, _
        Space$(32), _
        32, _
        IRO, _
        Response(1), _
        UBound(Response), _
        Timeout)

If rc = 0 Then
    'The ping failed
    Ping = False
Else
    'We could ping the address
    Ping = True
End If

        'Close ICMP
        IcmpCloseHandle hICMP
    Else
        'Unable to initialize ICMP
        Ping = False
    End If
End Function
```

inet_addr

Description

The inet_addr API converts an IP address in dotted decimal format (i.e.,
128.100.79.8) to a Long integer in network-byte order.

C Prototype

```
unsigned long inet_addr (const char FAR * cp);
```

VB Declaration

```
Private Declare Function inet_addr Lib "wsock32.dll" _
    (ByVal cp As String) As Long
```

Parameters

Parameter	Description
cp	A null-terminated string containing the IP address of the host you wish to resolve.
Returns	If successful, this API returns the IP address in network-byte order. Otherwise, it returns SOCKET_ERROR.

Example

```
Private Function Resolve(Host As String) As Long
    Dim he As Long
    Dim heDestHost As HOSTENT
    Dim addrList As Long
    Dim rc As Long

    'Attempt to resolve by IP first
    rc = inet_addr(ByVal Host)
    .
    .
    .
    'Return the address
    Resolve = rc
End Function
```

listen

Description

The listen API causes a socket to listen for connection requests from one or more remote computers.

C Prototype

```
int listen (SOCKET s, int backlog);
```

VB Declaration

```
Private Declare Function SocketListen Lib "wsock32.dll" _
    Alias "listen" _
    (ByVal s As Long, _
    ByVal backlog As Long) As Long
```

Parameters

Parameter	Description
s	Handle to a socket that will listen for connection requests.
backlog	The maximum number of connection requests that can be pending on this socket.
Returns	Returns 0 on success, or SOCKET_ERROR when an error occurs.

Notes

In many host applications a single socket is configured to listen for remote connection requests. When a connection request is received, a new socket is created, which actually accepts the connection request. This allows the original socket to continue processing connection requests.

Example

The following example allows a socket to listen and only allows five connections to backlog:

```
rc = SocketListen(mSocket, 5)
```

ntohl

Description

The ntohl API is used to convert a Long integer from network-byte order to host-byte order.

C Prototype

```
u_long ntohl (u_long netlong);
```

VB Declaration

```
Private Declare Function ntohl Lib "wsock32.dll" _
    (ByVal netlong As Long) As Long
```

Parameters

Parameter	Description
netlong	A Long integer in network-byte order.
Returns	A Long integer in host-byte order.

ntohs

Description

The ntohs API is used to convert a *short* integer from network-byte order to host-byte order.

C Prototype

```
u_short ntohs (u_short netshort);
```

VB Declaration

```
Private Declare Function ntohs Lib "wsock32.dll" _
    (ByVal netshort As Long) As Integer
```

Parameters

Parameter	Description
netshort	A short integer in network-byte order (little-endian).
Returns	A short integer in host-byte order (big-endian).

recv

Description

The recv API is used to read data from a socket.

C Prototype

```
int recv (SOCKET s,
    char FAR* buf,
    int len,
    int flags);
```

VB Declaration

```
Private Declare Function recv Lib "wsock32.dll" _
    (ByVal s As Long, _
    ByVal buf As Any, _
    ByVal buflen As Long, _
    ByVal flags As Long) As Long
```

Parameters

Parameter	Description
s	The descriptor of a connected socket.
buf	A pre-initialized buffer used to return the data from the socket.
buflen	The size of the buffer specified in the buf parameter.
flags	Not required. Set this to 0.
Returns	Returns the number of bytes received. If the call fails, the API returns SOCKET_ERROR.

Example

The following example loops through a receive buffer and builds up a string of data to be returned:

```
Public Function Read() As String
    Dim BytesReceived As Long
    Dim buf As String
```

```
        Dim buflen As Long
        Dim rc As String

        'Allocate a buffer
        buflen = 255
        buf = String$(buflen, Chr$(0))

        'Continue reading the data until the buffer is empty
        Do
            BytesReceived = recv(mSocket, ByVal buf, buflen, 0)

            'Add to the buffer
            If BytesReceived > 0 Then
                rc = rc & Left$(buf, BytesReceived)
            Else
                Exit Do
            End If
        Loop

        'Return the buffer
        Read = rc
End Function
```

send

Description

The send API sends data to a connected socket.

C Prototype

```
int send (SOCKET s,
    const char FAR * buf,
    int len, int flags);
```

VB Declaration

```
Private Declare Function send Lib "wsock32.dll" _
    (ByVal s As Long, _
    buf As Any, _
    ByVal buflen As Long, _
    ByVal flags As Long) As Long
```

Parameters

Parameter	Description
s	The descriptor of a connected socket.
buf	A buffer containing the data to be sent.
buflen	The length of the buffer specified in the buf parameter.
flags	Not required. Set to 0.
Returns	On success, this API returns the number of bytes actually sent. Otherwise, it returns SOCKET_ERROR.

Example

```
Public Function Send(Data As String) As Boolean
    Dim buf As String
    Dim BytesSent As Long

    'Send the data
    BytesSent = SocketSend(mSocket, _
            ByVal Data, _
            Len(Data), _
            0)

    'Return the result
    Send = (BytesSent > 0)
End Function
```

socket

Description

The socket API is used to create a new socket.

C Prototype

```
SOCKET socket (int af,
    int type,
    int protocol);
```

VB Declaration

```
Private Declare Function socket Lib "wsock32.dll" _
    (ByVal af As Long, _
    ByVal s_type As Long, _
    ByVal protocol As Long) As Long
```

Parameters

Parameter	Description
af	The protocol family. Set this to AF_INET.
s_type	The stream type. Use SOCK_STREAM for TCP connections and SOCK_DGRAM for UDP transmissions.
protocol	Unused. Set to 0.
Returns	If successful, a descriptor for the newly created socket is returned. Otherwise, the API returns SOCKET_ERROR.

Example

```
'Create a TCP connection
mSocket = Socket(AF_INET, SOCK_STREAM, 0)

'Establish a UDP connection
mSocket = Socket(AF_INET, SOCK_DGRAM, 0)
```

WSAAsyncSelect

Description

The WSAAsyncSelect API is used to establish an asynchronous handler for custom messages. For example, you can specify a message handler that is notified when a socket is created, destroyed, and when data is read. This API provides for asynchronous communication.

C Prototype

```
int WSAAsyncSelect (SOCKET s,
    HWND hWnd,
```

```
    unsigned int wMsg,
    long lEvent );
```

VB Declaration

```
Private Declare Function WSAAsyncSelect Lib "wsock32.dll" _
    (ByVal s As Long, _
    ByVal hWnd As Long, _
    ByVal wMsg As Long, _
    ByVal lEvent As Long) As Long
```

Parameters

Parameter	Description
s	The descriptor of an open socket.
hWnd	The handle to a message handler.
wMsg	The message to be sent to the handler.
lEvent	A combination of events that when raised, will send the message specified in wMsg to the handler in hWnd.
Returns	Returns 0 on success, SOCKET_ERROR on failure.

Notes

The lEvent parameter can be made up of one or more of the following constants:

FD_ACCEPT	Indicates that a message should be sent when a connection is accepted.
FD_READ	Indicates that a message should be sent when data is available in the socket.
FD_CLOSE	Indicates that a connection was closed.
FD_CONNECT	Indicates that a connection has been created.

If more than one event is specified they should be ORd together.

Example

The following example causes messages to be sent to a textbox control when the data is read or the socket closes.

```
        .
        .
        .
  'Go into asynchronous mode and trap
  'the Read and Close events
  rc = WSAAsyncSelect(mSocket, _
          txtRead.hWnd, _
          WM_LBUTTONUP, _
          ByVal FD_READ Or FD_CLOSE)

  If rc <> SOCKET_ERROR Then
      'Fire the Connect event
      RaiseEvent Connnect
      Connect = True
  Else
      Connect = False
  End If
        .
        .
        .
```

The simplest method to trap these messages is to pass a message to a Visual Basic control that already knows how to respond to it. In this case, we send a WM_LBUTTONUP message to a textbox control. When this message is sent, the MouseUp event will fire. Code can be placed in the MouseUp event that responds appropriately.

WSACleanup

Description

The WSACleanup API is used to shut down the Winsock session. This call is paired with a corresponding call to the WSAStartup API.

C Prototype

```
int WSACleanup (void);
```

VB Declaration

```
Private Declare Function WSACleanup Lib "wsock32.dll" () _
    As Long
```

Parameters

Parameter	Description
None	
Returns	Returns 0 on success, SOCKET_ERROR on failure.

Example

```
Private Sub UserControl_Terminate()
    'Close Winsock
    WSACleanup
End Sub
```

WSAGetLastError

Description

The WSAGetLastError API returns the last error that occurred while calling a Winsock API. You can call this API after many of the other APIs listed in this chapter if you desire more information about the nature of a failure.

C Prototype

```
int WSAGetLastError (void);
```

VB Declaration

```
Private Declare Function WSAGetLastError _
    Lib "wsock32.dll" () As Long
```

Parameters

Parameter	Description
None	
Returns	Returns the last network error that occurred.

Notes

After you have retrieved the error code and are done processing it, make a call to the WSASetLastError API and set the error code to 0.

Example

```
Dim rc As Long

rc = WSAGetLastError()
```

WSASetLastError

Description

The WSASetLastError API is used to reset the network error code after a call to the WSAGetLastError API.

C Prototype

```
void WSASetLastError (int iError);
```

VB Declaration

```
Private Declare Sub WSASetLastError _
    Lib "wsock32.dll" (ByVal iError As Long)
```

Parameters

Parameter	Description
iError	The error number to be set.
Returns	None

Example

```
WSASetLastError 0
```

WSAStartup

Description

The WSAStartup API is used to initialize Winsock. Each call to this API is paired with a corresponding call to the WSACleanup API.

C Prototype

```
int WSAStartup (WORD wVersionRequested,
    LPWSADATA lpWSAData);
```

VB Declaration

```
Private Declare Function WSAStartup Lib "wsock32.dll" _
    (ByVal wVersion As Long, _
    lpWSAData As WSADATA) As Long
```

Parameters

Parameter	Description
wVersion	The version of Winsock that will be used. The high-order word contains the major version number and the low-order word contains the minor version.
lpWSAData	A pointer to a WSADATA structure used to return information about Winsock.
Returns	Returns 0 on success, SOCKET_ERROR on failure.

Notes

Although it is a required parameter of the WSAStartup API, most of the members in the WSADATA structure remain for backward compatibility. Therefore, you won't need to populate it before calling WSAStartup. The WSADATA structure is included here for your reference.

```
Private Const WSADescription_Len = 256
Private Const WSASYS_Status_Len = 128

Private Type WSADATA
    wVersion As Integer
```

```
        wHighVersion As Integer
        szDescription(0 To 256) As Byte
        szSystemStatus(0 To 128) As Byte
        iMaxSockets As Integer
        iMaxUdpDg As Integer
        lpVendorInfo As Long
    End Type
```

Example

```
Private Sub UserControl_Initialize()
    Dim udtWSAData As WSADATA

    'Start Winsock
    If WSAStartup(&H101, udtWSAData) <> 0 Then
        'We couldn't initialize, so raise an error!
        Err.Raise SOCKET_ERROR
    End If
End Sub
```

Accessing TCP/IP Services

As mentioned earlier, there are numerous services available on the Internet. These include Whois, Ping, HTTP, FTP, SMTP, POP, Gopher, and many more.

In this section you will see how to use most of the Sockets control (provided in the WinsockAPI project included with this chapter) to access some basic TCP/IP services, such as Ping and Whois.

If you would like more information about these and other TCP/IP services and their implementations, access the Internet Requests For Comments (RFCs) on the Web at http://www.cis.ohio-state.edu/htbin/std/INDEX.std.html.

Pinging Another Computer

The most basic of TCP/IP services is the ability to ping another computer. Pinging computers works in much the same way as submarines ping each other. A signal is sent, and if it hits anything it bounces back. In a similar manner, a computer sends a signal to a target computer. If the target computer hears the ping it replies to the originating computer. If the originating computer receives a reply from the target computer, then it knows that the other computer is alive on the network.

One computer can ping another computer using the Internet Control Message Protocol (ICMP) within Winsock. The actual API that sends the ping signal is ICMPSendEcho. The following example shows how to initialize ICMP, send and verify the ping signal, and close ICMP:

```
Public Function Ping(Address As String, _
        Timeout As Long) As Boolean

    Dim IRO As ICMPReqOpt
    Dim Response(1 To 4096) As Byte
    Dim lAddress As Long
    Dim rc As Long

    'Start ICMP
    hICMP = IcmpCreateFile()

If hICMP <> INVALID_HANDLE_VALUE Then
        'Convert IP Address
        lAddress = Resolve(Address)

        'Build request packet
        With IRO
            .TTL = 64
            .tos = ICMP_ECHO_REQUEST
            .options = ""
            .optsize = Len(IRO.options)
            .flags = ICMP_FLAG_NO_FRAGMENT
        End With

        'Call the Ping API
        rc = IcmpSendEcho(hICMP, _
                lAddress, _
                Space$(32), _
                32, _
                IRO, _
                Response(1), _
                UBound(Response), _
                Timeout)

        If rc = 0 Then
```

```
            'The ping failed
            Ping = False
        Else
            'We could ping the address
            Ping = True
        End If

        'Close ICMP
        IcmpCloseHandle hICMP
    Else
        'Unable to initialize ICMP
        Ping = False
    End If
End Function
```

Performing a Whois Lookup

Another useful function performed on the Internet is a Whois lookup. The Whois service is used to look up domain name registration information. In the United States this service is provided by the InterNIC. This service is useful when you want to determine if a domain name is reserved or if you want to obtain the registration information for some reason.

The Winsock APIs provide everything you need to perform a Whois search. The steps to perform a Whois lookup are:

1. Connect to the InterNIC server (rs.internic.net) on port 43.

2. Send the name of the domain.

3. Read the reply from the server.

4. Disconnect from the server.

The following example is from the Sockets control in the WinsockAPI project. It shows how these steps are performed in code.

```
Public Function WhoIs(Domain As String) As String
    'Do this synchronously
    mAsync = False

    'Connect to InterNIC on port 43
    If Connect("rs.internic.net", , 43) Then
        'Get the info for the domain
```

```
        If Send(Domain & vbCrLf) Then
            'Read the reply
            WhoIs = Read()
        Else
            'We couldn't send the data
            WhoIs = ""
        End If
    Else
        'We couldn't connect
        WhoIs = ""
    End If
End Function
```

This method makes it easy to perform a Whois lookup. All you need to do is add the Socket control to a form and call the WhoIs method, passing it the name of the domain you want to look up. This method will return the server's response. As you can see, the code is simple:

```
MsgBox Socket1("sybex.com")
```

There are many other things you can use Windows Sockets to accomplish and many more APIs that can be discussed, but unfortunately to do so adequately would require a completely separate book! Examine the source code in the sample projects. There are a few goodies in there that are not covered in the text. In addition, you can add services to the Socket object as you learn more about Internet services.

CHAPTER
SIXTEEN

Putting it All Together

- The IChat Program

- The Basics

- Working with User Preferences

Now that you have learned many APIs and API programming techniques, it's time to see what the Windows API can do for you.

There are numerous applications, each one unique. Sometimes even the most simple applications require complex code. The example used in this chapter is one of those types.

The IChat Program

For this chapter you will utilize many of the classes developed in this book to build the chat program shown in Figure 16.1. This program, called *IChat*, allows you to configure various options, such as your chat name, window colors, speed dial options, and the port it uses to communicate.

FIGURE 16.1:

The IChat interface

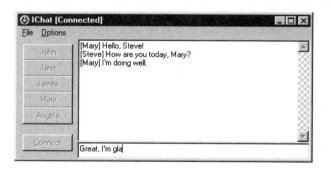

The port selection alone sets this chat program apart from many others. If you are behind a firewall and your chat partner is on the other side, you can configure IChat to utilize a port that accesses the outside world. For example, if you are only allowed to browse the Web, then you obviously have access to port 80. You and your chat partner can configure IChat to use port 80, thus using the http port as your ticket out of the protected network.

As I mentioned at the beginning of this chapter, IChat is actually a simple program, but relies on some APIs to make it work better. As we progress through this chapter, you will see how it uses some of the classes developed throughout the book to achieve functionality not available through intrinsic Visual Basic commands and controls.

By selecting Preferences from the Options menu you can tailor IChat to your liking. When you want to change your preferences you will do so from the Preferences dialog, shown in Figure 16.2. As you can see, you can change your chat name, the IP port that IChat uses, as well as the foreground and background colors of the receive window on the IChat interface.

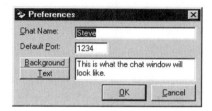

To keep this project simple, IChat has been limited to a single session. In doing so, IChat can be designed to work like a telephone. When you are not chatting it waits for someone to connect to you, or for you to connect to someone else. If you want to connect to someone, just click the Connect button and enter that person's IP address. If they have IChat running on their computer and it uses the same port as yours, then IChat will attempt to connect to their computer. If someone wants to connect to you, IChat detects this request and asks if you want to accept the call. This is similar to using your phone. When you hear the phone ring you have the choice to answer the phone or let it ring until the person hangs up.

In addition to making manual connections you can define up to five speed dial buttons. Do this by selecting Speed Dial from the Options menu. When you select this option IChat will present you with a dialog similar to Figure 16.3, which contains the settings for each speed dial button. Simply enter the name of the person and their IP address, then click OK. Once you do this, the speed dial settings will be saved to the registry and the speed dial buttons will be updated on the IChat interface.

Now that you have an idea of what IChat does, let's take a look at some of the code that makes it work.

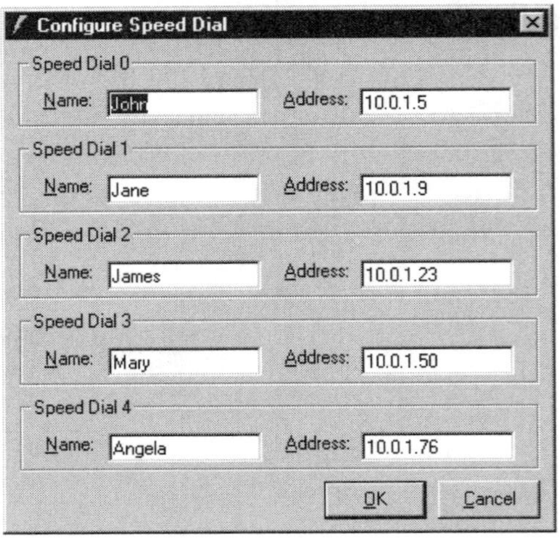

FIGURE 16.3:

Configuring speed dial

The Basics

Listing 16.1 shows the code required to initialize the application.

LISTING 16.1   **Loading the IChat Form**

```
Private Sub Form_Load()
    Dim i As Integer

    'Instantiate required objects
    Set dlg = New clsDialogs
    Set reg = New clsRegistry

    mConnected = False

    'Use asynchronous mode
    wsk.Asynchronous = True

    'Make sure that the registry
    'entries exist
    mChatName = reg.GetValue(eHKEY_LOCAL_MACHINE, _
```

```
            KEY_ICHAT, _
            KEY_CHAT_NAME)

    If mChatName = "" Then
        'Create default preferences
        mChatName = "User"
        mPort = 123

        'Save them in the registry
        SavePreferences
    End If

    'Load the user's preferences
    LoadPreferences

    'Go into listening mode
    Listen
End Sub
```

The first thing IChat does is set the WinsockAPI control developed in Chapter 15, *Internet Programming*, to asynchronous mode. This allows the text to flow freely between the two chat clients. Otherwise, you would have to read data in some other fashion. You could call the .Read method from a Timer event, but this would be a kludge and wouldn't look very professional, nor would it be efficient. Asynchronous mode works nicely for this method of communication.

The next step is to read the user's chat name from the registry. IChat uses the registry class developed in Chapter 11, *Programming the Registry*. If the user's chat name cannot be found, then IChat assumes this is the first time it has been used and proceeds to configure some default values. Then it stores these values in the registry by calling the SavePreferences subroutine.

Just before going into listening mode, IChat loads the user's preferences into memory by calling LoadPreferences. Once the preferences are loaded, IChat is ready to listen for a call.

Listening for a Call

For IChat to answer incoming connection requests, or calls, it must be configured to listen for them. This is done by calling the .Listen method of the WinsockAPI control.

Once IChat goes into listen mode it must enable the connection and option controls so the user can connect or change their preferences. These options are disabled while IChat is connected. Listing 16.2 shows the code that puts IChat into listening mode.

LISTING 16.2   **Listen Mode**

```
Private Sub Listen()
    Dim i As Integer

    If Not wsk.Listen(mPort) Then
        'Make sure the socket is disconnected
        wsk.Disconnect

        MsgBox "IChat could not listen!", _
            vbExclamation, _
            "Error!"

        'End the application
        Unload Me
    Else
        'Disable the transmit window
        txtTx.Enabled = False

        'Enable the connection options
        'and speed dial buttons
        cmdConnect.Enabled = True
        mnuFileConnect.Enabled = True

        LoadSpeedDialButtons

        'Enable the preferences
        mnuOptPrefs.Enabled = True
        mnuOptSpeedDial.Enabled = True

        'Disable the disconnect option
        mnuFileDisconnect.Enabled = False

        Caption = "IChat [Listening]"
    End If

    mConnected = False
End Sub
```

The code is fairly straightforward. If the call to the .Listen method fails, IChat will display an error message and terminate itself. If IChat cannot go into listening mode, then there is most likely a problem with Winsock or the computer's IP configuration.

If IChat goes into listening mode successfully it will disable the transmit window txtTx and enable the connection and option controls. From here you can either connect to another user or wait until another user connects to you.

Accepting a Call

When another client attempts to connect to your chat client the WinsockAPI control will raise the ConnectionRequest event, passing it the socket the request was made on. For the connection to be completed you must accept the connection request. Do this by calling the Accept method of the WinsockAPI control. Listing 16.3 shows how to answer a connection request from another client.

LISTING 16.3   Accepting a Call

```
Private Sub wsk_ConnectionRequest(Socket As Long)
    Dim msg As String

    msg = "Do you wish to answer the " & _
            "chat request?"

    'Prompt the user
    If MsgBox(msg, _
            vbQuestion + vbYesNo, _
            "Connection Request") = vbYes Then

        'Accept the call
        If wsk.Accept(Socket) Then
            'Configure the controls for chat mode
            StartChatting
        End If
    End If
End Sub
```

This code is very straightforward. When the ConnectionRequest event is fired, IChat displays a dialog asking if you want to answer the connection request. If you accept, IChat attempts to complete the connection by calling the .Accept method and passing it the socket that received the connection request. If the WinsockAPI control successfully accepts the connection, the connection and option controls are disabled by calling the StartChatting subroutine.

Connecting to Another Chat Client

Life would be boring if all you did was wait for someone to ask you to chat. As a result, you want to have the ability to initiate, or at least request, your own chat sessions. There are two ways you can request a chat with someone else in IChat. You can manually connect by clicking the Connect button or selecting Connect from the File menu. You can also click a speed dial button for one-touch access to your favorite chat partner.

When you click the Connect button, Visual Basic calls the Click event of mnu-FileConnect, shown in Listing 16.4.

LISTING 16.4   **The Connect Subroutine**

```
Private Sub mnuFileConnect_Click()
    Dim i As Integer
    Dim rc As Boolean

    'Get the address if a speed
    'dial was not selected
    If mAddress = "" Then
        frmAddress.Show vbModal
    End If

    'If the user selected a valid address,
    'then attempt to connect to it
    If mAddress <> "" Then

        MousePointer = vbHourglass

        'Stop listening so we can connect
        wsk.Disconnect

        'Attempt to connect
        rc = wsk.Connect(mAddress, , mPort)

        MousePointer = vbNormal
```

```
        'Were we successful?
        If rc Then
            mConnected = True

            'Configure the controls for chat mode
            StartChatting
        Else
            MsgBox "Connect Failed!", _
                    vbExclamation, _
                    "Error!"

            mConnected = False

            'Go back into listen mode
            Listen
        End If
    End If
End Sub
```

This code first makes sure that a valid address has been specified. If no address has been specified, then you prompt the user to manually enter the destination address. Once an address has been entered it gets stored in the mAddress variable.

After the user enters the address to connect to, you must stop listening for calls by disconnecting the WinsockAPI control. This has the effect of taking you offline by freeing up the port you are listening on. This port is needed to initiate a connection with another computer.

As soon as you disconnect, you attempt to connect to the remote host by calling the WinsockAPI's .Connect method. You must pass the address and port you want to connect to specified by mAddress and mPort, respectively. If the connection is completed successfully, then you must disable the connection and option controls by calling the StartChatting subroutine. If you cannot connect for some reason, you must inform the user and then go back into listening mode.

Speed dial is a smarter version of the Connect feature. All of the speed dial entries are read from the registry at startup. Then the .Caption property of each speed dial button is set to its corresponding speed dial name. If there is no name defined, then the word Unused is displayed on the speed dial button.

The speed dial buttons are a control array of Command Button controls. If the user clicks a speed dial button, the code in Listing 16.5 is executed.

LISTING 16.5   **Speed Dial Code**

```
Private Sub cmdSpeedDial_Click(Index As Integer)
    'Get the speed dial address
    If mSpeedAddress(Index) <> "" Then
        'use the current address
        mAddress = mSpeedAddress(Index)

        'Attempt to connect
        mnuFileConnect_Click
    Else
        mAddress = ""

        MsgBox "No speed dial address defined!", _
                vbInformation, _
                "Connection Failed!"
    End If
End Sub
```

Since each speed dial entry is stored in an array, use the `.Index` property of the Command Button to retrieve the address of the speed dial button. If there is an address defined for this speed dial entry the address is stored in the `mAddress` variable. Then you attempt the connection by calling the `mnuFileConnect_Click` procedure.

Sending Text

Now to the meat of the chat code. The bulk of the work consists of sending and retrieving text. In IChat, text is sent to the other client when the user presses the Enter key. This doesn't allow the other user to see what you are typing as you type it, but this technique minimizes the amount of editing code you have to write. For example, you don't have to write code to trap backspaces or cursor movements. Listing 16.6 shows the code that sends the text to the other chat client.

LISTING 16.6   **Sending Text**

```
Private Sub txtTx_KeyPress(KeyAscii As Integer)
    Dim buf As String

    'Store the buffer
```

```
    buf = "[" & mChatName & "] " & _
           txtTx.Text & vbCrLf

   If KeyAscii = 13 Then
        'Send the text
        wsk.Send buf

        'Add it to the local window
        With txtRx
            .Text = .Text & buf
        End With

        'Scroll the receive window
        Scroll

        'Clear the box
        With txtTx
            .Text = ""
            .SetFocus
        End With
    End If
End Sub
```

As you can see, sending the text is very simple. IChat traps every keystroke sent to the transmit window `txtTx`. Within the `KeyPress` event, use a buffer to prepend the user's chat name to the beginning of the message. Then add the message text to the end of the buffer. Finally, check to see if the user pressed the Enter key.

If the user presses the Enter key, send the buffer through Winsock to the other chat client. Then add the buffer to the end of the text in the receive window. As you may know, when you add text to a multiline Text Box control, the scrollbar will appear when there is more text than can be viewed within the viewing region of the control. Unfortunately, it doesn't automatically scroll. (Perhaps this would be a good property to add to a custom text box control!)

To allow the user to read the most current sentences, the receive window must be programmed to scroll automatically as text is added. Otherwise, the user would be forced to manually scroll the contents of the window during the chat session. This would make it difficult to chat and probably be very irritating to the user.

You could cheat and prepend the text to the beginning of the text in the receive window, but this would look somewhat cheesy, especially since every other chat program in the world scrolls downward. So what you do is use the SendMessage API to send the EM_SCROLLCARAT message to the receive window.

The EM_SCROLLCARAT message causes a multiline edit control (or text box) to scroll to where the carat is. If we place the carat at the very end of the text, then sending this message would cause the edit control to scroll to the end, revealing the last lines of text. Listing 16.7 shows how to accomplish this.

LISTING 16.7   **Scrolling the Receive Window**

```
Private Sub Scroll()
    Dim rc As Long
    Dim hOld As Long

    'Get the handle of the control
    'with the focus
    hOld = GetFocus()

    'Before we can scroll to
    'the carat, we must eneable
    'it by setting the focus
    With txtRx
        .SetFocus
        .SelStart = Len(.Text)

        'Now scroll to it
        SendMessage .hWnd, EM_SCROLLCARET, 0, 0
    End With

    'Focus back on the original control
    rc = SetFocusA(hOld)
End Sub
```

The first thing you need to do is get the handle of the control with the focus. Do this by using the GetFocus API, which was discussed in Chapter 8, *Working with Forms*. Once you have the handle you must move the carat to the last position in the receive window. Do this by setting the focus to the txtRx control and setting the .SelStart property to the last position in the control. Now that you know where the carat is, send the EM_SCROLLCARET message using the SendMessage API discussed in Chapter 3, *Windows Messages*. Once the scroll operation is complete, you must restore the focus to the previous control by calling the SetFocus API and passing it h01d. Visual Basic doesn't let you declare SetFocus because it is an intrinsic method, so declare the API using SetFocusA as its alias.

Receiving Text

Now that you know how the text is sent you can see what happens when IChat receives text. Since the WinsockAPI is set to asynchronous mode it will fire the DataArrival event when it receives data, as shown in Listing 16.8.

LISTING 16.8   The DataArrival Event

```
Private Sub wsk_DataArrival(Data As String)
    'Add the data to the local window
    With txtRx
        .Text = .Text & Data
    End With

    'Scroll the receive window
    Scroll
End Sub
```

When data arrives, all you need to do is append the data to the receive window. Then to make it visible you must scroll the receive window by calling the Scroll subroutine.

Working with User Preferences

What distinguishes IChat from other chat programs are its user options. Using IChat you can configure your chat name, IP port, receive window colors, and the speed dial buttons.

To make IChat smart, it would be nice to program it to remember the user's preferences. You could save these settings in an ASCII file, INI file, or database. However, the registry is a perfect location to store the user's preferences.

To access the registry use the registry class developed in Chapter 11, *Programming the Registry*.

Loading User Preferences

When IChat first loads up, it looks to see if any user preferences have been stored in the registry. If they have, then IChat will load them into memory so you don't need to tailor IChat again.

By default, IChat will set the chat name to User and the port to 1234. You should change these the first time you run IChat. Listing 16.9 shows how IChat uses the registry class to fetch the user's preferences.

LISTING 16.9   **Loading User Preferences**

```
Public Sub LoadPreferences()
    Dim i As Integer

    'Load the user's preferences from the registry
    With reg
        mChatName = .GetValue(eHKEY_LOCAL_MACHINE, _
                KEY_ICHAT, _
                KEY_CHAT_NAME)

        'Get the port
        mPort = .GetValue(eHKEY_LOCAL_MACHINE, _
                KEY_ICHAT, _
                KEY_PORT)

        'Make sure we have a valid chat name
        'and port
        If mChatName = "" Then mChatName = "User"
        If mPort = 0 Then mPort = 1234

        'Load the colors
        frmMain.txtRx.BackColor = _
                .GetValue(eHKEY_LOCAL_MACHINE, _
                KEY_ICHAT, _
                "BackgroundColor")

        frmMain.txtRx.ForeColor = _
                .GetValue(eHKEY_LOCAL_MACHINE, _
                KEY_ICHAT, _
                "TextColor")

        'Set the speed dial buttons
```

```
      For i = 0 To 4
         mSpeedName(i) = _
                 reg.GetValue(eHKEY_LOCAL_MACHINE, _
                 KEY_ICHAT, _
                 "SpeedName" & Format$(i, "0"))

         mSpeedAddress(i) = _
                 reg.GetValue(eHKEY_LOCAL_MACHINE, _
                 KEY_ICHAT, _
                 "SpeedAddress" & Format$(i, "0"))
      Next
   End With
End Sub
```

IChat stores all of its preferences in the IChat key under the HKEY_LOCAL-_MACHINE\Software sub-key of the registry. This allows the settings to be global to the computer. If you wanted them to be dependent on the current user you could modify the code to store the preferences in an IChat key under the HKEY-_CURRENT_USER\Software sub-key.

IChat first attempts to retrieve the user's chat name and IP port. If either of these settings is blank, then IChat uses the defaults User and 1234, respectively. These two settings are essential to the successful operation of IChat. Next IChat attempts to load the background and foreground colors of the receive window. Once these are loaded into memory, IChat attempts to load all five speed dial entries from the registry. These are stored in memory in the mSpeedName and mSpeedAddress arrays.

Changing the Appearance of the Receive Window

Not everybody likes black text on a white background. Many people like to customize their color schemes to suit their own preferences. As a result, you will want to add some functionality that allows the user to change the text and background color of the receive window.

To make it easy to pick a color, the color dialog would be a perfect tool since many users are familiar with it. For this project use the dialogs class developed in Chapter 6, *Dialog APIs*.

You can change the foreground and background colors of the receive window by selecting Preferences from the Options menu. Displayed on the Preferences dialog is your chat name, IP port, and color preferences. If you click either the Background or Text button, you can choose a color from the color selection dialog displayed by the dialogs class. Listing 16.10 shows the code for these two buttons.

LISTING 16.10   **Changing the Receive Window Colors**

```
Private Sub cmdBackground_Click()
    Dim col As Long

    col = dlg.GetColor(txtSample.BackColor, hWnd)
    frmMain.txtRx.BackColor = col
    txtSample.BackColor = col
End Sub

Private Sub cmdText_Click()
    Dim col As Long

    col = dlg.GetColor(txtSample.ForeColor, hWnd)
    frmMain.txtRx.ForeColor = col
    txtSample.ForeColor = col
End Sub
```

When you click the Background button you call the `.GetColor` method of the `clsDialogs` class. You pass the current background color of the receive window, which is used as the default color. The color you choose is returned from the method and stored in the `col` variable. Then you set the `.BackColor` of the receive window to `col` and the change is made! Setting the foreground color is identical to setting the background color, except you set the `.ForeColor` property.

Configuring the Speed Dial Buttons

The final feature covered in this chapter is how to configure the speed dial buttons. If you have numerous people you like to chat with on a regular basis you can program them into your speed dial buttons and IChat will remember them.

Since the speed dial settings are stored in arrays, they are very simple to use. Listing 16.11 shows the code that reads the settings from memory and stores them in the text fields on the Speed Dial Settings dialog.

LISTING 16.11   Loading the Speed Dial Settings

```
Private Sub Form_Load()
    Dim i As Integer

    'Configure the form
    For i = 0 To 4
        fraSpeedDial(i).Caption = "Speed Dial " & _
                Format$(i, "0")

        txtName(i).Text = mSpeedName(i)
        txtAddress(i).Text = mSpeedAddress(i)
    Next
End Sub
```

Listing 16.12 shows how the speed dial settings are saved in memory and in the registry. The first thing you do is store the new settings in the mSpeedName and mSpeedAddress arrays. This allows them to be used immediately in IChat. Then call the SavePreferences subroutine, which saves not only the speed dial settings, but all IChat preferences, to the registry.

LISTING 16.12   Saving the Speed Dial Settings

```
Private Sub cmdOK_Click()
    Dim i As Integer

    'Save the speed dial settings
    For i = 0 To 4
        mSpeedName(i) = txtName(i).Text
        mSpeedAddress(i) = txtAddress(i).Text
    Next

    'Save the preferences in the registry
    SavePreferences

    'Remove the form
    Unload Me
End Sub
```

IChat is just the foundation for a chat program. You can add your own functionality to it as you see fit. Some suggestions would be to use the wave player class developed in Chapter 13 to play a sound bite when a user wants to chat. If you wanted to get a bit more sophisticated you could add a button that sends a wave file to your chat partner and plays it on their computer! If you wanted to scale up IChat you could easily develop a directory application that accepts IP addresses from IChat clients. Then as each client starts up, it can read the addresses of who is currently using IChat. Viola! Instant buddy list!

There is no limit to what you can do, not only with IChat, but with all of your applications. By using the Windows APIs a whole new world of functionality is available to you. Have fun developing your next killer app!

APPENDIX

A

API Quick Reference

- Argument Conversion Table

- Virtual Key Codes

- Windows Messages

Argument Conversion Table

Table A.1 is an argument conversion table provided for your convenience.

TABLE A.1: Argument Conversion Table

If the API requires...	Declare it as...
ATOM	ByVal *argument* as Integer
BOOL	ByVal *argument* as Long
BSTR (VB String)	*argument* as String
BYTE	ByVal *argument* as Byte
BYTE *	*argument* as Byte
char	ByVal *argument* as Byte
char *	*argument* as Byte
DWORD	ByVal *argument* as Long
DWORD *	*argument* as Long
HANDLE	ByVal *argument* as Long
HANDLE *	*argument* as Long
int	ByVal *argument* as Long
INT	ByVal *argument* as Long
int *	*argument* as Long
LONG	ByVal *argument* as Long
LPARAM	ByVal *argument* as Long
LPBOOL	*argument* as Long
LPBYTE	*argument* as Integer
LPHANDLE	*argument* as Long
LPDWORD	*argument* as Long
LPWORD	*argument* as Integer

Continued on next page

TABLE A.1 CONTINUED: Argument Conversion Table

If the API requires...	Declare it as...
LPINT	*argument* as Long
LPUINT	*argument* as Long
LRESULT	ByVal *argument* as Long
LPSTR (C String)	ByVal *argument* as String
short	ByVal *argument* as Long
UINT	ByVal *argument* as Integer
UNIT *	*argument* as Long
WORD	ByVal *argument* as Integer
WORD *	*argument* as Integer
WPARAM	ByVal *argument* as Long

Virtual Key Codes

Table A.2 lists the virtual codes used when sending or reading keystrokes in the keyboard buffer.

TABLE A.2: Virtual Keys and Values

Virtual Key	Value
VK_ADD	&H6B
VK_ATTN	&HF6
VK_BACK	&H8
VK_CANCEL	&H3
VK_CAPITAL	&H14

Continued on next page

TABLE A.2 CONTINUED: Virtual Keys and Values

Virtual Key	Value
VK_CLEAR	&HC
VK_CONTROL	&H11
VK_CRSEL	&HF7
VK_DECIMAL	&H6E
VK_DELETE	&H2E
VK_DIVIDE	&H6F
VK_DOWN	&H28
VK_END	&H23
VK_EREOF	&HF9
VK_ESCAPE	&H1B
VK_EXECUTE	&H2B
VK_EXSEL	&HF8
VK_F1	&H70
VK_F10	&H79
VK_F11	&H7A
VK_F12	&H7B
VK_F13	&H7C
VK_F14	&H7D
VK_F15	&H7E
VK_F16	&H7F
VK_F17	&H80
VK_F18	&H81
VK_F19	&H82
VK_F2	&H71

Continued on next page

TABLE A.2 CONTINUED: Virtual Keys and Values

Virtual Key	Value
VK_F20	&H83
VK_F21	&H84
VK_F22	&H85
VK_F23	&H86
VK_F24	&H87
VK_F3	&H72
VK_F4	&H73
VK_F5	&H74
VK_F6	&H75
VK_F7	&H76
VK_F8	&H77
VK_F9	&H78
VK_HELP	&H2F
VK_HOME	&H24
VK_INSERT	&H2D
VK_LBUTTON	&H1
VK_LCONTROL	&HA2
VK_LEFT	&H25
VK_LMENU	&HA4
VK_LSHIFT	&HA0
VK_MBUTTON	&H4
VK_MENU	&H12
VK_MULTIPLY	&H6A
VK_NEXT	&H22

Continued on next page

TABLE A.2 CONTINUED: Virtual Keys and Values

Virtual Key	Value
VK_NONAME	&HFC
VK_NUMLOCK	&H90
VK_NUMPAD0	&H60
VK_NUMPAD1	&H61
VK_NUMPAD2	&H62
VK_NUMPAD3	&H63
VK_NUMPAD4	&H64
VK_NUMPAD5	&H65
VK_NUMPAD6	&H66
VK_NUMPAD7	&H67
VK_NUMPAD8	&H68
VK_NUMPAD9	&H69
VK_OEM_CLEAR	&HFE
VK_PA1	&HFD
VK_PAUSE	&H13
VK_PLAY	&HFA
VK_PRINT	&H2A
VK_PRIOR	&H21
VK_PROCESSKEY	&HE5
VK_RBUTTON	&H2
VK_RCONTROL	&HA3
VK_RETURN	&HD
VK_RIGHT	&H27
VK_RMENU	&HA5

Continued on next page

TABLE A.2 CONTINUED: Virtual Keys and Values

Virtual Key	Value
VK_RSHIFT	&HA1
VK_SCROLL	&H91
VK_SELECT	&H29
VK_SEPARATOR	&H6C
VK_SHIFT	&H10
VK_SNAPSHOT	&H2C
VK_SPACE	&H20
VK_SUBTRACT	&H6D
VK_TAB	&H9
VK_UP	&H26
VK_ZOOM	&HFB

Windows Messages

There are so many windows messages that it would have required almost a completely separate book to cover them adequately. Since most of the messages are named intuitively, they are listed in Table A.3. In addition, each message's value is listed so you don't have to search through the API Viewer or API Explorer to retrieve it.

TABLE A.3: Windows Messages and Values

Message	Value
WM_ACTIVATE	&H6
WM_ACTIVATEAPP	&H1C

Continued on next page

TABLE A.3 CONTINUED: Windows Messages and Values

Message	Value
WM_ASKCBFORMATNAME	&H30C
WM_CANCELJOURNAL	&H4B
WM_CANCELMODE	&H1F
WM_CHANGECBCHAIN	&H30D
WM_CHAR	&H102
WM_CHARTOITEM	&H2F
WM_CHILDACTIVATE	&H22
WM_CHOOSEFONT_GETLOGFONT	(WM_USER + 1)
WM_CHOOSEFONT_SETFLAGS	(WM_USER + 102)
WM_CHOOSEFONT_SETLOGFONT	(WM_USER + 101)
WM_CLEAR	&H303
WM_CLOSE	&H10
WM_COMMAND	&H111
WM_COMMNOTIFY	&H44
WM_COMPACTING	&H41
WM_COMPAREITEM	&H39
WM_CONVERTREQUESTEX	&H108
WM_COPY	&H301
WM_COPYDATA	&H4A
WM_CREATE	&H1
WM_CTLCOLORBTN	&H135
WM_CTLCOLORDLG	&H136
WM_CTLCOLOREDIT	&H133
WM_CTLCOLORLISTBOX	&H134

Continued on next page

TABLE A.3 CONTINUED: Windows Messages and Values

Message	Value
WM_CTLCOLORMSGBOX	&H132
WM_CTLCOLORSCROLLBAR	&H137
WM_CTLCOLORSTATIC	&H138
WM_CUT	&H300
WM_DDE_ACK	(WM_DDE_FIRST + 4)
WM_DDE_ADVISE	(WM_DDE_FIRST + 2)
WM_DDE_DATA	(WM_DDE_FIRST + 5)
WM_DDE_EXECUTE	(WM_DDE_FIRST + 8)
WM_DDE_FIRST	&H3E0
WM_DDE_INITIATE	(WM_DDE_FIRST)
WM_DDE_LAST	(WM_DDE_FIRST + 8)
WM_DDE_POKE	(WM_DDE_FIRST + 7)
WM_DDE_REQUEST	(WM_DDE_FIRST + 6)
WM_DDE_TERMINATE	(WM_DDE_FIRST + 1)
WM_DDE_UNADVISE	(WM_DDE_FIRST + 3)
WM_DEADCHAR	&H103
WM_DELETEITEM	&H2D
WM_DESTROY	&H2
WM_DESTROYCLIPBOARD	&H307
WM_DEVMODECHANGE	&H1B
WM_DRAWCLIPBOARD	&H308
WM_DRAWITEM	&H2B
WM_DROPFILES	&H233
WM_ENABLE	&HA

Continued on next page

TABLE A.3 CONTINUED: Windows Messages and Values

Message	Value
WM_ENDSESSION	&H16
WM_ENTERIDLE	&H121
WM_ENTERMENULOOP	&H211
WM_ERASEBKGND	&H14
WM_EXITMENULOOP	&H212
WM_FONTCHANGE	&H1D
WM_GETDLGCODE	&H87
WM_GETFONT	&H31
WM_GETHOTKEY	&H33
WM_GETMINMAXINFO	&H24
WM_GETTEXT	&HD
WM_GETTEXTLENGTH	&HE
WM_HOTKEY	&H312
WM_HSCROLL	&H114
WM_HSCROLLCLIPBOARD	&H30E
WM_ICONERASEBKGND	&H27
WM_IME_CHAR	&H286
WM_IME_COMPOSITION	&H10F
WM_IME_COMPOSITIONFULL	&H284
WM_IME_CONTROL	&H283
WM_IME_ENDCOMPOSITION	&H10E
WM_IME_KEYDOWN	&H290
WM_IME_KEYLAST	&H10F
WM_IME_KEYUP	&H291

Continued on next page

TABLE A.3 CONTINUED: Windows Messages and Values

Message	Value
WM_IME_NOTIFY	&H282
WM_IME_SELECT	&H285
WM_IME_SETCONTEXT	&H281
WM_IME_STARTCOMPOSITION	&H10D
WM_INITDIALOG	&H110
WM_INITMENU	&H116
WM_INITMENUPOPUP	&H117
WM_KEYDOWN	&H100
WM_KEYFIRST	&H100
WM_KEYLAST	&H108
WM_KEYUP	&H101
WM_KILLFOCUS	&H8
WM_LBUTTONDBLCLK	&H203
WM_LBUTTONDOWN	&H201
WM_LBUTTONUP	&H202
WM_MBUTTONDBLCLK	&H209
WM_MBUTTONDOWN	&H207
WM_MBUTTONUP	&H208
WM_MDIACTIVATE	&H222
WM_MDICASCADE	&H227
WM_MDICREATE	&H220
WM_MDIDESTROY	&H221
WM_MDIGETACTIVE	&H229
WM_MDIICONARRANGE	&H228

Continued on next page

TABLE A.3 CONTINUED: Windows Messages and Values

Message	Value
WM_MDIMAXIMIZE	&H225
WM_MDINEXT	&H224
WM_MDIREFRESHMENU	&H234
WM_MDIRESTORE	&H223
WM_MDISETMENU	&H230
WM_MDITILE	&H226
WM_MEASUREITEM	&H2C
WM_MENUCHAR	&H120
WM_MENUSELECT	&H11F
WM_MOUSEACTIVATE	&H21
WM_MOUSEFIRST	&H200
WM_MOUSELAST	&H209
WM_MOUSEMOVE	&H200
WM_MOVE	&H3
WM_NCACTIVATE	&H86
WM_NCCALCSIZE	&H83
WM_NCCREATE	&H81
WM_NCDESTROY	&H82
WM_NCHITTEST	&H84
WM_NCLBUTTONDBLCLK	&HA3
WM_NCLBUTTONDOWN	&HA1
WM_NCLBUTTONUP	&HA2
WM_NCMBUTTONDBLCLK	&HA9
WM_NCMBUTTONDOWN	&HA7

Continued on next page

TABLE A.3 CONTINUED: Windows Messages and Values

Message	Value
WM_NCMBUTTONUP	&HA8
WM_NCMOUSEMOVE	&HA0
WM_NCPAINT	&H85
WM_NCRBUTTONDBLCLK	&HA6
WM_NCRBUTTONDOWN	&HA4
WM_NCRBUTTONUP	&HA5
WM_NEXTDLGCTL	&H28
WM_NULL	&H0
WM_OTHERWINDOWCREATED	&H42
WM_OTHERWINDOWDESTROYED	&H43
WM_PAINT	&HF
WM_PAINTCLIPBOARD	&H309
WM_PAINTICON	&H26
WM_PALETTECHANGED	&H311
WM_PALETTEISCHANGING	&H310
WM_PARENTNOTIFY	&H210
WM_PASTE	&H302
WM_PENWINFIRST	&H380
WM_PENWINLAST	&H38F
WM_POWER	&H48
WM_PSD_ENVSTAMPRECT	(WM_USER + 5)
WM_PSD_FULLPAGERECT	(WM_USER + 1)
WM_PSD_GREEKTEXTRECT	(WM_USER + 4)
WM_PSD_MARGINRECT	(WM_USER + 3)

Continued on next page

TABLE A.3 CONTINUED: Windows Messages and Values

Message	Value
WM_PSD_MINMARGINRECT	(WM_USER + 2)
WM_PSD_PAGESETUPDLG	(WM_USER)
WM_PSD_YAFULLPAGERECT	(WM_USER + 6)
WM_QUERYDRAGICON	&H37
WM_QUERYENDSESSION	&H11
WM_QUERYNEWPALETTE	&H30F
WM_QUERYOPEN	&H13
WM_QUEUESYNC	&H23
WM_QUIT	&H12
WM_RBUTTONDBLCLK	&H206
WM_RBUTTONDOWN	&H204
WM_RBUTTONUP	&H205
WM_RENDERALLFORMATS	&H306
WM_RENDERFORMAT	&H305
WM_SETCURSOR	&H20
WM_SETFOCUS	&H7
WM_SETFONT	&H30
WM_SETHOTKEY	&H32
WM_SETREDRAW	&HB
WM_SETTEXT	&HC
WM_SHOWWINDOW	&H18
WM_SIZE	&H5
WM_SIZECLIPBOARD	&H30B
WM_SPOOLERSTATUS	&H2A

Continued on next page

TABLE A.3 CONTINUED: Windows Messages and Values

Message	Value
WM_SYSCHAR	&H106
WM_SYSCOLORCHANGE	&H15
WM_SYSCOMMAND	&H112
WM_SYSDEADCHAR	&H107
WM_SYSKEYDOWN	&H104
WM_SYSKEYUP	&H105
WM_TIMECHANGE	&H1E
WM_TIMER	&H113
WM_UNDO	&H304
WM_USER	&H400
WM_VKEYTOITEM	&H2E
WM_VSCROLL	&H115
WM_VSCROLLCLIPBOARD	&H30A
WM_WINDOWPOSCHANGED	&H47
WM_WINDOWPOSCHANGING	&H46
WM_WININICHANGE	&H1A

INDEX

Note to the Reader: Throughout this index **boldfaced** page numbers indicate primary discussions of a topic. *Italicized* page numbers indicate illustrations.

G

N

T

U

X

Y

Z

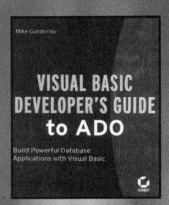

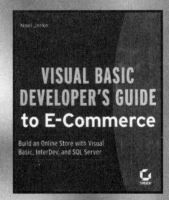